PROVIDENCE

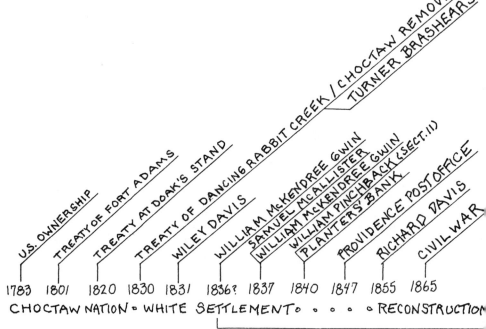

CHOCTAW NATION ▪ WHITE SETTLEMENT ▫ ▫ ▫ ▫ RECONSTRUCTION

PROVIDENCE

PROVIDENCE

WILL D. CAMPBELL

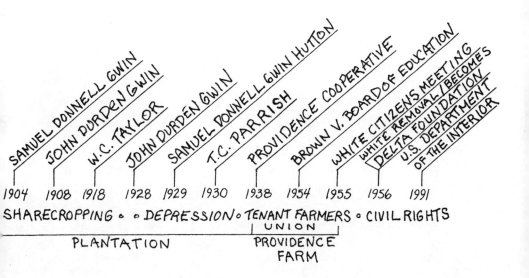

LONGSTREET PRESS

Atlanta, Georgia

Published by
LONGSTREET PRESS, INC.
2140 Newmarket Parkway
Suite 118
Marietta, GA 30067

Printed in the United States of America

1st printing 1992

Library of Congress Catalog Card Number: 91-77196

ISBN 1-56352-024-9

This book was printed by R.R. Donnelley & Sons, Harrisonburg, Virginia.
The text was set in New Baskerville by In Other Words..., Atlanta, Georgia.
Jacket art by Bonnie Campbell.

In Memoriam

Edward N. Akin
Thomas L. Connelly

Men of history

Acknowledgments

Many have helped. Too many to list. Those of libraries, archives, museums. Those who knew Providence firsthand and those who knew through oral tradition. I am grateful to them. I am especially indebted to two historians, Ed Akin and Tom Connelly, who aided and encouraged me at the beginning but did not live to see the ending. To them I dedicate this book.

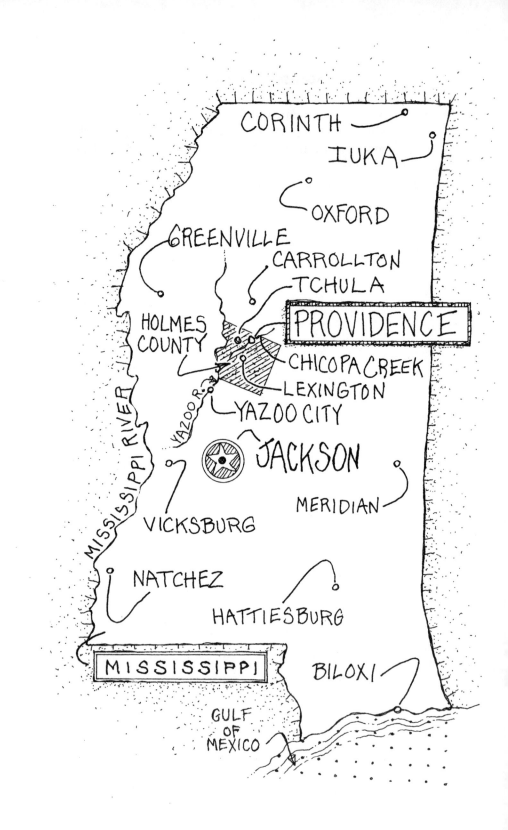

PROVIDENCE

CHAPTER I

. . . and God saw that it was good.

There is something about land. Something magisterial, at once basic and august. With all our technology and scientific know-how we have never been able to invent, manufacture, breed, or graft it. We can only discover, define its borders and its utility, or desecrate. We can never replace it with more of our own making.

This is the story of one parcel of that land, a place called Providence. Emphasis is on one section, a square mile, nucleus of the tract. One square mile. There are almost two hundred million of them on this planet's surface. I suppose that should make a single one seem of no account. But it doesn't. For in one important sense they are all equal, no matter where on Earth they may be.

In one of this nation's earliest documents, all human hierarchy was rejected when it was said that all human beings were created equal and endowed by the creator. I know of no document that establishes a hierarchy of Earth. Even so, we measure with our chains and transits and pretend there is a hierarchy.

I don't know who first started calling pieces of Earth sections, square miles, and acres. Or who began measuring. I know it hasn't always been so. There was a time when the Earth was one. There is a book a lot of us call Holy. It says, "In the beginning God created the heaven and the earth." That's the way the book starts. Then it talks about the land and water being separated, the land being called Earth, the water called Seas. But that's as far as it goes. It doesn't mention sections, miles, acres, townships, ranges. It does say that Earth should bring forth grass, trees, herbs. And

Earth has followed that command with exacting fidelity.

The notion that the Earth is simply "The Earth" didn't last long. That it didn't must have been a mistake, for we started fighting over it as soon as names were given to different parts. People of nations, continents, states, countries, hemispheres, counties, even sections and townships fight each other to call pieces their own. What good ever came of it?

We never ask Earth what is best. We have made those decisions. The Book talks about how two folks, Adam and Eve, thought they knew what was best and got in a lot of trouble. Then two of their children quarreled as to how Earth should best be used, for crops or cattle. One of them killed his own blood brother in the dispute.

When we started dividing Earth into pieces, we quit saying Earth. We never say "a section of Earth." It is always "a section of land." Then land came to mean dirt. And when something is dirt it is bad. Evil. Something earthy may be coarse, even vulgar, but not really bad. Dirt is bad. If something is bad, it can be fought over. Killed for. The Earth is the Lord's, the Book says. But we claim the land as our own.

The section that is the subject of this book was parceled and named late in history. It was among the last to be fitted. A little over 160 years ago. I suppose it was lucky until then. But it has had its trials since.

Section Thirteen. That's what it was named. Of Township Sixteen, North Range. In Holmes County, Mississippi, United States of America. North American Continent. Western Hemisphere. Planet Earth. One section. At times when I refer to Section Thirteen, it is a metaphor for Providence Plantation. Most of the time, though, it is literally the one square mile the measurers named Thirteen. No more. No less.

It has seen a lot. In a way its saga is the story of the nation. I'll tell it as best I can, based on what I know and what I have been able to find out.

Before beginning, the reason I believe all sections of the Earth are equal is because if one of them should be totally removed, from one layer to the other, all the way through the core of the planet, it would throw Earth off its axis. The planet would crumble into trillions of tiny pieces, spinning off into endless time from whence it came. One day some bright but feverish mind might figure out how to do that. We seem so disposed.

CHAPTER 2

I saw the place called Providence for the first time in the fall of 1955. It was an expanse of Delta land attached, as if riveted, to abrupt, craggy bluffs, each level a contradiction, each glacial formation easily distinguishable from the other. The man who introduced it to me was, I believe, one of the most gentle men I have ever known.

A. Eugene Cox.

He was done grievous wrongs during the years I was to know him, but I never heard him speak unkindly of anyone. Yet from the beginning I knew there was a toughness about him too. I did not know the source of it then, that he had been hardened by the West Texas winds of economic depression as a child, nurtured in the ways of charity there, then further seasoned by his years at Texas Christian University and the wretched poverty he found in his adopted Mississippi. He had become a blend of strength and gentleness, but on that wet October afternoon in 1955 I knew little more than his name.

I watched him walk hurriedly from a small, neatly painted frame building, approaching the car I had just wrestled up a rutted dirt driveway. A hefty bulge just under his left arm suggested he was armed. I tried to size him up as he came. He struck me as a man prepared to exert himself if the occasion beckoned.

"I'm Gene Cox," he said, stopping before he reached the car. "What can I do for you gentlemen?" He had not offered his hand.

My friend with me, G. McLeod Bryan, answered from the

opposite side of the car. "Hey, Gene. I'm Mac Bryan. You remember me. And this is Will Campbell. You know. From Ole Miss."

The man moved to the passenger side, stooped as if to get a better look. Suddenly he smiled, opened the door, and gave my friend a vigorous handshake, edging him at the same time underneath some nearby tree branches where they stood wrapped in somber conversation, the stranger occasionally looking back at me. I was uncomfortable and pretended not to notice him. After a few minutes they jostled in playful banter, shook hands again, and moved around to my side of the car.

Gene Cox laughed lightly, as if to apologize. "You boys come on in," he said, greeting me cordially.

I had watched him as they talked. He was a handsome man, of medium build but sturdy looking. I reckoned him to be about fifty years old. I had seen his piercing, inquiring eyes, partly shaded by bushy, uncropped eyebrows. His hair, starting to gray, was thick and well trimmed. It lay in tidy, parallel waves, like the rippling of pond water. He was a long-armed, rawboned fellow, with fair skin that appeared lightly tanned from the sun. He seemed the kind of man I instinctively trusted.

I had never been in Holmes County, Mississippi. I recalled the first 4-H Club in America had been founded there. I couldn't remember when. Around the turn of the century, I thought. I did know Holmes County was not a place notorious for its social radicalism. And the man I had just met, I was soon to learn, was an authentic radical. We followed him inside the building, obviously a medical clinic, which I found out later had once been a dairy barn. The place had an aura of friendliness. Yet somehow sad. I was introduced to Gene Cox's wife, Lindy, and their three children. They ranged in age from nine to fourteen. And to Dr. David Minter, his wife, Sue, and their three children. They were sitting in a circle in the doctor's office, as if in a formal seminar. They seemed subdued.

It was sixteen months after the Supreme Court had ruled that racially segregated public schools were unconstitutional. May 17, 1954. A day that would send tidal waves to be felt throughout the South for decades, claiming the attention and energies of the people as nothing had done since the Civil War. Most thinking persons had known the Court would, and must, rule as it did in the case of *Brown v. Board of Education*. Being under the scrutinizing eyes of emerging nations around the globe, few of them white, and faced with growing unrest within America's black populace, it had little choice. But few realized the stupendous import the decision would have. In its wake was an epoch of moral mischief, indescribable repression, social and political unrest, at times approaching anarchy. A recalcitrant white citizenry, invidious legislation, killings, riots, and vigilante judiciary would leave the body politic in sordid disarray. Words seldom heard before became commonplace: states' rights, interposition, nullification, massive resistance, miscegenation, amalgamation. The groundswell saw the region's most urbane and intelligent legislators and governors passing panic statutes as futile and ludicrous as a scholarly search for the hypotenuse of a circle.

The story we were about to hear from the little band huddled in a country doctor's office was prelude, portentous and dispiriting to a young man trained to bring good news to captives. It told me the South and the nation were moving into an era of domestic psychosis I had not imagined. It reminded me of a conversation three years earlier among a group of us Southerners about to graduate from Yale Divinity School. The major reason most of us went there was to get ready to work on the region's racial problems. As we talked about the case being argued before the Supreme Court, we almost resented the prospect that the matter would be settled by a brief Court decree, leaving us with no purpose back home. "So why don't we just stay here in New England where the summers are more pleasant?" we reasoned. I wondered if the others were now laughing too.

A week earlier I had read newspaper accounts of some trouble at a place called Providence Farm, a cooperative, interracial venture in rural Mississippi that I had never heard of. There had been a meeting of white citizens at the nearby Tchula High School.

Tchula, Choctaw word for red fox, was a town of less than two thousand people, two-thirds of whom were black. The news stories reported the meeting was convened following an incident in which four Negro youths, riding on the flat-bed of a farm truck on a brisk fall morning, had frightened a third-grade white girl waiting for the school bus near Providence Farm. She had thought they whistled or hollered at her as they passed.

The alleged incident occurred only one week after Roy Bryant and J. W. Milam had been acquitted in the nearby town of

Sumner by an all-male, all-white jury for the kidnapping and murder of fourteen-year-old Emmett Till. Emmett and his cousin, Curtis Jones, both from Chicago, were visiting relatives in Mississippi. They were staying with Mose Wright, Curtis's grandfather. Emmett reportedly had said, "Bye, baby," to a white woman after buying some candy in her store. He had been taken from Mose Wright's shack late at night, murdered, and thrown into the Tallahatchie River. At the trial, freed from fear by grief and anger, the grandfather of Curtis Jones stood in open court and defied what had been instilled in his people for centuries. When asked by the prosecuting attorney if he could identify the men who had come to his door that night and demanded the youth, he stood erect in the witness stand, pointed his long, bony finger at Milam, then at Roy Bryant, and uttered two words that would go down in the annals of courage. "Thar he." Though he soon left the state forever, his doughty stand became an ongoing precept for a generation of black citizens who would be similarly challenged during the long dark night of what we remember as the civil rights movement.

"Thar he." There should be a commemorative medallion with gold lettering. There should be a national holiday. September 20. THAR HE DAY, on the calendar. An old black man, boldly accusing two murderous white men with his entire world watching, the guns of ages pointed at his heart. Yes, there should be a day. For it was a beginning.

The little girl, frightened by the talk she had heard about the Till child's murder and the rumors of Negro reprisals, was crying when the bus arrived. The driver made her tell her teacher what had happened.

The news stories had said the school principal had called the sheriff and that he had promptly arrested the four boys. John Herbers, then a correspondent for United Press, wrote that the Negro youths were questioned for two hours by Sheriff Richard Byrd, County Attorney Pat Barrett, state legislator Ed White, and local businessman William Moses. No legal counsel and no parents were present. According to the newspaper accounts, most of the questions had to do with activities at Providence Farm, where the boys sometimes visited and played. The scared youths gave incriminating responses to leading questions. Things like, "Have you ever seen colored folks in the swimming pool?" When one answered "Yeahsuh," he was not allowed to explain that in the summer there was a day camp for Negro children and the campers went swimming. There were no white campers. The swimming pool, I learned, was nothing more than a dynamited hole below a cold, fresh-water spring. According to Mr. Cox, the only "mixed swimming" had been when a Negro nursemaid attending the Cox and Minter children went into the water with them to keep them from drowning.

The mass meeting at Tchula High School was held three nights after the youths were questioned. Newspaper accounts agreed that the White Citizens Council, an organization formed to preserve racial segregation shortly after the May 17, 1954, Supreme Court decision, was responsible for the meeting. W. F. "Bill" Minor, head of the New Orleans *Times-Picayune*'s Mississippi bureau, reported that Moses was head of the county chapter of the Citizens Council, County Attorney Barrett was president of the Lexington (county seat) chapter, and Representative J. P. Love led the Tchula chapter.

A tape recording of the interrogation was played to the approximately five hundred men and a few women present. Mr. Cox and Dr. Minter were questioned by the audience regarding their views and purpose. At the conclusion of what Editor Hodding Carter of the *Delta Democrat-Times* of Greenville described as a kangaroo court, a vote was taken, and Providence Farm was ordered to disband and the organizing families were ordered to leave the county.

The newspapers reported Providence as a cooperative venture where both whites and Negroes lived and worked together. Interracial. Cooperative. Incendiary words for a people long devoted and committed to what they knew as "the Southern way of life." Both words were sure to pique the passions of those persuaded already by their own history that God was the original segregationist, and reenforced by the years of Senator Joe McCarthy's preachments that a communist conspiracy was behind every effort to destroy ancient customs.

Although I had been on the staff of the University of Mississippi for more than a year, what I had seen in the papers was all I knew about Providence Farm. Dr. G. McLeod Bryan, a professor of philosophy at Mercer University, was on the campus as a visiting lecturer. When he told me he knew the Coxes and Minters, we decided to drive down to see them. Neither of us expected to find a situation of such dimensions.

Finding them at all proved to be a logistical problem. We knew the farm was located several miles off U.S. Highway 49, somewhere between the little towns of Cruger and Tchula. We could not reach them by telephone. The lines, we learned, had been cut following the mass meeting of the White Citizens Council.

"Most of Dr. Minter's patients are Negroes," Mac Bryan said. "When we get in the area, we'll ask a Negro family for directions."

"Things must be different in Georgia," I told him. "Folks here will know of the trouble and send us on a wild goose chase. He's their friend and they'll protect him. It's an old trick to confuse and divert deputies and bill collectors." We discovered after asking a few whites that we would fare no better there. No one would acknowledge that they had ever heard of Dr. Minter, though undoubtedly many of them had been at the mass meeting.

Mac suggested we find a physician in Cruger and ask for directions. "I'll introduce myself as 'Dr. Bryan.' I don't have to tell him I'm a doctor of philosophy. I'll tell him we went to school together, that I'm passing through and want to say hello. That way we won't have to lie."

Mac had told me that Dr. Minter went to the University of Pennsylvania. Mac had not. I told him that wouldn't work. He explained that some years earlier they had been in a seminar together in North Carolina. Something about farm cooperatives in the modern South. He wasn't too sure. So they really had, he insisted, gone to school together.

"What if he asks you where you went to med school?" I asked.

"Then I'll lie. I'll tell him I went to the University of Pennsylvania. No harm done."

"Unless he went there too. In the same class."

"Then, my friend, we're in trouble."

The trouble didn't happen. We stopped at a service station. I told the attendant I had a temperature and wanted to see a doctor. Both were true. I had a temperature of 98.6 and I did want to see a doctor. He pointed us down an unpaved street and said the doctor would be at the last house on the left. We found the doctor, lying on a cot on a sun porch in what seemed a pharmaceutical haze. Without getting up, he gave us detailed directions, spoke kindly of Dr. Minter, and wished us well.

The doctor had told us to cross three bridges several miles out of town on Highway 49 East, turn left on a narrow gravel road, and follow it until we came to a settlement. "You'll see a little white colored church as soon as you turn," he had slurred. As we drove away we joked about whether he meant a colored white church or a white-colored church.

"Let's look for a small church house painted white where Negro Christians gather on Sundays," one of us said, settling the matter. I recall a long silence after we left the busy highway, neither of us expressing our mounting fears.

The stretch of U.S. Highway 49 from Greenwood to Yazoo City runs almost parallel to the border of the Mississippi Delta. West of the road, all the way to the Mississippi River, lies that vast alluvial region famous for past floods, bountiful cotton crops from the labors of mules and sharecroppers and sometimes Parchman convicts hired out to plantation owners who lived in big houses in Clarksdale or Greenville, or in hamlets—Inverness, Sunflower, Pentecost, Merigold. And sometimes faraway places: New York, Paris, or London. The Delta. A place of mean poverty and garish opulence.

Soon to the east of the highway it ends. Whatever caused the Delta, that is as far as it goes. The land then climbs through the brush and up the rounded nates of the Loess Bluffs like the train of a nuptial gown, level satin trailing, moving precipitously up and across the arching spine and shoulders until it reaches the highest point of the bridal veil. It stops there as if some geological intrusion, some ancient and possessed mammoth dozer had, with an impetuous heave, pushed, in its madness, the glacial residue to some quarantine station, abandoning it there for changeless eternity, leaving fertile flat land behind for the favored bride who would then turn back to possess it, greedy and licentious, bequeathing the hills and cliffs to Loess vestals. The Bluffs.

It was on the edge of the Loess Bluffs that we found the dwellers of Providence Cooperative Farm.

After the children had been taken to one of the residences, and the small talk of the difficulty we had in finding them was over, the tale of Providence Farm and the mass meeting at the high school began to unwind, pieces fitting together like a Persian rug as one and then another spoke.

"Just where are we?" I asked, more to have something to say than really wanting to know.

"You're sitting right in the middle of Section Thirteen," Mr. Cox laughed.

"And where might that be?" I came back.

"Township Sixteen, Range One East," he said, treating it now as a serious question. "We have about four sections in all, but most of the buildings are on Section Thirteen."

At the time I didn't know, or had forgotten, that a section of land was one square mile. Six hundred and forty acres. And a township was thirty-six sections. I said, "That's a lot of land," anyway, still just to have something to say.

"We've done the best we could by it," Mr. Cox said. There was a tone of resignation in his voice. That, and his pained expression, told me that this man was in love with these acres. All of them.

"But now we'll have to go," Dr. Minter said.

"Why is that?" Mac Bryan asked.

"You can't practice medicine without patients," he said. "And they've blocked the roads, cut the phone lines. Negroes are afraid to come. Whites, even the poorest, won't come now."

"If it was just myself," Mr. Cox said, tentatively touching the bulge underneath his armpit, "I would get a bazooka and perch up on that bluff until they blow me away." His wife, Lindy, shook her head, smiling admiringly but not with approval. "But it's not just me. We have women and children here. Families." He sighed deeply and shook his head, appearing more stymied than defeated. "We'll work something out," he added after a long pause.

They began talking of the history of Providence Farm, of their personal histories, their hopes for a cooperative venture in rural Mississippi that would unleash the shackles that had continued to hold Negroes and poor whites in virtual peonage. They talked of Rochdale, the farm they had operated in neighboring Bolivar County when they first came to Mississippi in the 1930s.

"If the White Citizens Council had been around when we were at Rochdale, they might have had cause to complain," Gene Cox said. When I asked why, he responded that in the thirties, when the belligerent economy was like a coiled whip moccasin, striking its desperate and helpless victims at will, any promising stick was seized to flail the lunging viper. "We were pretty far to the left back then," he explained. Then, as if I were too young to remember or understand, he carefully explained the difference between socialism and communism. "We were never Communists," he told me. "The Commies hated the Socialists more than they hated capitalists."

For a long time he told background stories. He talked of H. L. Mitchell and Howard Kester, men who were already mentors for me. They had been involved in the Southern Tenant Farmers Union, an organization that challenged the sharecropper system and for a time seemed destined to change the face of the South. Kester had told me that during this time he wore a cyanide pellet around his neck which George Washington Carver, the eminent scientist of Tuskegee Institute, had given him in case he was captured by a mob intent on torture and slow death.

When the Civil War put an end to legal slavery, new structures took its place. The sharecropper scheme was inevitable. The plantation owners had the land; former slaves and poor whites had the labor. It seemed an equitable arrangement, and except for the human animal's propensity for evil it would have worked. Instead it became a ruthless and exploitative bastion of power and greed. Illiterate workers were cheated almost routinely. Any populist movement that sought to change the system was quickly put down by the gentry's careful manipulation of the issue of race. When poor whites were told that if they insisted in their egalitarian notions their daughters would be ravished en masse by black bucks, they quickly receded back into the prisonhouse of silence.

The Southern Tenant Farmers Union, under the influence of enlightened Socialists like Norman Thomas, evaded the trap. From the beginning it openly included Negro and white, male and female, among its members and in positions of leadership. Stripped of the weapon of racial fears, many large landowners turned to other measures, violent measures. Local legal apparatus were as much a part of the system as were gin belts, shotguns, and lynch ropes.

Eviction from the farms was one method of control that was available and legal. Families known to be members of or sympathetic to the Southern Tenant Farmers Union were systematically denied land to farm by the owners. By 1937 an estimated thirty-one thousand men and women had joined the union. The plantation owners saw the threat to the status quo, knew it was something they intended to stop. Men and women who had been plowing and hoeing for seventy-five cents for a ten-hour day were demanding five dollars. Cotton pickers wanted a dollar for each hundred pounds of cotton picked. To accentuate their solidarity, they were organizing strikes. Strikes by industrial workers were viewed with uncommon uneasiness by moneyed Americans in the 1930s. Pickets, boycotts, and work stoppages among farm workers were unheard of. Heightening the menace to white planters, Negroes and whites were defying laws and customs by meeting together. White women as part of it all were an added outrage.

All the prescriptions of the gentry, grass ropes, jailhouses, threats, and outrage could not say them nay. Arkansas, Mississippi, Louisiana were on the brink of violent revolution. "Roll the Union on!" filled the air. Tent cities sprang up for families kicked off the land with no place to go. Hunger was a reality, starvation a likelihood, mass murder an abiding threat.

It was such conditions that brought a little band of radicals, most of them fresh from university life, to Boliver County, Mississippi, in 1936. And then to Holmes County, Section Thirteen, Township Sixteen, two years later. When I asked why they chose Mississippi for such a hazardous venture in the first place, one of them laughed and said, "We thought Mississippi was safer than Arkansas." I laughed also.

I was having trouble making a distinction between Rochdale and Providence, so they gave a brief history of both places. For the first time I heard the name of Sam Franklin. Franklin was a protégé of Sherwood Eddy, internationally known scholar, leader of students in the Young Men's Christian Association, and a strong advocate of the socialization of all means of production. Franklin had also been a student of, and was a close friend of, Reinhold Neibuhr. In 1929 Sam and his wife, Dorothy, had gone to Japan as missionaries. During the five years they were there, Sam had come under the influence of Toyohiko Kagawa, a Japanese Christian who had organized for social justice in the slums of Kobe. Active in forming Japan's first labor union, Kagawa believed cooperatives were the answer to Japan's economic problems. When Sam Franklin fell into disfavor with his denomination's Board of Foreign Missions because of his Socialistic leanings, he resolved to find a place in America where he could work for economic justice among the poor. His friend Sherwood Eddy had told him if he found such a project he would offer financial support.

In early 1936 Franklin met with a small group in Memphis

committed to aiding the evicted sharecroppers and the Southern Tenant Farmers Union. Mr. Cox, who was telling the story, recalled the names of some who were present. "Have you met Mitch?" he asked Mac. That was H. L. Mitchell, then working with the farmers union which he and Clay East had founded near Tyronza, Arkansas.

"I believe Blaine Treadway was there," Mr. Cox said. "And John and Mack Rust." Blaine Treadway was a printer in Memphis. John and Mack Rust, like Gene Cox, were native Texans with populism in their veins. Mr. Cox explained that the Rust brothers designed a mechanical cotton picker but were never successful in marketing it.

"Bill Amberson was there too," Dr. Minter interrupted. William R. Amberson, we were told, was a physician and professor at the University of Tennessee in Memphis, and later at the University of Maryland.

"A Socialist doctor," Mr. Cox laughed. "Not many of them left."

"Don't forget the women," Mrs. Cox said. "I think Evelyn Smith was there." She told us Evelyn Smith was the office secretary for the Southern Tenant Farmers Union.

Sam Franklin talked with the group about his interest in farm cooperatives, based on what he had seen in Japan and Russia, which he had visited with Sherwood the year before.

After several investigative trips into Arkansas, where they found unbelievable suffering—including what was to become a celebrated case of peonage by a deputy sheriff who arrested evicted tenants for vagrancy, herded them into stockades, and forced them to cut firewood which he sold from his own wood yard—the group made plans for an experimental cooperative farm. Eddy contributed twenty thousand dollars he had in a trust fund, and in late March of 1936 they had purchased about two thousand acres of land in Boliver County, Mississippi, for approximately seven dollars per acre. The price included a number of mules and some farm implements. It was first called Sherwood Eddy Cooperative Farm but was incorporated as the Delta Cooperative Farm. For a post office address, they named the place Rochdale, taken from Rochdale Consumers Cooperative in England of a hundred years earlier.

"But it didn't work out," Mr. Cox told us. Despite the ease with which they found refugees anxious to move to the farm, and even considering the success of erecting buildings, organizing a cooperative store, and recruiting the services of a resident physician and nurse, the land was not suited for raising cotton.

"You boys know what buckshot land is?" Gene Cox asked. I did. It is sharkey clay which forms quagmires when it is wet and dries and cracks in the summer heat, almost as hard as concrete. "We didn't give up," he told us. "But after two years at Rochdale, we found this property over here in Holmes County and bought it for six dollars an acre." Rochdale was sold.

"So that's how you got to Section Thirteen," I said to Mr. Cox.

"Not quite," he said. "There's a lot more to the story."

Mr. Cox had volunteered to go to Delta Cooperative Farm at Rochdale soon after it was organized. At Texas Christian University he had met Sherwood Eddy, who had told him of the venture. Gene was a trained accountant and the farm needed someone to keep the books.

A few months later Lindsey Hail, who had been a student at Beaver College in Philadelphia and was a graduate of Massachusetts General Hospital School of Nursing, arrived to be the resident nurse for the farm. Miss Hail, called Lindy, was the daughter of missionaries to Japan. Her father died in an eruption of the Mount Asama volcano in central Honshu, Japan, when she was six weeks old. Her mother, also the daughter of missionaries to Japan, stayed on with her four children. Sam and Dorothy Franklin had known them in Japan. Lindy was eleven years old the first time she saw America. She lived in a cotton house with a small wood-burning stove for heat in that first harsh Delta winter she spent at the cooperative farm. Within seven months she and A. Eugene Cox were married.

On into the afternoon we heard the stories of what life was like in Mississippi in the decade of the thirties. Most of it was familiar to me. I was a six-year-old Mississippian when the thirties began. Almost ready for war when the decade ended. I knew the script.

"That's all pretty much changed now," Mr. Cox said, referring to nothing in particular. "The New Deal and the war changed all that." I assumed that he was talking about the Kingdom-of-God-on-earth ideology of their youth.

The conversation shifted suddenly back to the mass meeting of the White Citizens Council. "I really think they would have killed us," Dr. Minter said.

"Except for what?" Mac Bryan asked.

"Except for the schoolchildren," Mr. Cox answered. "There

was a ball game going on during the meeting. I reckon they thought we were important or they wouldn't have scheduled it while a football game was going on."

"Just about the time the vote was being taken on telling us to leave the state, the game ended and there were kids all over the schoolyard," the doctor said.

"Carol, our oldest daughter, was a cheerleader," Mrs. Cox put in. Her tone suggested she didn't want to hear again the part about one man saying what they needed to settle the trouble was two grass ropes.

The meeting had been convened by a local attorney, Edwin White, who, leaving his law books and his schoolboy recitations of the First Amendment behind, arose to address the crowd. What he offered was an interminable diatribe of Biblical proof texts, oblivious to any hint of love in that holy collection. When someone prompted him, he asked the pastor of the Tchula Methodist Church, a man who had been sympathetic to the Coxes and Minters, to give the invocation. Then he continued. Many years later I would be told by one of his legal colleagues, present at the meeting, that "Ed White was an oratorical firebrand. He just loved to make powerful speeches. He whipped the crowd into a frenzy. Most of them didn't know what was going on." Probably they didn't. One of the favorite tactics of the powerful White Citizens Council was to influence an uninformed populace with frenzied rhetoric.

After the two-hour recording had been played of the questioning of the four Negro youths, Mr. Cox and Dr. Minter had been allowed to make a statement of what Providence Farm was about. They talked of their Christian commitment and denied any violation of local mores or state laws.

"It's a busy practice, but not a lucrative one," Dr. Minter told them. When the attorney, also a member of the state legislature, asked him why a doctor with a degree from the University of Pennsylvania Medical School would locate in such a remote and obscure place when he could make far more money in a city, the doctor replied, "It's the kind of thing I like to do. I am motivated by religious conviction to heal body, soul, and mind." He tried to explain he wasn't interested in wealth. If anyone had bothered to ask, they would have learned that Dr. Minter came to Mississippi seventeen years earlier, soon after graduating from medical school. The Presbyterian Board of Missions had guaranteed him a salary the first year of up to one thousand dollars. That year he made $994, he told us. "They still owe you six dollars," his wife teased.

"No wonder they call you Commies," Mac Bryan laughed. "Any fool who chooses Jesus over dollars is subversive per se."

They said the most vituperative questioning had to do with segregation, although, they explained, race and subversion were used interchangeably. After trying to be evasive, Mr. Cox finally answered, "I think segregation is un-Christian."

A wave of angry boos greeted his words. One man, also a physician, jumped to his feet and yelled, "I've heard enough!" and left the meeting.

For raw courage, the affirmation of Gene Cox that night to an audience of several hundred men on a hostile mission must be ranked with the "Thar he" of Mose Wright a few days earlier. Perhaps both men were foolish, as the world measures foolish acts. But courage is not, in every case, directed by prudence.

A few others showed their mettle. A young planter stood up before the vote was taken and said by morning he might not have a friend left in the county, but that he intended to sleep well that night. "What you are doing here is wrong," he said. Then he turned and left the hall.

Another man, the Reverend Marsh Calloway, pastor of the Durant Presbyterian Church, took the floor and said he knew little about the activities of Providence Farm, but he knew the family of Dr. Minter. He said Dr. Minter's father was a Presbyterian minister; his brother had been a missionary to the Far East and was then a Presbyterian pastor in Texas. Dr. Minter's sister, Mr. Calloway told the gathering, was then a missionary nurse in Africa, married to a medical missionary. Such a pedigree did not assuage the passions of his fellow Christians. When he continued that what they were doing was un-American and un-Christian, someone yelled above the boos, "This ain't no Christian meeting, Brother." Mac Bryan said that was, no doubt, the understatement of the evening. Marsh Calloway's words that night would be among his last public ones in Holmes County. Dr. Minter told us the Session, the official body of the congregation, asked for his resignation almost immediately. "I'm sorry about that," Dr. Minter added. "We never meant to get anyone in trouble." I later learned that Mr. Calloway continued for several months to print bulletins, prepare sermons, and deliver them from the pulpit while he appealed his dismissal to the next judicatory level of his denomination. But only his wife was there to hear them.

Darkness comes early in October. We had planned to be back home by sundown. Instead we adjourned to the Cox residence where we ate supper, and the stories of Providence continued.

They talked of interesting guests who had come over the years. And more recently. It was the first time I heard David Halberstam's name. Just out of Harvard at twenty-one, he had come to West Point, Mississippi, to work for the local newspaper and learn about the South. It was a fortunate time to learn, for the times were perilous. In a perceptive article for *The Reporter* magazine, reporting on a murder trial of a white man who had killed a Negro in Tallahatchie County without provocation, he divided the white people of Mississippi into two groups: the good people and the peckerwoods. The good people, he said, would not resort to racial violence but would not take a stand to stop it. Someone had hung a row of dead crows on a barbed-wire fence on Providence land, possibly a youthful prank, possibly a symbolic act of intimidation. The young journalist had heard about it and in his article included the now classic line: "It is the peckerwoods who kill Negroes and the good people who acquit the peckerwoods; it is the peckerwoods who hang dead crows from the trees of a small town, and the good people who do not cut them down." Mr. Halberstam made several friendly and supportive visits to Providence following the mass meeting.

Another early visitor and well-wisher was Myles Horton, founder of the famed Highlander Folk School, a racially integrated adult education center near Monteagle, Tennessee. Four years after Providence Cooperative Farm was ordered disbanded, Highlander had problems of even greater magnitude. One of the most celebrated sets of photographs of the era was taken at Highlander by an undercover agent working for the governor of Georgia. Some of the pictures showed whites and blacks dancing together. Another one was of the young Martin Luther King, Jr., seated beside a writer for the Communist *Daily Worker*. That picture found its way to billboards, sponsored by the White Citizens Council, around the South. The caption read: "Martin Luther King at Communist Training School." That and similar rumors and propaganda resulted in the revocation of Highlander's charter and the seizure of its property. Dispossessed for a time for alleged subversion, Myles Horton moved to

Knoxville, later to New Market, Tennessee, and continued his work. "They called us Communists," I heard him say toward the end of his life. "But they misunderstood. Communism was always far too conservative for us. We were up to something a lot more radical than that. What we've always been after is democracy. And that's radical." I wondered if the same might have been said of Providence Cooperative Farm at its heyday. But that was my first visit. I knew nothing except what I had read in the newspapers and what I was hearing from those perhaps too close to be objective.

We sat into the night. A. Eugene Cox, Texas farm boy who went off to school and got ideas far ahead of his time. Lindy Hail Cox, whose spiritual ancestors were Japanese. Dr. David R. Minter, her colleague in a battle against poverty and disease in Section Thirteen, a veteran of a war against the people she loved. He with a brother as a missionary in China, our ally in that war but by 1955 also an enemy. With another sibling in Africa, ministering to the kin of the people they were serving here. Sue Wooten Minter, daughter of an Indiana businessman, she who had come for a summer work camp, taken a doctor for a husband and stayed on, bearing three children and working in the medical clinic as receptionist, office secretary, nurse's aid, and doing whatever was needed. G. McLeod Bryan, a teacher of philosophy in a Georgia Baptist college. And I, a child of the Mississippi yeomanry who had spent three years in the Pacific War against Lindy's people. An unlikely assemblage. Presbyterians, Disciples, Southern Baptists. In a house whose doors had been open to Protestants, Jews, and Catholics. Atheists and doubters. Foreigners and native born. Ecumenism had come to Mississippi in bootleg vestments.

Except for the subject and occasion, it was a traditional after-supper bit of Southern communing. Women in the kitchen; men with lighted pipes in the parlor, rocking and swapping innocent lies. But the gritty reality of the situation was not long in returning. When the women rejoined us, and the two couples fell to reminiscing on the early days of Providence Farm, the work and aspirations of young and foolish prophets, the magnolia blossom score into which we had temporarily receded, vanished.

I had been too young to know the hopes and dreams of the thirties they had known. Listening to their goals for a state I knew so well, it sounded at times like an effort at alchemy. I knew I was in the presence of good people, who, for the first time in their lives, were forced to drink from the bitter springs of defeat. Defeat not so much because they had failed, but because when the subject of race was at issue, the indurated hearts of the white citizenry, also good people generally, could not see the gold within the lode.

My own convoluted birthright struck me. I knew that those who had attended the mass meeting in Holmes County, Mississippi, where my new friends had been summarily tried, convicted, and sentenced to exile, were no different from those from whose loins I had sprung in Amite County, Mississippi. I knew their essential impulses were honorable. I knew it well. But how could eminently decent, spiritually knowing human beings become so quickly devoid of the civility they had taught me? What was there about black-white relationships, a cubist aspect of an otherwise benign culture? I was troubled in a fashion I had seldom known before.

I sat in awe of the banished four, their free-flowing saga at once inspiring and depressing me.

It was getting late. Susan, the youngest of the Minter children, about five, came and crawled into her daddy's lap. "Why are those men camped down by the road?" she asked. I couldn't hear what he said, but I watched his eyes well up as he hugged her tightly and kissed her. "Well, isn't the sheriff a nice man to be at the bottom of the hill to take care of us," the little girl answered.

Mr. Cox had stepped outside. When he came in he held up three fingers. It was a signal that three carloads of men, ostensibly there with the sheriff, a posse comitatus, actually some of the more zealous from the mass meeting, were there to further intimidate the families and any patients, or friendly outsiders, who might come. They gathered at dusk every day, built a campfire, talked loudly, and left their liquor and beer bottles, in this prohibition county and state, strewn about the area.

"Maybe we'll go to Arizona," Dr. Minter said, his words jumping ahead of my thoughts. "Bill has asthma and needs to be in a drier climate." Bill, the oldest of the Minter children at fourteen, was reading a school book in an adjoining room. "I'm a doctor. God knows I'm not in it for the money. There will always be patients." I saw his eyes glisten as they had when he was telling his little girl good night.

Still the stories continued. We heard graphic tales of the medical practice. Mrs. Cox and Dr. Minter took turns telling them, sometimes not clear if one case or another had happened at Rochdale or Providence. To me it made no difference. All of it was of the fabric of what I was already thinking of as "Section Thirteen."

There had been a program to control the scourge of malaria. The disease was so common, the chills and fevers so regular, it was part of the calendar of the victims. Nothing could be scheduled on their "chill day." There was a new drug, still in the experimental stage. Atabrine. I had taken it during my tour of duty in the South and Central Pacific and remembered it turned white skin yellow. The Winthrop Chemical Company had furnished it to the clinic as an experiment. It was highly successful. Their patients who took the atabrine had not one case of malaria from May to October, while the control group had the usual cases. The research was probably one of the reasons Dr. Minter was in charge of malarial control in New Guinea during the war and came out with the rank of lieutenant colonel.

Mrs. Cox told of a midwife bringing her a newborn baby, daughter of an unmarried girl. The child, weak from vomiting and diarrhea, was so dehydrated the skin had no resilience at all. Her eyes, sunk deep in her head, were partly open, frozen in place like a dead person's. Wrinkles in her face gave the appearance of a very old woman. Every rib stood out, and her abdomen looked like a round black drum. "She reminded me of a baby crow with no feathers," Lindy said. "I thought at first she was dead." The midwife had been feeding the child raw cow's milk, undiluted. And since the woman had no cow of her own, the milk was borrowed from different neighbors' cows, none of them tested for the dreaded tuberculosis so often transmitted at the time to infants through unpasteurized milk. Lindy Cox kept her in a basket at home, fed her a balanced formula from a medicine dropper. "I thought little Mildred might grow up to be another Marion Anderson," Lindy said.

"Did she?" Mac Bryan asked.

"No," she answered, smiling professionally. "Little Mildred didn't make it through infancy."

Dr. Minter lightened the conversation. "One of my early patients was a cow," he laughed. A man from off the farm came to ask him about a sick cow. When one of us asked what he had prescribed, he said he didn't remember but the cow survived.

Mrs. Cox remembered trudging two miles in mud almost knee

deep where a white family of twelve lived in one room and a lean-to. The mother had double pneumonia, and two of the children were also ill. There was no resident father. A sixteen-year-old boy had made the crop.

There was a luetic clinic, for venereal disease was rampant in the area. "Thank God for penicillin," the doctor said. And many cases of crippling polio. He expressed the same gratitude for Jonas Salk, whose vaccine was then promising to eradicate polio.

Mrs. Cox told of delivering a baby in the community late at night. For breakfast an older child had made biscuits by pouring milk directly into a barrel of flour, scooping up the portion the milk saturated, and baking it in the oven of a wood stove. There was also fried salt pork. When the child indicated she had nothing with which to cut the meat, a family member handed her a spoon he was using. There were no other utensils. Though the spoon was not washed, Lindsey Hail Cox would not offend.

On another occasion a man who had been deaf for some time came to the clinic. After examining him Dr. Minter took an instrument and pulled out globs of hardened wax, immediately restoring the man's hearing. News spread quickly around the countryside that the doctor over at Providence could cure the deaf. It took some time, he said, to get the word out that he could not perform miracles.

Finally it was time to leave, and we had to consider the matter of how to get by the posse at the end of the drive. Dr. Minter said he would drive my car, as if going to the clinic, then walk through the woods to his house. At first I took exception to the idea. "This is still the United States of America," I protested. The silent smiles at my naiveté suggested there might be some question about that at the moment.

Then our good-byes were quick but warm, like old friends who know they will be together again soon. I promised to come back on Sunday.

While we visited I had noticed the voices and laughter coming from the campfire grew louder, an effect, I supposed, of the hops.

It was nearing midnight, and a heavy fog had moved in from the Delta, making murky the edge of the Loess Bluffs where the settlement was located. As we eased down the mud-slick hill, Dr. Minter said, "Let me do the talking." We slowly approached a dozen or more dark figures, outlined by the lively blaze. Eerie streams of light, like fiery ropes, cut through the fog. Some of the men stood in the drive, blocking the way. A short, dozer-wide man whose face I could barely see through the beam of his flashlight peered through the open window, shining his light on each of us. Dr. Minter greeted him by name, then told him we were guests and he was going to the clinic. Another man moved close, said, "Wait a minute," and disappeared behind the car.

"Why didn't they ask who we were?" Mac Bryan said after they had motioned us through.

Dr. Minter said, "Probably afraid you're FBI. But they'll know come morning." I knew he meant the man behind the car was copying the license number.

"Section Thirteen," I said when we let Dr. Minter out and headed west toward U.S. Highway 49. "Whatever could God have been thinking about when he let things like that happen?"

"Freedom," Mac answered, weeping. And that was all he said for a long time.

The drive back to Highway 49 seemed much longer than when we came in. I imagined rifle barrels aimed at us from behind every tree and bank. I thought of all the things we had heard, remembering especially Mr. Cox's remarks when we saw a red-tail hawk swoop down and grab a medium-size black snake slithering across an open field as we were walking around the clinic in the afternoon. "Strange metaphor," he had said. When I asked what he meant, he laughed and answered, "Well, I'm a nature buff, you know. Those hawks are getting rare. But plenty of snakes." He laughed lightly and picked up his gait. "Somehow I feel like the snake. Yet we're the endangered species." His remark jarred me as the hawk flew away with the dangling rope writhing in his beak. I reckon he means liberals in Mississippi are getting rare, I thought.

As I turned right on the paved highway and headed north, gaining speed but still respecting Mac's silence, I wondered what it all meant. Who were those five hundred people at that school-house? I had thought earlier that they were basically decent human beings. Like the ones I had grown up with in Amite County. Now I was having second thoughts. Thoughts about original sin, a doctrine I had been taught but never really believed before. Probably some were there from simple bore-dom, hungry for sport. Not really bad but tediously slow of courage. I had found myself supposing they were all from the gentry class. I knew that was not the case. Many of them were poor laborers and sharecroppers, men who were little better off than the Negroes they were there to oppose. Called "rednecks" by the insensitive, they had competed with the Freedmen following the Civil War, and the competition for bread and status had never abated. The accused before them had intended to be their friends, to offer them hope. It is the tragedy of the poor, white, rural working class of the South, those called rednecks, my people, to choose the wrong enemy. They had no stake in the Civil War and nothing to be gained by opposing the Supreme Court decision of May 17, 1954, outlawing segregation in public school education. Yet here they were, like a dying man railing and cursing at the bedside physician, blaming him for his plight, while he stands, patient and implacable, understanding but saddened by the illogic of the scene.

But what of the others—those present from sheer meanness, with satchels of mischief in their souls? Just wicked. I could find no sympathy for them. Still I was haunted by the thought that all of them were there out of certainty that their cause was just, right, and necessary, with minds muzzled by something as deep and faraway as the Edenic fall and as near at hand as the rhetoric of election year.

"And grace," Mac said after more than half an hour, as if it followed immediately the last word he had spoken.

"What?" I said.

"God was thinking of freedom. And grace." I didn't understand what he was talking about—that God made us just as free as He is, for to have done otherwise would have left no place or reason for grace. Even after I understood I still knew I wouldn't have done it that way. I would have devised some invisible tether, or perhaps a proxy god to jerk folks around and make them behave. Then reality returned. If I were that proxy god I wouldn't know who should be jerked around. Of those I had just met I knew little. Of the five hundred I knew nothing at all.

"It's the beginning of something big," Mac said when he was completely composed. How little we knew how big it would become. It was the beginning of the Second Removal of the people of Section Thirteen. The First Removal came 125 years earlier, almost to the day, at the signing of the Treaty of Dancing Rabbit Creek when, for similar reasons, the Choctaw Nation was forced to give up and leave. It was the beginning of two decades

23

of chaos and violence the professor of philosophy and I could not even imagine.

Next morning the chancellor called. He said a state senator was on campus and had asked, "What the hell was one of your men doing in Holmes County last night?" He told me not to leave my office, that someone would be over to talk to me. He said, "We don't want you to think we're afraid, but the White Citizens Council is a powerful outfit right now. We have to give them an answer."

"Yes, sir," I said. "I reckon we do."

CHAPTER 3

Best go back to the beginning. At least as far back as history will take me. Back to the land of the Choctaws, the land of my own birth. I remembered a historical marker on the edge of my father's farm in Amite County, Mississippi. It is on Highway 24, between McComb and Liberty, six counties south of Holmes. I had paid it no mind; just another marker for geriatric tourists from up North to stop and read. I knew it had something to do with the Choctaw Nation.

My father was beyond ninety and in rapidly declining health. I would begin there. Perhaps he knew stories. His mind was still clear. At least I could read the sign.

It would be the first of many trips I would make, by car, bus, and airplane, in search of the original owners of Section Thirteen, people I should have known but didn't.

I found my father sitting on the front porch of his farmhouse, the same house I was born in sixty-five years earlier. A few hundred yards from where he had been born and raised.

After a brief visit, we fell to talking about the old days. I recalled that the county I intended to write about, Holmes, had been named for David Holmes, governor of the Mississippi territory when my father's people arrived from Georgia and later first governor of the state of Mississippi. He was not a peaceful man. Our county, Amite, had been named by the French because of the cordial reception the Choctaw Indians had given them. *Amite.* While the word was in my mind, I went inside and checked the ragged old dictionary our father had bought when his children were young.

AMITY *n. pl.* -ties. Peaceful relations, as between nations; friendship. (Middle English *amite*, from Old French *amitie*, from Medieval Latin *amīcitās* from Latin *amīcus*, friend.)

Reading the definition gave me a soothing, warm feeling. Yes, yes. That is what the old man sitting on the front porch is like. Yes, yes. We of Amite County have always been a people of amity. Quickly the thought of ghastly violence during the sixties against black people in our county who wanted to register to vote flushed the notion from my head. Back outside I asked my father if there had been any Indians in this neighborhood when he was a boy. He said he didn't remember any. He did, however, recollect his mother and grandfather talking about the Indians. They had encountered many along the way from Georgia. And here as well.

"Were they friendly?"

"Oh yes. They said they were as nice as they could be. Never gave them any trouble. Said they helped them get settled when they got here." The feeling of *amīcitās* came back for a moment.

I asked him if he would like to ride up the road with me, that I wanted to read what was on the historical marker. He went inside, got his hat, and we got in the car. As I started the engine he said, "Of course, you know I'm like Grandpa Bunt, always ready to burn the other fellow's gasoline. But far as that's concerned, I can tell you what's on the marker if that's all you want to know."

I turned the motor off and got my pen as he recited the exact wording:

CEDED BY CHOCTAWS AND CHICKASAWS
IN FORT ADAMS TREATY, 1801,
CONFIRMING EARLIER BRITISH
TREATY. CONTAINED MOST OF
PRESENT WARREN, JEFFERSON,
CLAIBORNE, ADAMS, FRANKLIN,
WILKINSON, AND AMITE COUNTIES.

"Is that it?" I asked.

"Well, up at the top it says, 'Old Natchez District.' And an outline map of Mississippi. Down at the bottom it says, 'Mississippi

Historical Commission. Nineteen fifty-two.'"

I was confused. "Nineteen fifty-two? I thought that marker had been there all my life. I was twenty-eight years old in 1952."

He laughed. "Sometimes I wonder which one of us is getting old."

"Both of us," I said. "You always told us we were all the same age."

"Let's ride over to Liberty," he said. "The marker is just two hundred yards up the road. We'll stop and you can read it for yourself."

He had every word correct and the counties in order. I commented on his amazing memory but he wouldn't have it as anything special. "I've passed that sign enough times to know how much it weighs," he said.

"Then our farm was included in that treaty?" I asked. "Our place is in Amite County."

"Son, I thought you went to college. You didn't read the sign. It said *most* of Amite County was in the treaty. The line started right at our property line. Not that it was our property then. The treaty was from that point west to the Mississippi River at Natchez."

"Most of seven counties," I said. "That was a lot of land."

"Yes," he said in a low, soft voice, not laughing anymore. It was as if he was feeling bequeathed transgressions, sins we did not commit but which were now ours to acknowledge and atone for. "The fathers have eaten sour grapes and the children's teeth are set on edge," I remember thinking.

I had decided to research the history of Section Thirteen, Township Sixteen in Holmes County. This was the appropriate place to begin. On the property line of my father's farm. Which, though not lost by the Choctaws in 1801, would be a few years later. It soon belonged to some white people from Georgia. My people. Appropriate also because, I was to learn, this treaty was the beginning of the end for the Choctaws. It was the first time they ceded a parcel of their homeland to the United States. Here they gave up 2,641,920 choice acres. There had been a bad crop year, and during the famine the Choctaw farmers had bought supplies on credit at the trading posts they had allowed the government to build on their land fifteen years earlier. The debts were canceled at the Treaty of Fort Adams.

The historical marker did not tell the story entire. While the treaty did confirm earlier British lines, it also cost the Choctaw

Nation more than two and a half million of its most fertile acres. Perhaps there is no such thing as unmodified history. Maybe the whole truth is too forbidding to the soul of a nation.

The road we were riding was more than a hundred miles from Section Thirteen in Holmes County. But it was the trail to follow. The scent blew hot and cold. Many things would happen along the way. We would bury our father two miles east of the line of the Treaty of Fort Adams. I would abandon the project several times, start again. The publisher sent my agent a contract, along with a research grant. After my father died I sent the money back. Of the many things he had taught me, honor was high on the list. It wasn't fair to spend money I was doing nothing to earn.

The story chased and obsessed me. I began reading books on the history of the Choctaws. Angie Debo, Horatio Cushman, Grant Foreman, Charles Kapler, Robert Cotterill, Mary Elizabeth Young, Arthur DeRosier, Jr., and many others. All fine historians. All in agreement that what was done to the Choctaws was one of the darkest blots in America's history.

I spent time in archives and state libraries in Tennessee, Mississippi, and North Carolina. I made numerous trips from our home in Tennessee to Holmes County and Section Thirteen in Mississippi—looking, listening, learning, being there, flirting with the ghosts. I got a manual and audio cassette of the Choctaw language and began learning words and phrases, falling in love with the lyrical voice of the woman on the tapes, fantasizing her exquisite visage.

Old assumptions had to be abandoned. Things I thought had happened didn't. At least, not the way I had learned them. A people I had thought of as nomadic semisavages turned out to be a gentle, highly developed society—peaceful, democratic, ambitious, lovers of life and liberty, addicted to the land of their ancestors. I learned also there was not always warfare and strife between the European settlers and the original inhabitants they found. Although the behavior of the Spanish, French, and English had been reprehensible at the policy level, there were, in each era, those of the rank and file who became friends and neighbors with the native Choctaws. While Hernando De Soto, in search of gold in 1540, would disgrace the Spanish throne with the bloody rout at what is now Mobile, that would not be the total picture during the three hundred years that followed. Certainly the French and English who came later were motivated by mercantilism, a form of emerging capitalism, and devotion to worldly goods seems always to claim ascendancy over virtues of the heart, but there were from the beginning those whites who rose above the courts of evil. They did not prevail. Mercantilism proved little better friend to people of the soil than the feudalism it had replaced. Feudalism had its serfs; mercantilism had its slaves, field hands, and finally sharecroppers. Always someone at the top, many at the bottom, few in between. In Europe and the New Country.

Opinions of old heroes had to be revised. Old enemies reconsidered. Even Thomas Jefferson, one I had admired for many reasons—among them that in response to the prompting of two of my Baptist ancestors, John Leland and Isaac Backus, he and James Madison had been the strongest advocates of civil and religious liberties and were responsible for the First Amendment. My assumption was that Jefferson was friendly to the people Europeans had found when they came. Even though it was true on the surface, I was unsettled to see documentation by Arthur DeRosier, Jr., that Jefferson had encouraged the Choctaws to run deeply in debt at the trading posts because, he said, they were then willing to lop off the debts with cessions of land. He openly called it bribery and said bribery was preferable to war. No doubt it was, but in addition to his advocacy of extortion, he later said if that policy did not work he was prepared to push a constitutional amendment to remove the Indians by force to the West. I had admired his advocacy of civil liberties for those who had recently arrived on this continent. Now I must deal with his espousal of cattle drives for those whose lands we arrogated.

Conversely, I was perplexed to learn that John C. Calhoun, whom I had known mainly through his political rhetoric on the matter of slavery, and whom I had deemed the sire of racist demagogues of my own time, had been a leader in urging fairness and moderation toward the Choctaws and other southeastern nations when he was secretary of war under James Monroe. I had not looked beyond his sea-granite eyes. Perhaps only the poets ever do.

Finally I would learn that little has changed at either the national or local level in our attitude and actions toward those whose nation we appropriated. Mammon prevails; ideals become blurred even to the righteous when silver is the prize.

On the journey I met many of the distant past. Choctaws and

white settlers, vassals and potentates. Those whose god was clearly mammon, those who strived to serve a true God, and those who confused the two. Names I did not know, many of which I could not pronounce. Chiefs like Puckshunubbee, Mushulitubee, and Pushmataha. Ordinary folk like Oaklaryubbe, Ishtehaka, and Tieberboomah. Big Axe, Red Wolf, and Living War Club.

It was the young who spoke loudest to me and who kept coming back. Their names are legion, their deeds harder to come by in the annals of history. I cannot here recount all their names nor transcribe all their dreams and yearnings.

A few stand out. Luther Cashdollar is one. Jesse Furver another. As individuals, they are an invention. Yet they are as real as neighbors next door. I spent time with them and know them well—what they looked like, thought like, smelled like. And when I meet them in the Great Beyond, I shall embrace them and address each as Brother. I gave them names to keep the journey in a tractable arena. The stories they tell are true. As a white American, I would be more at peace with my history if they were fiction. But they aren't.

I met Luther Cashdollar, a Choctaw youngster, at a mission school not far from the Yalobusha River in the Western District of the Choctaw Nation. Eliot Mission School was established by Presbyterian missionaries in 1818. Luther entered a few years later. I was interested in the school because Presbyterians were most prevalent among those who had founded and operated Providence Farm in Holmes County. Luther Cashdollar was said to be the brightest student in the short but distinguished history of Eliot School. I wish I could have known him then, instead of 160 years later.

I came across Jesse Furver one day while going through some records in the Holmes County chancery clerk's office that Mrs. Jamie Moore had graciously made available to me. And later on a solitary and sultry evening at Section Thirteen, where I had camped for the night awaiting any soul from the past who might come by to pass some time with me. Was it mere fantasy that I spoke with him that night on the banks of Chicopa Creek? Did I dream, aided by my evening toddies, that a callow young man with a cowlick and modest frame had spent some time with me and told me his story? Who's to say?

I followed these two a long way and learned much from them. I watched their friendship deepen as they outgrew childish ways and took their places in a world for which the times, though not their years, had prepared them. I tracked them through fields and forests, watched their toil and capers while summer's sun had its day, and finally, when winter clouds shadowed them, felt their pain.

Getting to know Luther Cashdollar gave me an aching appreciation for his people. Getting to know Jesse Furver brought both pride and remorse about my own people. Knowing the two together gave me new insights about the numbered days of us all, in the knowledge that no civilization as we know it lasts for long, and that any intentional community formed by the notion of Manifest Destiny writes its own epitaph with sword for quill and blood for ink.

Sometimes, when sitting alone in the woods on long summer days, I still miss those two, and imagine I hear their cries.

It was late summer of 1827, another year when nothing slept, and independence was a continuing theme. Isabella Hardenburgh, a slave woman of thirty-seven years, had just been freed in New York by that state's Emancipation Act, a warning shot across the bow of the ship of slavery. She would change her name to Sojourner Truth and begin a crusade that would leave her a saint in the hearts of generations to come. In the Battle of Nabrarino, the French, English, and Russian fleet had intervened in the Greek war for independence, destroying the Turkish-Egyptian fleet. Joseph Smith discovered the gold plates that became the Book of Mormon, and a German scientist named Friedrich Wohler produced aluminum, destined to become the sustainer of soft-drink makers and the curse of latter-day environmentalists.

The first time I encountered Luther Cashdollar and Jesse Furver together, they were romping around in a cleared area beside a small pyramidal cloth tent. The tent belonged to Dr. Alexander Talley, a physician and Methodist preacher who would soon begin a camp meeting for the white settlers and Choctaws on the edge of the Loess Bluffs in the Western District of the Choctaw Nation.

Each boy carried a dried slippery elm limb about three feet long. They were playing stick ball, swinging and hacking at a dried sycamore seed case, trying to knock it through a hoop they had woven from broom sedge. They were a team, battling an imaginary team they pretended was defending the goal. A tan and white bench-legged feist named Cito, the Choctaw word for big, ran with them, barking in unison with their swings. They screeched and complained good-naturedly when they stumbled or tripped over the frolicking dog, sometimes falling over him on purpose, making him part of the game. He soon caught the seed case with his teeth, breaking it into bits, the fragile, tissue-like pieces scattering with the wind. Luther Cashdollar, the larger of the two boys, heaved Jesse onto his shoulders so he could pull a green sweetgum ball from a low-hanging limb.

"If'n we bust this'un we'll git a hickernut," Jesse Furver yelled as he slid from Luther's back.

Luther Cashdollar was a full-blooded Choctaw lad of about fifteen. Jesse Furver, about the same age, was the son of a white settler couple who farmed on Choctaw land a few miles from the small settlement where Luther lived with his parents. The settlement, bordering Chicopa Creek in Chief Greenwood Leflore's district, consisted of a few families who had come from the Eastern District of the nation to hunt and trap the prolific wetlands. Instead of returning at the end of the season, which generally lasted several months, wives and children with them to assist in jerking the meat, tanning the hides, drying fruits and berries, they simply stayed on, cleared land, planted crops, raised their families. Their village was on the very edge of the Loess Bluffs, overlooking the vast expanse of wilderness leading to the Mississippi River.

Luther Cashdollar was darker than most Choctaws. His silky black hair, braided until recently, hung in long, undulating strands, covering his ears and upper back. The whites of his eyes appeared disproportionately large as they outlined the flashing black irises that glowed with intensity in the excitement of their game. Or whenever he was challenged. His substantial biceps tapered to small wrists, and even smaller hands. He wore un-dyed, hand-woven pants and shirt with a drawstring for a belt.

Jesse Furver, though tanned and freckled by the sun, seemed ashen beside Luther. His blond hair, weather yellowed, was a little shorter than Luther's. Except for a tidy cowlick, which seemed pasted at the very center of his forehead, his hair bounced and waved as he ran.

Jesse was small for his age. He was short and on the chubby side. For some reason, when they looked at him, some people thought he was not very smart. Luther, perhaps intuitively, perhaps because they had been best friends and playmates all their lives, knew better.

Jesse could not run as fast as Luther, and his swing with the stick was not as swift. Luther appeared not to notice, never commented on it. On the other hand, he never intentionally let Jesse outdo him in a contest. Each carried his own weight and did the best he could. Jesse's pants and shirt were identical to Luther's. Neither boy wore shoes.

The summer of 1827 had been hot with little rain. Chicopa Creek, where the two boys often fished and bathed, was almost dry. Fish in deeper spots in the creek bed, which still held water, panted at the surface for oxygen.

They tired of playing and stretched out underneath a clump of small cottonwood trees. Cito walked across the chest of first one and then the other, licking their faces. The dog belonged to Luther but showed no partiality.

"*Laspah toffa,*" Jesse said.

"Yes, hot summer," Luther answered, smiling approvingly at Jesse's Choctaw.

Luther had learned to speak good English at the Eliot Mission School and wanted Jesse to know his language too. Sometimes they would play school, with Luther as teacher. From childhood he had possessed some of the eloquence for which the Choctaws were well known among Europeans who continued to encroach upon them. This natural bent had been encouraged, honed, and tuned by his teachers at the Eliot Mission School. Jesse loved to hear him launch into a lengthy oration Luther had memorized from Chief Pushmataha or one of the other great chiefs.

Jesse had never been to a formal school. His mother had taught him to read and write, but he knew nothing of grammar, history, and little of arithmetic. Though his parents cautioned him about the things Luther might teach him, especially about Choctaw and white dealings, Jesse looked forward to their time together.

Eliot School had been established in 1819 not far from where the Yazoo River joined the Yalobusha. John C. Calhoun, secretary of war, had encouraged plans for the education of young Choctaws. Thomas Jefferson had advocated it more than a decade earlier but apparently saw it more as a means of effecting removal of the various nations to the west, more as expediency than obligation. Calhoun saw it as a dictate of conscience, and with the encouragement of Greenwood Leflore, a half-French Choctaw who would later become chief of the Western District and for a time chief of the entire Choctaw Nation; Pushmataha, chief of the Southern District of the Choctaw Nation; and others invited a Presbyterian missionary, Cyrus Kingsbury, to build the school.

An earlier beginning had been a prayer meeting in New England in 1806 when three Williams College students met in a haystack and came from their prayers determined to civilize and Christianize the heathens near at hand and far away. It was the spawning of the American Board of Commissioners for Foreign Missions, an agency that would sponsor many missions and schools to the Choctaws and other tribes and nations.

More than three hundred Choctaw boys and girls applied for the first class at Eliot in 1819. Only eighty were admitted. Luther Cashdollar entered in 1824 and, according to Kingsbury, was the smartest student to attend the school in its short history. Within three days he had mastered the alphabet, and two months later he could read as well as his Lancastrian teachers, those who were also students but advanced enough to teach the new ones. Although the mission schools concentrated on a vocational type of education, feeling such subjects as the classics, foreign languages, and higher mathematics were not appropriate for the aboriginal mind, exceptional students were sometimes singled out for those subjects also. They were given special attention by sympathetic teachers.

Luther excelled in language, history, literature, and Bible studies and was a hard worker in the fields and shops as well. Though advanced in those things, at playtime he became a frisky and prankish child.

By the early nineteenth century, a few of the brightest students from the Southern nations were being sent back east for university education. Cyrus Kingsbury, before Luther had completed his second year, had already made arrangements for him to attend Brown University, where he had gone, and hoped Luther would then go to Andover for theological studies as he had done. Kingsbury and the other teachers recognized in Luther those qualities they had come to the frontier to nurture. His statuesque frame was a picture of health and hope; his mind was brilliant, though impenetrable to anyone except the few he chose to let enter. Cyrus Kingsbury and Jesse Furver were among the few.

Luther and his sister had been taken to the school by their aged grandfather, who told Mr. Kingsbury, "I now give them to you, to take them by the hand and the heart, and hold them fast. I will now hold them by the end of their fingers." Two deerskins were paid for their tuition.

The school was supported by the federal government, the Choctaw Nation, and the American Board of Commissioners for Foreign Missions. Though Luther's father, Bolokta, had wanted his children to attend, he was suspicious of the missionary motive, resented the teaching of English to the neglect of the Choctaw language, and refused to be converted or to change his name to English.

A black-maned, blaze-faced sorrel mare hitched nearby nuzzled Jesse's ribs. "Go on, hosi̷," he giggled, pushing her away.

"Yeah, go on, issobah," Luther said, standing up and turning away to hide his smile, not telling Jesse hosi̷ meant bird. Luther felt a small lump on the mare's back, looked at Jesse as if to confirm a diagnosis. When he nodded in agreement, Luther took the lump between his thumbs and mashed, popping the larva of a botfly from its base underneath the horse's hide. He grimaced at the string of bloody pus that came out with the larva, wiped it off with a green leaf, ground it underneath his leather-tough heel, and sat down. "That thing looks like a grubworm," he said. "Wolves aren't supposed to get ripe till winter."

The horse, named Fičik for a blaze on its face looking like a star, belonged to Luther, but both boys rode it. Generally together. They had ridden it to the campsite, following the banks of Chicopa Creek that paralleled the settlement. There was a thin leather rein around her neck. No bridle or saddle.

"Wherebouts did you git named Cashdollar?" Jesse asked. It was as if he had never thought about it before.

"Where'd you get your name?" Luther said, jostling him playfully.

"My mama and papa give it to me," he said. "But yo papa's name ain't Cashdollar. So wherebouts you git it?"

Luther explained he was given the name at the mission school when he was baptized. "There was this Irish, or maybe she was from Scotland, lady there. She was sort of a missionary too. I reckon she liked me. And that was her name. Lilly Marie Cashdollar. She cooked and sewed and told us about Jesus and let me study extra things."

They watched a flock of turkey buzzards soaring nearby, searching for carrion. The birds drifted in the wind which had settled to a gentle breeze, not once flapping their wings or straying outside the circle formation. They moved so slowly and precisely they seemed fixed on a spindle, moving a little lower with each rotation. The boys could see the naked heads of the vultures, looking like pieces of the red clay they sometimes helped Luther's mother dig from a clay bank on the lowest part of the Loess Bluffs for making pottery.

"Wonder what them things is after," Jesse said.

"Maybe us," Luther said, sighing, without expression. Jesse thought he was making a joke, but Luther didn't laugh. So he didn't. "You know what they like to eat the most?" Luther asked. He said it hurriedly, as if to cancel what he had just said. "They like to eat dead skunks the most. They'll eat a dead skunk before they'll eat chicken."

"Why they just eat dead stuff?" Jesse asked.

"And I'll tell you something else. If you get close to them they'll throw up on you. They'll eat all that rotten skunk and then throw up on you if you get too close. But Dr. Kingsbury told us not to say throw up. He said white people back where he came from didn't say that." Jesse appeared baffled, like he didn't understand why Luther was talking so fast, seemed piqued, and wondered why he didn't answer his question.

"Why they eat just dead stuff?" Jesse asked again.

"He said back where he came from, in New Hampshire, white people said, let's see. I think it was re-gurg-u-tate. Something like that."

"My papa calls it puking," Jesse said, not asking his question again.

Luther didn't respond, just stood watching the vultures who were by then at treetop level. Suddenly, though, he began speaking again, like he had just heard what Jesse had asked. "They eat dead things because their claws aren't made like hawks and eagles and such. They can't use them to kill live things."

"Their feet deformed? Like me, I reckon," Jesse said.

"Nothing wrong with your size and nothing wrong with buzzards' feet," Luther said, looking him sternly in the eyes. "Everything is made the way it's made and that's the way it's supposed to be. Buzzards aren't supposed to kill with their feet and we aren't supposed to be the same size."

"Well, s'posed or not, I'm a runt. My papa says I'm a runt."

One of the buzzards pulled its wings in quickly and dropped out of sight. One by one the others did the same.

While the two boys were talking, people had been arriving for the camp meeting from each direction of Chicopa Creek. There was about an equal number of Choctaws and whites. Men, women, and children. Most of the white settlers came in wagons. The Choctaws walked or were on horseback. Dr. Talley was there, and two men with him were showing people where to hitch their wagons, and in the case of the Choctaws, where to tie their horses and spread their blankets. White settlers were guided to one area, Choctaws to another.

"Let's go see what them buzzards are after," Jesse said.

"Yeah," Luther answered. "Papa said Chief Leflore won't be here until tomorrow. He always interprets for the preacher. I wish they would let me do it but they won't. Papa said Chief Leflore won't stay out here in these woods with the rest of us. He'll get here just in time for the preaching. Papa and my uncle say the chief is rich. He won't stay out here. So let's go see what those buzzards are after." Sometimes Jesse would repeat what Luther had just said, using his correct grammar. Jesse had heard his parents and other white settlers criticize Luther for "talking like he's as smart as white people." Jesse wished he could talk pretty like Luther.

The sun had disappeared behind the clearing. Low clouds had rolled in from the Delta swamps and a light fog hovered over the area. "We'd better hurry," Luther said. "Buzzards don't eat after dark. They always go home before dark."

The air was heavy as they moved down the hill toward the creek bed, Cito right behind them. Despite the moisture of the fog, breathing was more difficult for them, almost like trying to breathe in a vacuum. They held onto each other as they lumbered along, briars tearing at their clothes, the warm misty air a ghostly breathing on their faces, the luminous rays of the sun breaking through the clouds dancing through the bosky slope in strobic bursts.

"Wait!" Luther whispered, jerking Jesse to a halt, then dropping to his knees. Cito stopped beside him.

Jesse motioned that he had not heard anything.

Luther pulled him down beside him and pointed. There were

the buzzards. A bustling, hissing mass of beaks and feathers.

The two boys edged closer. In the midst of the hopping vultures they saw hundreds of dead fish. Of many sizes and colors. Carp, eels, catfish, sun perch, minnows, and buffalo. In life, friends, or natural enemies. They had become trapped in a shallow spot in the creek. When the water dried up, they died in the sun.

Luther and Jesse watched the carrionic banquet, watched as the hungry birds tore into the bloated dead, sometimes taking but one bite before jumping to another, the crepitation of the gas-filled bellies sounding like blowguns.

Suddenly Jesse broke the hold Luther still had on his sleeve. He ran wildly toward the gorging birds, screaming, flailing his arms. The startled vultures sat immobilized as Jesse landed in their midst, then could not escape his rage. Kicking, grabbing, stomping, he scattered them in every direction. Wings seemed paralyzed as they struggled to gain altitude, spewing their putrid fare as they fled.

Luther had not moved. He just hunkered there, watching Jesse's frenzy. He seemed to sanction and understand what he was seeing. When the last one was gone, Luther stood erect, called Jesse by name, then moved slowly and calmly to where he stood. "I did what I could," Jesse said as Luther patted his shoulder. Luther did not answer and said nothing as they made their way back to the campsite. Both boys appeared to understand.

As they walked they heard the ominous hooting of a great horned owl far away, too early in the evening. Nearer by the last evening music of a bluebird, the angry canting of a blue jay, and the chirps of what sounded like a thousand sparrows with their seeming predilection for optimism, as if testing a God on record as marking their fall, altogether a mingling clamor staking its primeval claim.

They passed the last of summer's wildflowers: spider lilies, dock-leaved smartweed, pokeweed drooping with their purplish-ink berries, cloverlike heads of rosy milkwort, and bear grass with its tall dome-shaped blossoms rising out of a cluster of a hundred bayonets, blooming far out of its season.

Two young boys. Walking along. One knowing a bit more than the other. One suspecting a lot and feeling almost more than he could stand.

Getting a non-Choctaw name and learning to speak the English language with the tongue of a New England gentleman were not the only things Luther had garnered from the Eliot Mission School. Cyrus Kingsbury, the stern Calvinist, was steeped in his own history and religion and worked hard to plant both in the minds, and hearts, of the young Choctaws who came to him for learning. Yet he patiently heard the stories of their history and religion, adapting their myths to his myths, certain his myths were eternal truth, just as certain that theirs would not long survive in the white heat of his God's word.

But he listened. Sometimes before speaking. Listened to their account of Choctaw creation at Nanih Waiya, a mound few of them had ever seen but of which they all knew well.

The earth had once been a great plain, they told him. A supreme being came and constructed a huge mound. Inside it humans were formed. One by one they emerged from a tiny hole, dried themselves on the rampart, and scattered into tribes. The Muskogee went east, the Cherokee followed, became lost because of a great fire, and headed north and settled. The Chickasaw stopped near the Cherokee. Last were the Choctaws, who, when dried, chose to stay near Nanih Waiya. When enough people had emerged, the supreme being stamped the hole with his foot and told those he had created they would live always. Not being sure that they had heard him correctly, they asked him to say it again. Angered that his creatures had questioned the creator, he revoked the blessing. Death became a reality.

It was not far from Cyrus Kingsbury's story. He told them of Adam and Eve. They too were created from the earth, questioned their God, and suffered a similar penalty.

And another of their legends: Their people had once lived far, far toward the setting sun. There they had suffered persecution, defeat, and captivity. A great national council was held where it was unanimously decided they should remove to a new land. Two brothers, Cahta and Cikasah, accepted by all for their skills in war and wisdom in matters of controversy, were selected to lead them. Their medicine man, also the prophet, had it revealed to him by the Great Spirit that the direction of their journey would be indicated by a pole set in the midst of their encampment. The pole was set in the ground in the evening. When morning came it leaned in the direction of the sun's rising. Each morning they followed the leaning of the talismanic pole. Weeks. Months they wandered. Deserts, mountains, waters, and forests did not stay them. Coming to the edge of a vast, flowing water, they supposed it was the end of their pilgrimage. Morning proved them wrong; the pole still pointed east. Rafts and canoes were constructed for the crossing, and within weeks all were on the other side Through it all the bounty of wilderness game sustained them. At the banks of a smaller river, the Yazoo, a torrential rain delayed them. For days and nights the flood beat upon them. Yet each morning the pole stood rigid and erect, unaffected by the raging water, no longer leaning eastward, pointing only to the sky. Cahta and Cikasah declared they had arrived.

Cyrus Kingsbury sought to emend the tale with the Genesis and Exodus account. Cahta and Cikasah became Moses and Aaron. The far distant land to the west was Egypt, the displaced nomads the children of Israel. The magical pole became the pillar of fire guiding the people from captivity; the mighty Mississippi, the Red Sea; Yazoo country, the Promised Land. Nanih Waiya was the mountain where Moses talked to God; the Yazoo rains, the flood of Noah.

Each comparative story brought them closer to Jesus. The Choctaws knew already of creation and sin. Salvation was on the way.

The camp was neatly arranged around the tent and meeting area when the two boys got back from the buzzard venture. A few of the white and Choctaw men talked in small groups, but most stayed with their own people.

Huge red oak logs, previously split in halves and hewn smooth with broadaxes to serve as seats, had been pulled into place. They had been arranged in rows, six on each side of a wide aisle. One for the white settlers, one for Choctaws. There was a more narrow aisle in the middle of each section. Men and women did not sit together. A rude triangular pulpit, fashioned between two logs, faced the long benches. Directly behind it was Dr. Talley's tent, bedroom for the preacher—a sort of vestibule to this simple edifice of the Lord.

"Let's run over to the old mound," Luther said when they had both spoken to their parents. "We still have time."

He hurriedly untied Ficik, jumped on her back, and pulled Jesse up behind him. With a quick jerk on the rein to the right and a firm kick on her side, Luther whirled the pony around and headed away from the camp. After a sharp slap on the flank from

Jesse, she broke into a rough trot, changing then to a rocking gallop, Cito yelping and nipping at her heels. They did not slow down until they reached the bottom of the mound.

Leaving her hobbled, the rein around a fetlock, they tried to outrun each other to the top. The untended mound was covered with weeds, bushes, and full-grown trees. It was not a large mound, about fifty yards square. It was one of the favorite spots for the two boys. It was here Luther told Jesse the stories of the Ninah Waiya mound, more than a hundred miles away, describing what he remembered of it in detail. And of Cahta and Cikasah, fathers of the Choctaw and Chickasaw peoples.

"My papa says yo folks buried in this thing," Jesse said as they meandered around the top of the mound.

"No one is buried under this mound," Luther said. "This thing was built, well, Dr. Kingsbury said, maybe ten thousand years ago. He said that was before the Choctaws got here."

"Well, that's what my papa tole me. He says bone-pickers put 'um in there."

Luther laughed, perhaps appalled again at how little the whites knew of the Choctaw Nation's history. He recited the Choctaw words for bone-pickers. "*Na foni ayyowah.*"

Jesse tried to repeat the phonetic sounds, making Luther laugh again. "I saw a bone-picker one time," Luther said. "Old fellow. Came to our house when my grandpa died. Said Grandpa would want to be buried the old-time way. Papa said he and my uncle gave him something to eat and sent him away." Luther picked a scarlet-bright berry from a black alder bush nearby, thumped it over the edge of the mound. "Gone as that berry," he said, watching it disappear. Then he described the burial custom of his people when white people first came to Choctaw land.

When someone died, the body was covered with a blanket or bear skin and placed on a high scaffold. Benches were built around the scaffold. Each day members of the family would cover their heads, sit on the benches, and bewail the dead. When a number of corpses had been placed there, and the flesh was decayed and falling off the bones, the bone-pickers were notified. Together they set a day for the official burial. The bone-pickers dispatched their messengers to all the communities and villages where bodies were waiting. The messengers gave the family a bundle of split canes, no bigger than a broom-straw. Each day the mourners threw one stick away as they accompanied the bones to the bone house, a central location where the bones were kept until they were buried or placed in a mound. They arrived when the last stick was gone; it was the Choctaw way of counting time.

Before that day arrived, however, the work of the bone-pickers—actually bone gatherers, because their function was to clean and gather the bones for burial—must be performed at the respective homes. They had fingernails four to six inches long, used as instruments to pull the shriveled and decayed flesh from off the bones of the deceased. When this was accomplished, the bones were washed thoroughly and placed in a coffin. On the appointed day for the mass interment, processions from all the houses made their way to the bone house and placed the coffins on the mound. After long and sustained weeping and wailing, the coffins were covered, each ceremony bringing the mound higher.

"Let's go home," Jesse said when Luther had finished his graphic story. Jesse seemed sorry he had mentioned the subject of bone-pickers at all.

"I'm just telling you what my papa told me. That's the way he said it was done. I never saw it." Luther told Jesse that now they buried dead folks the way white folks did, only in a sitting instead of stretched-out position.

"Who is your uncle?" Jesse asked.

"You know Uncle Brash," Luther said. "He lives right across the woods from us. When he's not gone. You've seen him a thousand times. He translates for the government."

"Oh yeah," Jesse said. "But he don't never talk to me. I think he don't like me."

"Papa says he likes the chief too much. Says Uncle Brash wants to be white."

"I'm white," Jesse said, bringing one hand up close to his eyes, rubbing the skin.

"Nothing wrong with being white if you're white," Luther said, thumping another berry off the mound. "Uncle Brash gave up his Choctaw name. My papa won't let them change his name. I'm proud of him."

"You ain't got no Choctaw name," Jesse said in a confused tone.

"Sure I do. Tunapinachuffa. That's my name."

"I can't even say that word," Jesse said, then stumbled awkwardly over it.

"That's why they gave me Luther," he said, laughing and slapping Jesse sharply on the back, then serious again. "But I will be Tunapinachuffa again soon. When they take us away."

Neither boy spoke for a long time after that. They stood like carved totems, outlined against the sky. From where they stood they saw a small whirlwind in the distance, gaining momentum as it moved. Leaves and dust swirled round and round, climbing higher until it blew itself out toward the sun. Luther seemed glum as he watched it disappear.

Before they started back down the mound, Luther pulled a folded piece of paper from his pocket, studied it for a minute or more, then handed it to Jesse. "You understand all this?" he asked. It was a circular advertising the camp meeting.

> CAMP MEETING
> *A Camp-Meeting will be holden under*
> *the superintendence of the Rev.*
> *Alexander Talley, to begin on*
> *Tuesday, the tenth day of August*
> *on the Chicopa Creek Camp-Ground, five*
> *miles North of Tchula, and continue*
> *four days, on the land of Amos*
> *Northcutt.*

"All but one word," Jesse said.

"I'm not talking about the words. I'm talking about why they would say that land belongs to Mr. Northcutt."

"It belong to yo papa?" Jesse asked, his voice getting louder when he didn't understand.

"Not my papa. Well, yes, my papa too. And me. All of us. Nobody owns the land. Everybody owns the land. Papa says Uncle Brash claims it but he doesn't own it by himself."

Jesse still didn't understand.

"It's Choctaw land. Nobody owns Choctaw land. Not even Choctaws. It belongs to the Great Spirit." Luther stumbled over the words "Great Spirit," thought for a moment, and went on.

For the next few minutes he was no longer the Christian Luther Cashdollar. He was Tunapinachuffa the Choctaw. He told again the legends of his origin, described the long, arduous wanderings of Cahta, the people bearing the ancestral bones to be placed in the bowels of Nanih Waiya for all times. He stood on this unnamed mound and recited words he had heard since infancy, words of Cahta's prophet Book Bearer standing on the leaning mound, Nanih Waiya, and announcing, "I give you these hunting grounds for your home. The land, the forests, and streams are yours. When you leave them, you die." He had not screamed the words, actually had almost whispered them, but his skin glistened with sweat, neck veins bulged, and his dark eyes glowed with the intensity of one completing the most spirited harangue. It was if something had prompted him, had jarred him to reality from a protracted and evasive fantasy.

He continued to stand, looking down at Jesse sitting as his audience. "Why must the tongue of the white man be forever forked with guile?" Jesse felt as if he were watching an old man. It was as if Luther had rehearsed what he was saying. Jesse had never heard him speak this way. It made him feel uncomfortable, as if he had somehow erred.

"Three hundred years ago De Soto the Spaniard came. With horses we had not seen before, steel we could not match. Our chief, Tuscaloosa, befriended him. As reward he demanded our women, slew our warriors, and left sickness from which we did not soon recover." Luther spoke like a seasoned orator who had made this same speech many times before.

"The French came. The English came. We bade them well, fought their wars, shared our goods, worshiped their God, took their names, bore their children." He raised his voice and gestured wildly over the mound's top and the country below, as if his lone listener had suddenly become a multitude.

"Forty years ago we treated with them at Hopewell. We journeyed to South Carolina to discuss our lands on their terms. There we gave them rights to establish trading posts in our nation. In return they promised peace and friendship forever. They agreed that any who wandered within our boundaries would be subject to our laws and not theirs. It was not the first of many lies."

"I ain't s'posed to talk about this stuff," Jesse mumbled to himself. "My papa tole me." But he continued to sit transfixed on the mound top as Luther spoke with the sagacity Jesse heard nowhere else. Luther spoke of white souls trashed with avarice, of demeanor only God could pardon, digressing often to dispel some notion many whites had about the Choctaws, or to explain some long-abandoned custom. Somehow Jesse did not hear what Luther was saying as words of anger. More as protection from some far-off memory, standing there like a bronze statue, never once fading into incoherence. Jesse felt and believed it all.

Jesse had heard his father refer to Choctaws as "flatheads." It had been centuries since Choctaw mothers had bound their offspring's head with sandbags for the first year, causing their foreheads to develop in a sloped shape. Luther compared it to the white women's custom of binding their bodies with corsets. He said Cyrus Kingsbury told them one such custom was no worse than another.

Luther mentioned Andrew Jackson on the banks of the Yazoo River but did not explain. He was referring to the meeting Andrew Jackson had convened in 1819 with the Choctaw chiefs to try to convince them to migrate west of the Mississippi. The year before, John C. Calhoun, as secretary of war, had appointed Jackson and two others as a delegation to explore the possibility of removal. But he had instructed the three commissioners to be polite, to demand nothing, and if the chiefs resisted, to thank them for their kindness and leave the Choctaw Nation immediately. It was a brief meeting; the Choctaw chiefs declined forthwith even to discuss removal. Chief Pushmataha delivered a powerful oratorical summary to the delegation in response to Jackson's ultimatum, a stinging insult which Jackson never forgot. Andrew Jackson, the frontier hero, did not hold with the idea of "asking" Indians anything. Negotiate, or else!

Luther pretended now to be the great Chief Pushmataha as he pressed on, still more as teacher than angry victim. "Six years ago we fought for you against our own kinsmen, the Creeks, on the Black Warrior River. Three years ago we stood with you against your people the British at New Orleans. At Fort St. Stevens you promised we would be forever friends; that never again would your United States be allowed to mistreat us."

Luther, his hands clasped behind his back, pranced about the area, his voice rising steadily now, answering, in the words of Pushmataha, the threats and cajoling of Andrew Jackson, which Luther had heard so many times he knew them by heart. "And now you tell us of the rich lands across the river you wish generously to give us." He paused briefly, wiping the sweat from his brow with his shirt sleeve, glowering at Jesse as if Jesse were Andrew Jackson. Jesse watched him, uneasy with the changed expression. "I am well acquainted, my old comrade-in-arms, with the country contemplated for us. I have often had my feet sorely bruised there by the roughness of its surface."

When Luther finished he pretended to break camp and ride away, just as he imagined those attending the aborted scheme of Jackson had done. Then he sat down in front of Jesse and in his normal voice told him of the Treaty at Doak's Stand signed in 1820. Like a child sharing a secret with a playmate, he talked of the more than five million acres his people had ceded to the United States in exchange for land in Arkansas, land already claimed by white settlers, and of the deception and trickery perpetrated upon his people by Andrew Jackson. Jesse had no idea what all of it meant but he felt comfortable with his friend. Although Luther Cashdollar did not know it at the time, Andrew Jackson, stung by the rebuff on the Yazoo River and soon to be president of the United States, would know no peace until his baleful purpose had been effected.

"How you know all this stuff?" Jesse asked as they made their way down the mound.

"How do I know?" Luther said. As they jumped as one on the back of Fičik he whooped, "*Chahta hapia hoke!*" Racing in the direction of the camp, he screamed it over and over, alternating from Choctaw to English, the galloping hooves of Fičik and the yelping of Čito seeming in cadence and unison. "We are Choctaw! *Chahta hapia hoke!* We are Choctaw! *Chahta hapia hoke!*" Jesse picked up the chant and they continued until they reached the campground.

Luther and Jesse sat on the back row of the split-log benches. They had been laughing and talking as they waited for the campers to finish the morning meal and convene for the first preaching service. Through the tent flap they could see Dr. Talley and Greenwood Leflore, along with a stout Choctaw man, sitting on the ground enjoying a social smoke of the pipe. The fragrant smoke of the tobacco laced with sumac leaves drifted through the opening, and Jesse and Luther leaned forward to catch it in their nostrils. As the fifty or so men, women, and children began to file down the aisle and take their seats, one of the exhorters—assistant preachers whose job was to encourage those who began to catch the spirit, or attend them when the spirit possessed them, for they sometimes fell to the ground in the throe of conviction, jerking with convulsions—approached the two boys and told them they were sitting on the side reserved for Choctaws. Without thought or hesitation, they moved together to the opposite side. Just as everyone was in place and Dr. Talley and Leflore were leaving the tent and taking a stance side by side behind the tree-anchored pulpit, the exhorter spotted Luther's father and said something to him. Bolokta, obviously annoyed, moved hurriedly to where the two boys were sitting. He whispered something to Luther, moved away. Luther went with his father back to the row of Choctaws. Jesse, not understanding Bolokta's Choctaw words, that he had told Luther that he and Jesse could not sit together, followed. When the two boys were seated again, Leflore and Dr. Talley looked at each other in mild confusion. Although Leflore spoke both languages, he was there in the role of interpreter and probably didn't feel comfortable giving a command. Dr. Talley probably feared an offense to one side or the other. Neither man moved to enforce the customary seating arrangement.

Chief Leflore tried to break the impasse. He looked sternly at Jesse's father, holding the gaze as long as there was eye contact, until Lonnie Furver turned his eyes away, knowing the look was a flag of hostility, yet tinged with uncertainty. Torn between obeying the command of a Choctaw and having his boy sit for hours in a Choctaw assemblage, he did nothing. There was a rustle of murmuring complaint on the part of some on each side of the aisle. Others tried to stifle a giggle. Luther and Jesse sat in composed innocence. Finally Reverend Isaac Smith, a Revolutionary War soldier who had been with George Washington at Yorktown and who had been invited to the meeting by Dr. Talley, intervened. The opinions and utterances of old men were trusted most by the Choctaws, and Isaac Smith was an old man. He stepped from inside the tent where he was waiting to be introduced, gave a jovial bow to the congregation, then moved quickly to where the two boys sat. Putting a hand on each boy's head, as if in the company of angels, he announced in a humorous yet earnest tone, "And a little child shall lead them." Greenwood Leflore, though he did not seem to approve, interpreted the words. When Father Smith, as he was called because of his years, disappeared inside the tent, the meeting began.

Leflore, a colonel in the U.S. Army as well as chief of the nation, had in fact camped with the others during the night, despite what Luther had said to Jesse. "This must be an important meeting," Luther remarked when he saw the chief's tent pitched directly behind Dr. Talley's.

Greenwood Leflore was dressed in a fashionable calico morning gown, standing one step ahead and to the side of Father Smith. Father Smith, the oldest of the guests, spoke first. His message came in short paragraphs, each one containing something about the plan of salvation. At the end of each paragraph, Leflore would interpret, expanding and embellishing the words. His interpretations were actually expository sermons, using what the preacher had said as a text. The deep resonance of his voice and the eloquence of his words, accentuated by timely inflections and compelling gestures, made him seem more of a Methodist preacher than chief of a nation.

When Alexander Talley preached, he dwelt longest on the Great Father's love for his children in sending his son to earth to die so everyone might be saved. Some of the Choctaw men seemed confused. They talked aloud among themselves, asking each other if the chief was telling them they and their land would be saved from white intruders by Jesus dying on a cross. The men passed a pipe, each man taking a deep pull before passing it on to the next one.

Greenwood Leflore was not a professing Christian at the time. Born of a French father, Louis LeFleur, and Choctaw mother, Rebecca Cravat, niece of Chief Pushmataha, he had adopted the language and culture of both. At the age of twelve his father, by then a successful tavern keeper in the Choctaw Nation, had allowed him to go to Nashville with Major James Donly, who had a government contract to carry the mails between Nashville and Natchez on the Natchez Trace, a road made possible by the Treaty of Fort Adams in 1801. Leflore was educated in Nashville, at seventeen married the fifteen-year-old daughter of his benefactor, returned to the Choctaw Nation, and at twenty-two was elected chief of the Western District. Though never popular with many of the full-blood tribesmen, he became a powerful man at an early age. Despite the fact that he was not then a Christian, he was zealous in his assistance to the missionaries.

Jesse and Luther listened intently with the others to the preaching, Jesse not understanding the translation, Luther understanding both. Occasionally he flinched at words he felt Greenwood Leflore was ascribing to the preacher. And once he asked Jesse if he had ever thought about becoming a Christian and being baptized. When Jesse didn't answer he whispered, "I wonder why Chief Leflore is so anxious to Christianize all us

Choctaws except himself." He said it as if he knew the answer. Jesse didn't understand.

Between 1801 and 1830, the United States succeeded in getting more than twelve million acres of Choctaw land. After each treaty the Choctaws were told they would never be asked for more, that there would be peace, and that white settlers would not be allowed to encroach upon their remaining lands. But as the year 1830 began, there was a great clamor, largely fed by Andrew Jackson, who had become president of the United States the previous year. The uproar among the whites now was for every last bit of land belonging to the Choctaw Nation. And for every last native of the nation to be removed west of the Mississippi River.

"I think we might have to move," Luther Cashdollar said to Jesse Furver one morning as they sat beside a bubbling spring, taking a break from their chores on hog-killing day. Hog killing was an annual affair for the two families. It was also something of a social event.

The day before the two boys had hunted the herd of hogs in the Chicopa Creek swamps. Hogs were the only thing of value that Hernando De Soto had contributed to Choctaw culture when his party came through in the sixteenth century. Swine brought along for food on the hoof escaped in the swamps and fattened on the beech masts, as did the hogs of Bolokta and Lonnie Furver. They were turned loose in the swamps in the late fall to feed and fatten from the bountiful crop of masts that completely covered the ground underneath the giant beech trees that thrived in the humid lowlands of the Choctaw Nation. When the weather was cold enough for butchering, the hogs were herded home. Shoats, both barrows and gilts, would be slaughtered. The boars and older sows would be kept for spring breeding. All of them, some so fat they had to stop often to rest, carried the earmarks of one family or the other. Two small v-clips in the right ear meant they belonged to Bolokta. Those with one clip in the left ear belonged to the Furvers.

"My papa said we're going to kill the sows and boars this year too," Luther said. "He said we might not be here next year so there is no use in keeping them. Said we might leave them for Uncle Brash though. Uncle Brash says he isn't going to move."

Jesse had heard the talk of Choctaw removal at home and among other white settlers, but he wasn't supposed to talk about it with Luther. Sometimes he did anyway. Before he could answer this time, the men had called them back to work.

While the men continued their work, women had tossed the first ribs and backbones cut from the slaughtered hogs into a large pot of briskly boiling water. Thrown in with them were dozens of banahas, a mixture of previously cooked dried beans and corn meal wrapped firmly in corn shucks. The meat and banahas were eaten with sweet potatoes, baked in the ashes around the cooking pot.

"Wherebouts you gonna move to?" Jesse asked in late afternoon when the work was all done. They were sitting beside the spring eating the last of the backbone and banahas. Cito sat directly between them, turning his head to first one and then the other for a morsel of the meat, refusing the banaha when Luther tried to trick him with it.

"West, I suppose." Luther said, throwing a section of backbone as far as he could for Cito to fetch. "Toward the setting sun." He turned facing the sun, which they could barely see above the treetops, and bowed low. "That's all I know."

CHAPTER 4

Jesse and Luther were in the deep woods on the bluff behind the settlement. They had made bows from willow branches and were pretending to be ancient hunters. Although it had been many years since the Choctaws had used arrows as weapons for war or hunting game, Luther knew how to fasten the flint points and flight-stabilizing feathers onto straight slippery elm or willow shafts and make swift-flying arrows. The arrow points and spearheads were easily found, often littering the ground in open fields, dating back thousands of years to a people differing more from the Choctaws Luther knew than his people had ever differed from the encroaching European whites.

Sitting on the trunk of a longleaf pine tree that a tornado had blown down three years earlier, they listened to Cito chasing a rabbit in the distance.

"*Abi. Yanaš. Tapa. Paska. Apa.*" Jesse enunciated each of the Choctaw words painstakingly, grinning, his eyes seeking Luther's approval. Luther repeated each word in English as Jesse said them in Choctaw. "Kill. Buffalo. Cut. Bake. Eat." His tone seemed to marvel that Jesse's pronunciation of Choctaw words was better than his English. But he didn't say it. He just laughed, pleased that Jesse could imagine past days when they would have been hunting buffalo instead of rabbits. "Yeah. We'll eat the buffalo," he said.

"He's treed," Luther said when the barking sounded from one spot. They knew the rabbit had run into a hollow log. They would poke a long stick with a forked prong on the end into the hollow.

When the stick hit the rabbit, one of them would twist until the fork caught in the rabbit's skin enough to pull it out. If either family needed the rabbit for food, they would kill and dress it. If the meat was not needed, they would turn it loose, holding Čito until the rabbit got away. Jesse had learned the Choctaw rule of never killing anything unless it was needed.

Before they got to the dog, Luther stopped suddenly, fell to his knees, then put his right ear to the ground, motioning for silence. Jesse watched at first, then dropped and listened as Luther did.

"That way," Luther said, standing and pointing deeper into the forest. "Three men."

"Let's go," Jesse said, turning back toward the settlement.

"No," Luther said, moving on.

They had found the dog and were pulling the rabbit from the log when three men came through the trees toward them.

"Let's go," Jesse said again.

"*Chahta hapia hoke!*" Luther said, loud enough for the men to hear.

"Yeah. *Chahta hapia hoke*," Jesse whispered. Then in English. As a question. "*We* are Choctaw?"

They had turned the rabbit loose and Luther was holding Čito by the loose-fitting thong around his neck as the men came close. Čito was struggling and barking, trying to get away.

One of the men was carrying a three-legged device the boys had never seen before. Another was pulling a long chain. They couldn't see the end of it and Luther said, "I wonder what he's leading," as they came closer. The third man carried a thick writing tablet looking like the ledgers they had seen at the trading post.

"You boys hunting bears?" one of the men asked, patting Čito on the head, looking at the bows they had leaned against a tree and nodding at the bamboo quiver strapped on Luther's back.

"Buffalo," Luther answered.

"Not any buffalo left in these woods," the same man said.

"I know," Luther said. "Bear either."

With a sardonic smile, the man winked at the other two. "Don't worry though, Little Bolokta. Where you're going there's lots of buffalo. Bears too. So I've been told."

"My name's Luther. And we're not going anywhere."

"Whatever you say," the man said.

"I'm Mr. Payten," the one with the writing tablet said. "Mr. J. B. Payten."

"I greet you," Luther said, giving a courtly bow and extending his hand. The man turned away, pretending not to see the offered courtesy.

"I'm Luther Cashdollar. And my friend here is Jesse Furver." None of the men answered. Jesse stood behind Luther, watching, saying nothing. Cito moved back and forth between the three men and the boys, as if defending them.

"We're surveyors," Mr. Payten said, although the boys had not asked what they were doing. "We're making maps, plats, measuring all this land, dividing it into townships, sections, all that." He was leaning against a black oak tree, writing as he talked.

"Why?" Luther asked. He moved close enough to see what was being written.

"So people will know who owns which land. The government will be giving patents."

"What's a patent?" one of the men heard Jesse whisper to Luther.

"Decree of the king," the man laughed.

"The Great Spirit owns the land," Luther said. "The Great Spirit provided it for the children of Nanih Waiya to live forever."

"Whatever you say," the man with the chain said in the same condescending manner as before. Then his tone changed abruptly, as if suddenly threatened by this brazen young Choctaw. "This land belongs to the United States. So get your scrawny red ass off it!"

"Let's go," Jesse whispered to Luther, tugging at his sleeve. "We ain't got no king."

"There's been a treaty, boy," Mr. Payten said, like he was trying to soften the slur.

"I was there," Luther answered, both defiance and resignation in his voice. Luther knew the surveyor was referring to the Treaty of Dancing Rabbit Creek, but he said nothing further to him. Instead he looked at Jesse, frowned, shrugged, turned away. He started to leave with Jesse, then stopped when Mr. Payten began reciting his field notes as he wrote them down.

"Township Sixteen, Range One East, Choctaw Cession of 1830." On the paper his words were abbreviated. T 16 R 1 E Choctaw Cession of 1830.

"Let's go," Jesse pleaded. Luther did not answer. He stood

listening as Mr. Payten went on. Thinking thoughts neither Jesse nor the three men, perhaps no white man at all, could ever fathom, suddenly knowing what he did not want to know and for the very first time believing what had been to him unbelievable, feeling pangs as piercing as the flint points in his quiver.

"Run from the sixth milepost on the standard parallel. Variation of the needle eight minutes, three seconds. Forty chains. True point of one-quarter section at cottonwood tree thirty inches circumference."

Mr. Payten waved the other two men back to work. Luther and Jesse watched and listened as they called back and forth.

"North to end of Chicopa Bayou tributary. Eighty chains to black jack twenty inches circumference. Enter heavy ash and cottonwood, and undergrowth. Fifty chains to black jack thirty inches circumference. . . ."

"What's he talking 'bout?" Jesse asked. Luther still didn't answer.

They stayed on for half an hour or so, following from a short distance as the men moved.

"That's all for Section Thirteen," Mr. Payten called to the other two, motioning them back.

"Well, boy, if the squaw asks where you've been, you know what to tell her," the chainman said.

"He means the land where we're standing is Section Thirteen," Mr. Payten said, patting Luther gently on the head as he walked by.

"Thank you, sir," Luther responded. "Thank you a lot."

"Maybe we should have gone with Tecumseh," Luther said when they began making their way back to the settlement. "Maybe the great Pushmataha was wrong."

Pushmataha was well known by all the white settlers, had been to the Furver home many times. But Jesse had never heard of Tecumseh so Luther explained. He told him Tecumseh was a Shawnee chief who had visited the Choctaw Nation less than twenty years earlier. He had come to try to convince the Choctaws and all the Southern tribes that their only hope of surviving was to refuse to cede any more land, refuse to sign any more treaties, and to join with him in an all-out war against the United States. Luther knew the story because his father, Bolokta, and his uncle had been at the council meeting when Pushmataha had advised his people not to join in such a war.

Cyrus Kingsbury, knowing the esteem of the young for their dead chief, used the incident to illustrate the merit of peace in his informal talks with the students at Eliot Mission School. Luther knew the chief had not been the irenic spirit Cyrus Kingsbury pictured. Bolokta had fought with Pushmataha in both the Creek War and against the British in the War of 1812. Luther knew the stories. Jesse had heard them from him.

"There's been a treaty," the surveyor had said. Yes, there had been a treaty. Luther had been there as his father's personal interpreter because Bolokta did not trust the government interpreters nor his own chief, Greenwood Leflore, to be precise. But there had been other treaties. Luther knew them all. From his studies at Eliot Mission School and from the many conversations he had heard from his elders. As they walked along, through woods they had just been told would be forever known as Section Thirteen, he told his white friend of each one. Treaties, of land and woods that had never been named before because that which belonged to the Great Spirit should remain as nameless as the Great Spirit himself, as hidden and awesome as the God of the white man who told Moses through a burning bush His name was I AM WHO I AM.

Luther spoke calmly of Hopewell, where, in 1786, a nation only ten years old treated with a nation of ancient vintage, promising protection and for that pledge being ceded seventy thousand acres of land. "Too little to miss," Luther said.

He moved quickly in his treaty review to Fort Adams and 1801, a year when a severe famine—caused in part by the excesses of European interlopers—struck the Choctaw Nation. The Choctaws traded Thomas Jefferson more than two and a half million acres of land and the right to build a road through the nation, a road that would reach from Nashville to Natchez. The government built trading posts along the road, where Choctaws could barter peltry for salt, powder, and shots, but where their peltry was seldom sufficient, so debts were incurred, debts that both the government and the trading company knew the Choctaw Nation would not be able to pay. But credit would be quickly granted, and in exchange the nation received two thousand dollars and some blacksmith tools.

Jesse Furver, who no more felt enemy to Luther Cashdollar than to his own sister, heard the story of Hoe Buckintoopa and Mount Dexter, where, in 1803 and 1805, Jefferson's government paid the trading company money the Choctaws owed, promised a small annuity, and was ceded a total of almost five million acres of valuable land, land for which the white settlers continued to clamor.

Luther was no longer calm. Jesse thought he sounded the way he had on the mound that day, when they were about to attend Reverend Talley's preaching service. And on other occasions when Luther turned lecturer and preacher. Jesse had heard the stories before. As the urgency in Luther's voice continued, in the mode of a professor doing a quick review of a year's study to a class, preparing them for tomorrow's final exam, Jesse listened. He heard Luther talk again of the great Pushmataha's bravery in helping the United States defeat the Creek Nation on the Black Warrior River in Alabama. And of the thousand Choctaw warriors, his father one of them, who had raced with Andrew Jackson to New Orleans and helped in the battle that would speed Jackson on his way to the presidency. With insight beyond his years, and bitterness Jesse could hear but not appropriate nor comprehend, Luther told him of how quickly and without warning had come the notion that all his people should be removed far, far away from the land of their ancestors' bones.

It was the same Andrew Jackson beside whom Pushmataha and his warriors had fought who met them at Doak's Stand and, after the most unspeakable bribery and intimidation, exacted the first treaty calling for their removal. This despite the fact that after each treaty along the way they had been promised goodwill, coexistence, and protection from white encroachment or foreign aggression.

Luther wondered aloud how it happened that on a trip to Washington for the purpose of clarifying the Treaty of Doak's Stand Chief Puckshunubbee had died mysteriously and that the greatest of all chiefs, Pushmataha, had died of croup while there.

Still maintaining the tenuous balance between mentor and friend, Luther recited words from Pushmataha's last speech as he addressed the secretary of war at that fateful gathering:

I can boast and say, and tell the truth,
that none of my fathers, or grandfathers,
nor any Choctaw, ever drew bows against
the United States. They have always been

friendly. We have held the hands of the
United States so long that our nails are
long like the talons of a bird and there
is no danger of slipping out.

Luther told of the grandiose funeral service on Christmas Day, 1824, for the fallen chief. Two thousand people had followed his casket down Pennsylvania Avenue in the mile-long procession. Following ardent praise from Andrew Jackson and others, Pushmataha was buried in the Congressional Cemetery. "Even so," Luther said, "Nanih Waiya is without his bones. So still he knows no peace."

Luther recited some words the great chief had uttered just before he died in Washington:

I shall die, but you will return to our brethren.
As you go along the paths, you will see the
flowers and hear the birds sing; but
Pushmataha will see them and hear them no
more. When you shall come to your home,
they will ask you, "Where is Pushmataha?"
and you will say to them, "He is no more."

They had moved out of range of the voices of the surveyors and were sitting on a mat of grass almost within sight of the village. Čito had chased a fox squirrel, and it had run up a poplar sapling while the dog was barking up a different tree twenty feet away. Jesse had drawn his bow and was taking careful aim. "Leave her be," Luther said, as if he did not want his words interrupted. He had saved his major eloquence for the treaty he had recently attended with his father. His voice no longer loud, in a tonic accent he launched into an extended and impassioned chronicling of the Treaty of Dancing Rabbit Creek. The feist dog was still sitting on its haunches, barking up the same tree.

They sat facing each other, Jesse sitting in innocence, the guilt of his skin to indict him, yet indemnified by the strong bond of love.

"There were about six thousand of us who went," Luther began. "We camped on the little creek where the rabbits dance." Jesse smiled at the picture. Each person was allowed a pound and a half of beef, a pint of corn for each day, and a quart of salt. "We

57

ate well."

At times his shrill voice cracked with emotion. He told Jesse the Christian missionaries, his old teacher and mentor Cyrus Kingsbury among them, were expelled from the campgrounds. Gamblers, prostitutes, and whiskey could remain. Whiskey enough to soften the resolve of the most intrepid opponent of the removal treaty.

To Jesse the story was just another adventure. Still he somehow felt a part of the bruise deep within the spirit of his buddy. He had heard the talk at home and from other white settlers. He had not understood why they wanted Choctaw families who had been good neighbors, who had so often befriended them, moved far away. He knew nothing had changed between him and his friend.

Luther told him how the campground had been arranged. At first Jesse thought it was like the Methodist camp meetings of Alexander Talley, but he was confused when Luther told him no missionaries were allowed to attend and gambling tables and whiskey were present. At other times Jesse had trouble distinguishing between the various treaties. Each time, Luther patiently explained.

Greenwood Leflore and the people of his district camped together, Luther told him. On the high ground on the Big Rabbit Creek. Jesse remembered how Leflore, there to interpret for Reverend Talley, had slept away from the others on the banks of Chicopa Creek. Chief Mushulitubee and his people were just below Chief Leflore at Dancing Rabbit Creek, and Nittakacaffa's district was further down. Mushulitubee, who had served in the army and had led his warriors in the War of 1812, was dressed in his military uniform. "He thought that would gain him favor with the secretary of war who was leading the treaty talks," Luther said. He said his papa had told him that. Nittakacaffa wore buckskin Choctaw clothing. Greenwood Leflore wore a fancy civilian suit. "He is not a good man," Luther said. "My papa says the chief is not our friend."

Each day was described. "On the very first day, on Saturday, they told us what they wanted. They said they wanted all Choctaws to move west of the Mississippi River."

The Choctaw Nation had been given the western land ten years earlier, at the Treaty of Doak's Stand, but when Pushmataha convinced the government of what he had told them at the time, that settlers were already there, they were promised land farther west.

"For two days our people talked among ourselves. Then talked with the government people. I heard all of it. I stayed right beside my papa and told him every word the white men said. Just like they said it."

Luther picked up a stick and showed Jesse how they had voted. "On Wednesday, after everyone who wanted to speak had been heard, we were sitting in this big circle. If you wanted to vote for moving away you hit the ground with the stick when it got to you. My papa did not strike the ground with the stick, just passed it on to me. I didn't strike the ground. Just one Choctaw struck the ground with the stick. I didn't know him and my papa didn't know him and we never want to see him again. When he struck the ground he said, '*Yakni kanči lishkeh.*'" Luther quickly interpreted. "'I am for selling the country.' That's what he said."

Luther folded his hands and rocked back and forth. A deep humming, wailing sound came from his throat. Jesse followed the rocking and tried to make the same sounds.

When Luther began speaking again, he no longer stressed particular syllables in the pitch-accent fashion. Almost a monotone. He told Jesse how they had been threatened with war from President Andrew Jackson and the United States if they did not agree to move: they would be ruined. The commissioners said if the Choctaws did not agree, they would return to Washington and leave them with nothing but starvation and destruction.

"'*Hakčoma kiho šakka,*'" Luther quoted one of the chiefs as saying, "'Let us all smoke tobacco.' My papa passed the peace pipe with a silver stem to me and I smoked tobacco just like they did." He said it proudly. A rite of passage. He could attend the treaty council and interpret for his father. He could smoke tobacco with them as they meditated and contemplated. And he was just as helpless as the rest.

He talked of the beauty of looking between the trunks of the tall trees, the ground underneath them covered with clean leaves and straw, and watching the clouds that blew in on the fourth day hovering over their encampment along the river banks, folding in on them like a mother spreading a blanket over her young for the night. And then the new harangue of the uniformed officers with the coming of morning.

By the end of the week most of the Choctaws who had not favored the removal, who were determined to stay on their native lands, near the bones of their ancestors at Nanih Waiya where they had been first created, left the treaty grounds and went home. "We have voted once. We have voted twice. We have not struck the ground with the stick."

But some had remained. Luther Cashdollar's tale continued. Luther Cashdollar the Christian. Speaking now in the vein of Tunapinachuffa, the precocious but dispirited Choctaw.

Greenwood Leflore promised to present a modified treaty the next day. The revised article he brought seemed to favor the Choctaws. Any family head who wished to remain in Mississippi and become a citizen of the state, complying with its laws and yielding to its will, would receive one section of land. Each unmarried child over ten living in the household would receive a quarter of a section.

There were hitches, however, to the generous article. Application must be made within six months from ratification of the treaty. They must then live on the property for five years before a deed would be granted.

After three more days of negotiation—consisting mainly of Secretary of War Eaton's threats that if they did not sign the president would laugh at their adversity, more drunkenness, more bribery, and more concessions of additional land to Greenwood Leflore and a few others—the treaty was signed.

Of the six thousand Choctaws who gathered on Friday, September 17, 1830, 173 signed the Treaty of Dancing Rabbit Creek on Monday, September 27. Of those, 163 had signed with an X mark.

His story ended, Luther lay on his back, staring straight up. Cito had given up on the squirrel and was stretched out beside him.

He repeated what Pushmataha had said on the eve of his death in Washington. He lay there for a long time after he finished, neither of them saying a word. Finally Luther broke the silence. "When you shall come to your home, they will ask you, 'Where is Luther?' and you will say to them, 'Luther is no more.'"

Jesse heard his words but did not understand. He knew about the treaty now, knew it meant the United States wanted all the Choctaws to move away so the white settlers could have their farms and timberland. But he thought it would be easy for those like Bolokta to stay where they were by a simple signing.

Luther knew and understood, intuited the outrage of things to come. Was it not the learned pedagogues of Eliot who had instilled in him their Calvinist doctrine of man? Had they not told him "there is none righteous, no not one?" So why should he be surprised when it was the hand of Preacher Alexander Talley, who had talked so much of sin, that had penned the treaty of deception at Dancing Rabbit? He was not surprised. Not at the preacher. Not at the chief. He had heard them well. He recalled Simon, the Cyrene. And was grateful for his young friend who, unknowingly, was helping him to bear his cross. He knew of David and Jonathan also. Of friend closer than blood.

It would have been in Luther's favor if that had been all he knew. But he knew too that past deceptions were prelude, portending calamity beyond perception and endurance.

William Ward had been a kindly Choctaw agent. It would be he who would be charged with registering claims for land. And it would be he who would conduct the business in an intoxicated fog, losing records, using applications for toilet paper, catering to the land speculators who would soon make great fortunes on the land of the hapless natives, confusing, discouraging the illiterate Choctaws until they despaired of trying, so that when the last chapter was written not one section of land promised under the terms of Article 14 of the treaty would remain in Choctaw hands. And somehow Luther knew Chief Greenwood Leflore knew, knew that Article 14, which he and Reverend Talley had designed and which appeared on the treaty grounds in the handwriting of the preacher even though all missionaries had been expelled, was but a caul protecting a dead fetus.

Knowing, he lay there, exhausted by the events of the day and the telling of the tale.

"Luther is no more." The words were stuck in Jesse's mind and would not go away. He was as drained by Luther's cram-course review as the schoolmaster who lay prostrate beside him. Was Luther speaking of dying? Of leaving? Or was he telling him all that, reminding him, positing it in the deepest recesses of a white mind so firmly that generations to come could never forget? Jesse could not bring what he was feeling into focus. He had known grief. He had known aloneness and blight of mood. What he felt now was alien to his being, like some parapet of passion that he strained to see over but that protected him from nothing.

To the right of where they sat was the beginning of a newground where Luther and Jesse had planned to plant beans and pumpkins. Their fathers had let them plant small plots together since they were little boys. Three years earlier they had girdled the trees with broadaxes. The first year the trees died, the second they dried of all moisture, and the third they partly rotted. The last step was to pile fat pine around them and set them on fire. They had been burning for more than two weeks, sputtering and fading in torrents of rain, then flaming again from deep within the solid hearts when the rains subsided.

Jesse's mind did not deal with such refined metaphors. Yet in this moment the newground reminded him of the words that continued to haunt him. "Luther is no more."

The two boys liked newgrounds and were happy when Bolokta and Lonnie agreed for them to clear one on their own. It was a beginning. They had looked forward to its completion. When winter was banished and spring hovered with teasing pear blossoms, slipping up on summer, luring farmers to their chores, they would turn the rich humus soil and begin the cycle. The newground they sat beside was almost ready, the fire eating now into the deepest roots in the bowels of Section Thirteen.

The sun had gone down and they sat in half darkness. A mama skunk with a column of her babies passed nearby. Čito started to give chase. Luther called her back. The mother saw them, hesitated, then rushed on, judicious with her odious defense. The boys did not comment. What she was about was as much a part of their world as the rivers, fields, and woods. They would not bother her and she would not bother them. She was leading her children to danger, into the maze of burning stumps. It was for their good. She would station each of them in a different spot and leave them. But only for a little while at first. She would soon come back and take them to the safety of their home. The next outing would be longer, the next one overnight. Finally she would abandon them forever, leaving each one on its own, alone, because they were no longer hers and in her love she would set them free. The two boys watched the stripped, furry lines disappear in the flickering haze.

Čito became restless. She whined and traipsed around the area. She would run a short distance in the direction of Luther's house, as if trying to lead them, then try to edge her way underneath Luther's body. He hugged her close, as if his strong and caring hands could stay the distant lightning.

"It's going to storm," Luther said. "She always does that when a storm is coming." Jesse asked him how a dog could tell. "They just can. They know more than we do."

"Will you keep Cito?" Luther asked when darkness had completely engulfed them. "When Luther is no more?"

Jesse did not answer at first. Hearing the words again made him want to cry, the way he used to do when he got hurt, and the way he had done when his baby brother had died. But he was six years old then. Now he was almost seventeen.

He wanted to hold Luther close, hug him the way Luther was hugging Cito. And the way they had done when they were little children, or even when they were older and Luther would come back from the mission school. But big boys didn't do that. They had been taught.

He reached out in the darkness and touched Luther. He could not see him through the darkness. His hand fell on Luther's chest and for a short-lived minute he felt the pounding of his heart. Jesse's own heart was pounding too. He was strangely afraid. He didn't know why. He stood up quickly, stumbled into the darkness, then turned back. "*Chahta hapia hoke,*" he whispered. And left.

CHAPTER 5

Lonnie Furver's grandfather had come to Virginia from England as an indentured servant following the Puritan Revolution. His great-grandfather had sold his son's indenture to a ship's captain to pay his own way out of debtor's prison when the boy was sixteen.

After a seven-year term of bonded servanthood as a blacksmith and plantation worker, he moved to the small town of Smarr, Georgia, where he eventually had his own shop. He married late, and Lonnie's father was born in 1710, when the old man was past seventy.

Lonnie was the last of eleven children, born when his own father was old.

When Lonnie was grown, slaves did most of the work of artisans, and if a white man were not a landholder he faced a precarious future. Lonnie, along with his young bride, joined an ox train to the Mississippi territory intending to homestead. Inadvertently the wagons stopped in what was still part of the Choctaw Nation. No one told him to leave, so he cleared land, got along moderately well with his Choctaw neighbors, eked out a living, and stayed on.

Jesse was not really afraid of his father, but they were not close. When Jesse was a little boy, smaller than other children his age, his father would make fun of him in front of adults to make them laugh. Jesse learned to hide in the woods when company came to avoid the humiliation. He spent a lot of time alone. He liked to go to Luther's house because no one there made fun of him. Even before Luther went to the mission school and learned good

English, they spent a lot of time together. Jesse's father didn't approve, but there were no other white children nearby so he didn't stop him.

Jesse met little resistance when he asked his father if they could keep Čito. At first his father told him he would agree to keep the dog if they could keep Fičik too. He said the dog and pony were good friends and ought to stay together to keep each other company. When Jesse told him the Choctaws moving west were allowed to take their livestock with them, Lonnie Furver said Čito was a good squirrel and rabbit dog so they would keep her.

Keeping the dog was but the first of Jesse's questions. He waited until the whole family was present at supper to ask the important one. Since his father had wanted to keep Fičik because she was a companion to Čito, although Jesse knew that wasn't the real reason, and since the pony belonged to Luther, if they could keep Luther they would also have the pony. Logic does not always prevail. Jesse's mother, Tracy Mai, was a gentle woman and had always been protective of Jesse. His sister was soon to be married and he thought that might help his case, that she would say Luther could take her place. Jesse thought he had a perfect plan.

No one spoke for a long time after Jesse asked if they could keep Luther as well as Čito. Tracy Mai sat looking at her husband, her eyes doing the talking. She was sure what his answer would be but thought a sign from her might help. Bettye Pearl, the daughter, stifled a giggle at first, then fell silent, gazing through the open shutter at nothing in particular. Jesse pushed the beans and boiled okra back and forth across his plate, not taking a bite.

Lonnie went on with his supper, saying nothing, as if a question so senseless did not require an answer. When he finished and started to get up, his wife said, "Ain't you going to answer the boy?"

"Don't be silly, woman!" he snarled, getting up. "There's been a treaty!" When his wife started to say something else, he interrupted. "That boy of yorn ain't never been right nohow." No one answered.

Bolokta and Luther would never know if Greenwood Leflore would own their land, now Section Thirteen. It was widely known he had no intention of migrating under the terms of the Treaty of Dancing Rabbit Creek. By that treaty he had been given twenty-four hundred acres of land and was already on his way to amassing a vast fortune. By various methods of chicanery, some intratribal, some in concert with missionaries who seemed more in his employ than as advocates of the lowly Galilean, sometimes in collusion with Agent William Ward and the powerful land companies that had been waiting impatiently for the treaty to be completed, poised like panthers about to spring upon some unsuspecting prey, he would soon have one of the largest plantations in the ceded sector.

Soon after the Dancing Rabbit Creek treaty was signed, arrangements began for mass removal. A scouting party composed of the chiefs of the three districts, plus four mingoes from each district, were supposed to explore the areas beyond the Mississippi where they were to be moved. George Gaines, a white businessman trusted by the Choctaws, was the leader. He convened Chiefs Nittakacaffa and Mushulitubee, along with their captains. Bolokta was not a mingo of the Western District, but his brother was. His brother had chosen to try to remain and had asked Bolokta to go with the exploration party in his place. When Bolokta left to rendezvous with the others, he told his wife he would be back within a day. When she asked him why, he said he was sure Leflore would not go. He was right. When Bolokta and the others rode up to Leflore's yard, the chief greeted them in an almost jovial fashion. Juggling his guilt with intermittent giggles, he teased and cajoled, seemingly unmindful of their anguish, explaining that he was afraid to leave just yet, that the whites might take an unfair advantage of his people while he was away, no more convincing to the mingoes than the bluff of an aging ram vaguely remembering rutting days.

The half-breed chief who had so diligently sought to Christianize his people would cast his lot with the white half of his bloodline. He would stay on. Stay on to own fifteen thousand acres of rich land and many slaves, Africans whom he would seek to convert with the same sedulous zeal as he had his own people. To give a county and a city his name. Stayed on to serve in the infant state's senate, where on one occasion, peeved at the flaunting of scholastic prowess by some of his colleagues who would sometimes cite long passages in Latin, he arose one day and gave an hourlong speech entirely in Choctaw, stopping in its tracks further displays of erudite pomposity. Remained to build the elegant Malmaison, a fourteen-room mansion furnished with damask curtains hanging from gilded cornices, glittering chandeliers, seamless, handwoven carpets, and the finest furniture to be purchased in all of France. Staying, too, to see his prestige in the white citizenry turn to contempt, his empire reduced to little, when he opposed the Civil War. Then to die sitting on his front porch, facing the expanse he had betrayed his people to possess, wrapped in a Union flag. But before the tide of his personal fortune had ebbed, the tribulations of the people he wronged at Dancing Rabbit Creek would be etched on the pages of ignominy.

The place where Jesse and Luther stood now, the scene itself, was but a piteous prologue to the story. They were grown men now. This was as far as I could go with them. I had followed them as they traipsed the length and breadth of Section Thirteen and miles on each side. There had been summers filled with work and fun; tilling the fields, frolicking on the banks and splashing the waters of Chicopa Creek. Lolling in noonday sun and chasing low-flying winter clouds. They went fishing, hunting, and attended Methodist camp meetings of Reverend Alexander Talley. But mostly, they just loved one another.

Now they were standing on a loading dock in Vicksburg, on the opposite side of the river where the legendary chiefs, Čahta and Čikasah, seeing the talismanic pole still leaning eastward, had built rafts to reach the land of Nanih Waiya, fleeing persecution then as now. Cows, hogs, horses, and teams of oxen, yoked and hitched to iron-wheeled wagons, stood in serpentine formation waiting to be loaded. Behind them were scores of men, women, and children, all scantily dressed for this cold beginning of a bitter journey. They were huddled close together, the children squatting, men and women encircling them to stay the fierce winds. Many of the women were crying. The men did not weep. But from their ranks Jesse and Luther could hear the most doleful lamentations, deep dissonant groans and muffled sounds of indignation and abdication.

Luther had found Fičik and was feeding her acorns he had picked up on the long trek from Section Thirteen to the Mississippi River at Vicksburg. He and Jesse were patting and rubbing the aging mare affectionately. A young but sickly ox had just died, still in its yoke, and two other oxen were dragging it by the neck to the edge of the bluff where it would be rolled into the dark waters of the mighty river. One of its horns dug into the ground, leaving a deep gash in the earth, making the pulling more difficult, resisting even in death. Luther and Jesse blocked the scene from

Fičik's view. Throughout the trip they had tried to act casual, as if they were on a journey everyone had made, as if what was happening was not the calamitous thing it was.

All efforts to rescind the oppressive terms of the treaty made where the rabbits danced had ceased. The proud and mighty Choctaws were defeated. Heartbroken and weary, they had prepared themselves for the removal journey as best they could, packing the few meager possessions they were allowed, selling to the eager settlers what they could not carry. They did not know what lay in store, knew nothing of the land to which they would be taken by the soldiers. They knew only that the last hope of remaining with the bones of their ancestors was no more.

Luther's old teacher, friend, and mentor, Cyrus Kingsbury, had gone west with an earlier party. He had assured his students a new school would be built and they could continue to learn. He again encouraged Luther to prepare to go to Brown University when things were more settled, told him he carried a letter of admission with him.

Luther had asked him to get a job for Jesse as assistant escort with the cavalry on the overland trip to Vicksburg. They had ridden together on the week-long journey.

These were their final moments, each glance and gesture brimming with pangs of affection. The grizzly steamboat had moved into place to receive its human cargo. The animals were being loaded onto barges. For a moment Luther thought of paintings he had seen in Bibles at Eliot Mission School of the loading of Noah's ark. The mounted troops moved nervously, sympathetically, around the area, a peculiar advocate for, "We hold these truths to be self evident . . . ," giving more commands to each other than to the vanquished and desolate mortals awaiting a fate imposed by a people they had befriended for three centuries. Strange or not, it would be the soldiers who would show the greatest degree of clemency, salvaging such dignity as they could for their doomed charges.

The steamboat *Brandywine* sounded a long blast of its whistle, brusque as the sound of hell's nurses. Bolokta came to where they were standing, said something in Choctaw, and moved back to the group.

"He says it is time to go," Luther said.

Each one stood gazing intently at the face of the other, as if studying and memorizing every marking, each blemish and line wrought ahead of its time, as if some last-minute epiphany would reveal something of the other they had not known before. The very air between them was the breathing of mercy and grace. They did not cry. They had been taught.

"Stay," Jesse pleaded, taking him by the arm. "We can hide you." They had heard the stories of some of the Choctaws hiding in the wilderness, refusing at the last to leave. And they had witnessed a number of men, and sometimes whole families, breaking ranks and deserting the caravan, disappearing into the heavy thickets, chancing survival like wild animals in these woods they knew rather than face the 550-mile jaunt through wilds unknown.

"No," Luther said, his eyes still fixed, voice resolute. "My people are going. *Chahta hapia hoke.* I will go with them."

Jesse made no further protest. "Then good-bye, my dear friend," he said, and extended his hand.

He was not aware and Luther did not notice that Jesse's enunciation was perfect. What Luther did notice was that Jesse seemed suddenly taller. Their hands clasped on a level. As if in this moment of parting some long-sought miracle had, without notice, made its visitation, unleashing a stunted growth.

They shook hands like old men at a graveside, firm, somber, and immutable. Luther turned and joined the shuffling line moving toward the gangplank. He was as quiet now as the others. As if he wanted these moments with his friend to be the last thing he remembered as he took the final step from his homeland.

When he moved away, Jesse went methodically about the chores assigned him, preparing for the return trip to Leflore's district. His eyes did not follow Luther. He fixed his mind on the little dog Cito his father had permitted him to keep. He tried to think of nothing else.

A large crowd of white settlers from the Choctaw Nation, men, women, and children of dubious bloodlines, had gathered to view the leaving of these of a near-pure breed. Jesse heard them break into a wild hurrah, slapping each other on the back, some throwing hats in the air, when the *Brandywine* weighed anchor and began the slow movement into the Mississippi's current, straining against the flow as it made its way upstream toward the Arkansas River. He knew that Luther was hearing what he was hearing, the muted echo of sadness. He hoped he could not hear the cheers.

The Choctaws were gone. Their land remained. And even as the last whistle sounded and the last smoke of the *Brandywine* disappeared in the dark February clouds, the jubilant throng dispersed to stake their claims. Section Thirteen was part of the bounty.

Luther and Jesse never saw each other again. Two months before the removal party reached its assigned destination, Luther Cashdollar died in a cypress swamp in Arkansas. A soldier Jesse had known when he worked for the cavalry told him about it ten months later, when the troops came back to conduct the last group to the West. The soldier was not sure whether it was of cholera or exposure. He said they had to wade for thirty miles through waist-deep water, their bodies sometimes breaking thin layers of ice as they went. Many people were sick. He did not know where Luther was buried. Or if he had been buried at all. Sometimes, he said, the dead had to be left to sink in the jungle of cypress knees where they died.

The soldier told Jesse he was sorry.

CHAPTER 6

In my quest for facts and lore concerning Section Thirteen and Providence Plantation and Providence Farm, I had learned much by following the trails of Luther Cashdollar and Jesse Furver. More than I had ever known about those who dwelt on the hills and valleys I had plowed as a boy and looked upon as my own birthright. Now I had to turn elsewhere, for my two young friends were gone.

I went again to the court records of Holmes County, searching and asking questions, finding cooperation, openness, and hospitality at every turn. But I sometimes came with questions to which there seemed no answers.

My initial inquiry had to do with the first non-Choctaw owner of the land. The court record showed the first grantor to be the United States. The grantee was Turner Brashears. Who was Turner Brashears? No one seemed to know or choose to guess. I was intrigued by the name: Brash ears. Where were those ears now to hear my questions? I knew Brashears was a well-known name in my part of Mississippi, though there were various spellings.

I drove to Jackson, Mississippi, and located Mrs. Elaine Ellington, an elderly, intelligent, and alert woman who had been chancery clerk of Holmes County for many years. Prior to that she had been deputy clerk under Parham Williams, Sr., father of an old friend who had been a student when I was on the staff at the University of Mississippi in the mid-fifties. My son had been one of his students when Parham was dean of the University of

Mississippi Law School. Currently dean of Cumberland School of Law at Samford University, he had told me Mrs. Ellington was the most knowledgeable person alive on Holmes County land history. She was living in an elegant retirement home in Ridgeland, just outside of Jackson. I told her I was writing a history of Section Thirteen. With what appeared to be a spark of recollection and suspicion, she quickly asked, "Which township and range?" When I told her Township Sixteen, North Range, she sat in sparring silence for a moment. I assumed that she knew my mission had something to do with the turmoil surrounding Providence Farm in 1955, for that had been the most controversial event in Holmes County during her years in the courthouse. Neither of us seemed ready to commit.

A woman of obvious high class and culture, she was polite but formal as we talked of related things. She continued to be obliquely inquisitive of my purpose no matter the turn of the conversation. We talked of early Mississippi history, and of Parham Williams's success as a legal scholar and teacher. Buford Ellington had been governor of Tennessee more than thirty years earlier. I recalled that he was a native of Holmes County, Mississippi. I bluffed that I knew she was related to him. "He was my husband's brother," she said, smiling, the kind of smile that cautions one against further dissembling. "And he made you a fine governor," she added. I concurred.

Finally she asked me directly, "Mr. Campbell, exactly what is your interest in this land?" It was a fair question. And one I would be asked by almost everyone I interviewed from then on. I knew I had to risk offending her by confessing my long association with her radical neighbors. As sophisticated and bright as she was, she was a child of the same racist age as I, and I had no way of knowing her opinion on a subject still as volatile in Mississippi as racial integration. But I had no choice.

I told her in detail of my first visit to Providence Farm thirty-five years earlier. "I've kept in touch with them ever since," I said. Her face showed no expression as I spoke.

When I finished, she walked to the far side of the large room, opened a drawer in a well-preserved antique bureau, and removed an oblong cardboard box looking like the ones fine jewelry comes in. She opened it and held it for me to see. Inside were about twenty shiny, finely polished rocks of many colors. She watched my face and handed me the box, waiting. It was, I thought, a test.

I had seen such rocks before. After Mr. Cox left Providence and moved to Memphis, he used to walk the dry bed of Chicopa Creek on his frequent visits, filling his pockets with rocks. Back in Memphis he had rock-polishing tumblers with various grits of emery and a cleaning solution. Starting with the rough rocks of Providence, in three weeks he would have the glass-slick stones that he generously gave away. They seemed a fine parable of what the folk of Providence had been about. He called them worry rocks, never mentioning the metaphor. "When you are worried about something, just take this rock out of your pocket and rub it," he would advise. Many he fashioned into pendants or key rings. Once I was with him at Providence and watched as he selected hundreds of the creek rocks, with the same care as a mother choosing her baby's first shoes, explaining to me the thousands of years it had taken for them to become the geological gems they were. I found it sad, reminding me of the stories of captured Africans scooping up handfuls of dirt and sand from the shores as they were about to be loaded on the slave ships, eating it so a part of their native earth would go with them.

The woman standing there seemed to sense my mood and broke the stare. She turned to the double window and looked down at the spring blossoms in the English garden below. She said nothing of the stones. Instead she began pointing to various trees and plants, asking if I knew what they were and how big they would grow, testing me further, I thought, for they were species anyone familiar at all with Mississippi flora would know.

When she turned back she spoke softly. "Mr. Cox gave them to me. He was a nice man." I felt somehow more comfortable. Without another word, she took one of the glossy stones from the box and handed it to me to keep.

As she carefully placed the box in its place, I began searching my briefcase for maps, plats, and notes. As she sat down, not waiting for a question, she said, "That land once belonged to Louis LeFleur."

I was astounded. It was what I had hoped to find from the beginning, yet strangely was not one of the questions I had planned to ask her. If Louis LeFleur, the French trader, then doubtless his son Greenwood Leflore, the Choctaw chief who had betrayed his people.

"Are you sure?" I almost shouted.

"I'm as sure as forty years in the chancery clerk's office will permit," she answered.

"Then what about Greenwood?" I hurriedly pressed on.

"Louis LeFleur's last will and testament is in the Holmes County Courthouse," she said, still matter-of-fact. "If my memory serves me correctly, it doesn't specify which land went to each of his children. As I recall, it says after his debts for other lands were paid, and slaves provided for, his holdings were to be distributed evenly among his children."

"You mean, uh, I mean you mean I can actually read Louis LeFleur's will?" My excitement seemed now to amuse this unflappable public servant of many years.

"It's there," she said. "Public record."

I asked her if she would assume Greenwood Leflore once owned Section Thirteen. "Chancery clerks learn early not to surmise," she answered, laughing lightly now.

"But you *are* telling me Louis LeFleur owned it." She didn't answer, as if the matter had been closed when she told me the first time. Instead of answering, she explained that Holmes County had been formed in 1833 from parts of two other counties, Yazoo and Carroll. She said records prior to that, if they existed, would be in one of those courthouses. That part of Holmes, she said, was in Carroll County. "They have two county seats, one in Carrollton, one in Vaiden." She said it was possible there would be more detailed records there.

I unfolded the land records Mrs. Jamie Moore had copied for me in Holmes County. I pointed to the first entry, Turner Brashears. Mrs. Ellington shook her head. "I really can't help you on that." She said she had no way of documenting who Turner Brashears was. I needed badly to know. Before I could continue the story of Providence, it was important that I identify him.

Mrs. Ellington pointed to the second entry after Turner Brashears. William McKendree Gwin. It was my next question. I knew the Providence Farm I had known had been Providence Plantation, the Gwin place. There still remains at the end of the long cement walk leading from the Providence schoolhouse and community center, where the plantation house had stood, the high step from which women mounted the sidesaddles, or stepped from the carriages. The ceramic lettering GWIN is still in place. In searching the titles of the years from the Treaty of Dancing Rabbit Creek to 1938, when the land became Providence Farm, the Gwin name appeared frequently—from December 1836, when a Wiley Davis conveyed it to William McKendree Gwin, until October 1930, when John D. Gwin sold it to T. C. Parrish, who eight years later sold it to Delta Cooperative Farm, the legal entity of Providence Farm. My research had not established a nexus across the century of Gwins. I suspected one existed.

Mrs. Ellington said there were Gwin relatives living in Jackson who might be able to help me. She gave me the name of Mrs. Erin Lail, who, she said, had been a Gwin from Holmes County.

Back in my hotel I decided to work on Turner Brashears before proceeding with the Gwin family. I called the chancery clerk's office in Vaiden. I identified myself to the woman who answered the phone and told her what I was trying to find. She responded in the fashion of one reporting the most horrendous news. "I wish I could help you, hon, but the Yankees came down and just burned everything up." It was if she had moments before witnessed a tornado ripping through town and I was the first one she could tell. I told her I was sorry to hear about it. She rushed on. "Oh, it was just awful. Everything! Every last thing burned up!" I told her again that I was sorry. "I just hope nothing like that ever happens again in my lifetime."

I said, "Yes ma'am. I understand. Once in a lifetime is enough for that sort of thing."

Some of the distress and urgency of her voice left as she continued. "But we have a brand-new courthouse now and we're mighty proud of it. I wish I could help you, hon, but we don't have any records earlier than when they came down." I told her again I was sorry to hear about the old courthouse and glad they had a new one. She said she just worked there and offered to let me talk to the chancery clerk but assured me that what I was trying to find was not there. I thanked her, and she said she had enjoyed talking with me.

Stymied in my pursuit of Turner Brashears, I walked to the Mississippi State Archives to see what they had on the Gwin family before calling Mrs. Lail. Finding no genealogy on any Gwin named, discouraged and bored, I asked for something on Louis LeFleur or his son, Greenwood Leflore. In LeFleur's file was a copy of his will, taken from the records in Holmes County. It contained exactly what Mrs. Ellington had told me.

I wondered why there was a copy of the supplementary articles to the Treaty of Dancing Rabbit Creek in the genealogical file of Louis LeFleur. Thinking it might further document Mrs. Ellington's certainty that Section Thirteen had once been in LeFleur's family, I glanced over the supplementary articles to the treaty. I found nothing of interest and was about to close the folder. The supplementary articles simply named individual Choctaws who were to be given sections of land. The reason stated was, "As evidence of the liberal and kind feelings of the President and Government of the United States the Commissioners agree to the request as follows. . . ." There followed a lengthy list of names, most of them familiar to me from previous reading: Peter Pitchlynn, G. H. Harkins, Jack Pitchlynn, Hopoynjahubbee, Onorkubbee. The list continued. It contained three Leflore brothers, but not Greenwood.

I skimmed over Article 2, which began, "And to each of the following person's there is allowed a reservation of a section and a half of land, (to wit) James L. McDonald, Robert Jones, Little Leader, T. Magagha and. . . ." Suddenly my eyes stopped and I gasped. The last name on the list: "and Turner Brashears."

The elusive Turner Brashears was a Choctaw, maybe a mingo, and as such had been given 960 acres of land by supplementary act of the Treaty of Dancing Rabbit Creek. As welcomed and startling as this information was, taken alone it did not establish that he was the Turner Brashears listed in the court records as the first owner of Section Thirteen. The last sentence in Article 2 did, for it stated: "The two first named persons, may locate one section each, and one section jointly on any unimproved and unoccupied land . . . ; The others are to include their present residence and improvement." I had learned earlier of "floating claims." Some Choctaws, and others, were given the right to possess a section wherever in the nation they chose, so long as no one else had established a claim on it. This had allowed favored chiefs and mingoes who lived on piney woods land to own rich delta acres. Others were given only a claim to the land on which they presently lived. Turner Brashears was in that category. And the land records established clearly that he had been given Section Thirteen, along with 320 acres surrounding it.

My luck had changed. I had located the first individual owner of Providence Farm. My next thought was startling. My legendary character Luther Cashdollar spoke often of an "Uncle Brash." Had I found him as well? The similarity of the two names gave me pause. I let it pass as coincidence. At least for the moment.

Still there was little to celebrate. Under the terms of the Treaty of Dancing Rabbit Creek, before a Choctaw given such claims was entitled to a deed in fee simple, he must reside there for five years. Obviously Turner Brashears did not meet that requirement, for long before five years had expired the land was no longer in his name.

Some confusion lingered. On one line the record shows the transfer from Turner Brashears coming in 1846. But this is not possible for, according to the same records, by that date the land had belonged to William McKendree Gwin. The chancery clerk's assumption is that the date was miscopied when the records were transferred from the original book to the present one. A fire, this one not by the Yankees, had damaged court records in the 1890s.

What became of "Uncle Brash," Turner Brashears? The court-house record showing him to be the grantee from the U.S. government reads, under the "Acknowledgment," "letter." Apparently "letter" was the term used to convey, but not quite convey, the property promised to Choctaws who wished to remain after the treaty of 1830. Obviously Turner Brashears did not remain for the required five years and never received a deed in fee simple to the property where he lived. When Brashears, the new grantor, transferred the property to Wiley Davis, the new grantee the following year, under "Acknowledgment" the word "defect" appears. Under "Remarks" the notation states, "Wife's signature does not appear on deed. . . ." Did Wiley Davis, as was so commonplace at the time, simply declare Turner Brashears was not the legal owner to the property because the grantor, in this case the U.S. government, did not have his wife sign the deed, a requirement of law? In that case "defect" was an abbreviation for "defective." Whatever, Wiley Davis is listed as the first non-Choctaw owner of Section Thirteen, followed almost immediately by William McKendree Gwin.

In a later conversation with Samuel James Wells, a historian whose Ph.D. dissertation at the University of Southern Mississippi had been "Choctaw Mixed Bloods and the Advent of Removal," I learned that the Brashears family was well known in the Creek, Chickasaw, and Choctaw tribes. They were widely scattered, and the given name "Turner" was common. One Turner Brashears furnished liquor to the Chickasaws at Muscle Shoals, Alabama, in the early 1790s. Another Turner Brashears, or the same one, had a trading stand northeast of what is now Jackson, Mississippi. Another, or the same one, helped the Spanish with maps and treaties, and a Turner Brashears went to Washington with the Choctaw chiefs as interpreter in 1804. Any one of these things might have been enough to entitle him to the land which was to become Providence. Still, the treaty stated that a Turner Brashears lived on Section Thirteen in 1830. It is not likely that a mixed or full-blooded Choctaw of such accomplishments would have been living on the edge of these remote bluffs in 1830 when he had access to land along the Tennessee River in Alabama, a trading post on the Natchez Trace, or even a spread in northern Florida. So what am I to conclude about the Turner Brashears who was given Section Thirteen under the terms of the Treaty of Dancing Rabbit Creek? Did he join his brother Bolokta in Oklahoma? Did he become a sharecropper on the property after it passed to William McKendree Gwin? Did he disappear into the wilderness to live off nuts and berries and wild game, as did thousands of his kinsmen? Or did he immediately sell his claim to Wiley Davis and move to Port Gibson or some other town and live as a white man? I do not know. Professor Wells is of the opinion that there was but one Turner Brashears. Perhaps he did not physically dwell on the land given to him by the treaty. Maybe the father of Luther Cashdollar lived and farmed there while Turner Brashears was running his trading stand, interpreting for whites, or pursuing other interests. That would account for the mysterious and elusive character Luther described as his Uncle Brash. Something still troubled me. Luther had been my invention. Now I had discovered a historical character who seemed to be the person my phantom had talked about. I decided not to try to sort it all out, content to wait for the rest of the story. Speculation is akin to dissembling. Or, *what is truth?*

What was certain was that in 1837 a number of lawsuits were filed against the estate of Wiley Davis, then deceased, for selling five sections of land that he said he had purchased from Choctaw claims under the articles of the Treaty of Dancing Rabbit Creek. The plaintiffs claimed Wiley Davis had acquired the land from the Choctaws by duplicity. Was Section Thirteen, given to Turner Brashears by the treaty, one of those sections? The record is not clear but perhaps so, for Samuel McAllister, who is listed as buying Section Thirteen from William McKendree Gwin on

February 1, 1837, then selling it back to him on June 7, 1837, was one of the plaintiffs.

And what of Louis LeFleur and his ownership of the property? The likelihood is he claimed the land through some trading-post deal with the tribal council. Turner Brashears did have a brother who lived on and worked the land and was thus entitled to it under the terms of the treaty. Louis LeFleur owned it in the context of the day. But not in fee simple.

Was Chief Greenwood Leflore once the titular master of Section Thirteen? There are two answers to the question. That it was part of the Choctaw land over which he reigned as chief there is no doubt. That he ever held a legal title to it under the laws of the state of Mississippi is open to serious question. Without exception, of the dozens of local citizens of the area I visited, everyone was of the opinion he did. Folklore has established it as true. No available written records establish it as fact. Oral tradition is generally convincing to me. But because the chancery court records of Holmes County are among the most detailed and meticulous I have ever examined, I must demur from my usual instinct. One other thing was established by my locating Turner Brashears. My resources had not agreed as to which treaty this part of Holmes County had been ceded under. Some were sure it was the cession of 1820 and Doak's Stand. Others were just as sure it was Dancing Rabbit Creek in 1830. All old maps I examined showed it right on the line. Since the court records show that Turner Brashears received Section Thirteen, Township Sixteen, North Range by supplementary article of the Treaty of Dancing Rabbit Creek, the matter is settled. Section Thirteen came in the cession of 1830, the Treaty of Dancing Rabbit Creek, not the 1820 treaty.

Then what of Luther Cashdollar's vivid memory and description of Doak's Stand? Since Chicopa Creek was on, or very near, the dividing line, there had to have been the quandary of not being sure whether their farm was included.

By then I had lived with my search for more than a year and had made many trips to Mississippi. This was the most successful discovery I had experienced.

In 1836 there came upon the scene of Section Thirteen one of the most remarkable families I encountered on my journey. My learning that story came about in as strange a manner as my find of "Uncle Brash."

Mrs. Erin Gwin Lail, whose name had been given to me by Mrs. Ellington, was at the start as curious about my intentions as Mrs. Ellington had been. And then, equally as cooperative and helpful. "I don't know how you're going to get a story out of that piece of ground," she insisted. "There never was much to it. Just some poor land that nobody seemed to want for very long at a time." I told her I was convinced there is a good story in every section of land in the world.

She told me something of her own history and I shared some of mine. She was interested that I had once been chaplain at Ole Miss. She had been a Chi Omega at the university and we talked about some of her sisters of that sorority, living and gone on.

After a lengthy conversation she said, "Now I have a cousin here in Jackson who can tell you more than you will ever want to know about the Gwin family and Providence Plantation." She said she would call him and see if he would talk to me. She was obviously devoted to him but wasn't sure I would share her regard for him. She told me he was one of the smartest persons she had ever known. She added that some people considered her cousin weird. I told her there were those who considered me weird, that I wore the badge proudly and I looked forward to meeting her cousin of similar rank. Before saying good-bye, she predicted her cousin and I would be instant best friends.

Within five minutes I received a call from Charlton Hutton. He proved to be as exceptional as his cousin had described. At seventy-nine, he seemed to have almost total recall, as he began a recitation of the Gwin dynasty in epic dimensions—names, dates, places, events. Nothing about him bespoke his years. His wit, keen intellect, whetted appetite for sharing facts and philosophy, plus the abundance of information that rolled forth with oratorical magnificence made him a researcher's dream. Trying to make notes as he talked on the telephone, on the other hand, made him a scribe's nightmare.

Charlton Hutton, son of the minister of the First Presbyterian Church of Jackson, Mississippi, James Hutton, who held the reins of Calvinist orthodoxy in central Mississippi for four decades. Prior to going to Jackson, James Hutton was pastor of the First Presbyterian Church of Lexington in Holmes County, closest neighbor to the Presbyterian church where Reverend Marsh Calloway stood in his pulpit Sunday after lonely Sunday, with only his wife as congregation because he had stood up at the mass meeting in Tchula when Dr. David Minter, son of another Presbyterian minister, and Gene Cox were risking their lives for taking what today would be a modest stand against racial injustice.

Charlton Hutton had also been a Presbyterian minister, pastor of the Reynolda Presbyterian Church in Winston-Salem, North Carolina, and teacher in a private academy. He resigned when still a young man to return to Jackson to care for his mother when his sister died. For forty years he has immersed himself in his world of philosophy, theology, history, cultural causes, and an individualized ministry of teaching and good works.

"Was William McKendree Gwin of the nineteenth century a progenitor of the Gwins of later years who owned Providence Plantation, later Providence Farm?" I asked.

"Indeed he was. I can document it for you in one or several ways." I said I would settle for one. As we talked I could hear him shuffling papers. As he continued I knew why some people considered him eccentric. The man is uncommonly brilliant, I remember thinking. For two days I waited for him to deliver books and documents to my hotel. During the wait there were numerous telephone conversations with him. Those conversations were the beginning of an exhaustive, and sometimes exhausting, inquiry into the life of William McKendree Gwin, owner of Section Thirteen soon after the removal of the Choctaws.

His father, a Welshman named James Gwin, born and reared in Virginia, had fought in the Revolutionary War. He came to Tennessee from North Carolina in 1791 along with a wagon train of twenty families. There, just north of Nashville, near where I now live, James Gwin prospered as a planter of tobacco and cotton. He also had a reputation for fighting Indians in Kentucky and Tennessee. Two of his closest friends were William McKendree and Andrew Jackson. McKendree, who became the first American-born bishop of the Methodist church, would give James Gwin's fourth son his name. Jackson, when he became seventh president of the United States, would start two of Gwin's sons on the road to fame and fortune.

Following the model of his neighbor William McKendree, James Gwin became a Methodist clergyman. But adhering to the example of his other close friend, Andrew Jackson, he never gave up fighting. In the War of 1812 he was Jackson's chaplain and went with him to New Orleans. Though Gwin was noted for his forceful pulpit performances, General Jackson, perhaps feeling more in need of firepower than prayer and exhortation, placed the preacher in charge of fourteen hundred sharpshooters in the Battle of New Orleans.

William McKendree Gwin was not drawn to either vocation. Instead, after receiving a classical education in his father's plantation home, he became a lawyer and established a practice in Gallatin, Tennessee, near Nashville. He felt unsuited for courtroom work because he considered himself a timid and inept public speaker.

He turned to medicine and attended Transylvania College in Lexington, Kentucky, at the time the most noted college west of the Alleghenies. His yen for adventure, along with a sharp nose for financial possibility, led him to Vicksburg, Mississippi. And soon thereafter to Mount Salus, now Clinton. With Jackson as president, his inflexible views on the removal of the Choctaws certain to open millions of territorial acres to settlers and speculators, thousands were migrating to the Yazoo Valley and surrounding areas just as predicted by Robert J. Walker, a man Gwin did not know but with whom he would one day be associated in an immense land-speculating venture, and whom he would make a senator. At a gala reception in a Natchez hotel to celebrate the removal of the Choctaws, Walker, addressing the jovial assemblage, said, "The stream of emigration will flow from every section of the south and west. Kentucky's coming, Tennessee's coming, Alabama's coming, Carolina's coming, Georgia's coming, Virginia's coming, and they're all coming to join the joyous crowd of Mississippians, who will bid them welcome to our new domain." Dr. William McKendree Gwin was among those who came, and his practice flourished.

He was the second of three physicians to be associated closely with the area of Section Thirteen and Providence. Dr. Alexander Talley, though remembered best as a Methodist missionary to the Choctaws and white settlers, was also a doctor. When Dr. Gwin studied at Transylvania, the thesis he submitted for graduation was "Syphilis." It was the treatment of that disease, brought to the Yazoo Valley by De Soto's troops, that greatly occupied Dr. David Minter, the third of the physicians who would breath the air of Providence and treat the sick of the area.

The restless spirit of William McKendree Gwin survived little longer in medicine than it had in law. However, changing vocations with such frequency in the land of King Cotton did not infer emotional instability. Few men grew gray in their first profession, for to be a planter was the ambition of all. The bar was populated with young men; judges were often under thirty, explaining why in neighboring Tennessee the bar at the time, with names like Grundy, Whitesides, Crabb, Bell, Foster, Fogg, and many others, was famous for its competence throughout the Union, while in cotton-dominated Mississippi few lawyers were known beyond their court jurisdiction.

Physicians, who made money faster than lawyers, were generally even younger. Though keeping their titles, as soon as they had acquired enough money to buy a few hundred acres of rich alluvial land and some slaves, they removed the syringes, elixirs, and fever thermometers from the little black bags and replaced them with land deeds, slave-auction handbills, and blueprints for baronial mansions befitting the planter and his lady. Gwin was of the breed, and his mission was soon accomplished.

His friendship with his father's old comrade, General Jackson, had continued. And in 1833 President Jackson, as a favor and reward to his neighbor, chaplain, and troop commander, appointed William McKendree Gwin as U.S. marshal for the Mississippi District, a highly lucrative and politically influential position. Jackson had previously named William's brother, Samuel Gwin, as register of the Land Office at Mount Salus, a position of similar magnitude. Both appointments were vehemently opposed by Senator George Poindexter of Mississippi, on the grounds that neither man was from Mississippi. The power of the president prevailed, and both appointments were confirmed by the Senate, although as a compromise Samuel Gwin was transferred to the new land office at Chocchuma, an even more enviable post.

The appointments would alter the lives of both men. To one it would bring an early death. To the other a rise to vast wealth and political prowess. The two were instantly the greatest champions of Andrew Jackson in the state to which they were newcomers.

Poindexter's savage denouncement of the appointments led to his defeat when the Gwin brothers brought out Robert J. Walker, a Pennsylvania native with little more identity with the state than the Gwins. The acrimony generated by that campaign terminated in a duel between Samuel Gwin and Judge Isaac Caldwell, law partner of Poindexter, in which both men were shot down. The judge lived two hours. Samuel Gwin was shot in a lung and survived for about a year.

For William McKendree Gwin, the appointment as U.S. marshal placed him in a position to acquire large land holdings, including Section Thirteen, to which his kin would relate at various times for a hundred years. It also sent him on a rapid course to prominence in national and international affairs. It was he who, representing Andrew Jackson, spent many weeks with Sam Houston in Nacogdoches, where the plan for the independence, recognition, and annexation of Texas was fashioned and subsequently followed as closely as events permitted, including war. In Texas, at one point in his life, he would own 600,000 acres of land "at and around" the three forks of the Trinity River. In Mississippi it was he, more than any other man, who was responsible for new coalitions that reorganized parties in Mississippi and made Andrew Jackson the popular man he became there.

Although many of the new planters lost vast sums of money for themselves and their investors in the financial crash of 1837, when plantations purchased earlier for thirty dollars per acre sold for sixty-five cents an acre, Gwin became a wealthy and powerful man in Mississippi. Partly because of his keen intellect, partly because of his close association with his father's old comrade-in-arms, Andrew Jackson, whose success in ousting the Choctaws made quick financial and political fortunes possible.

Overcoming somewhat his dread of public speaking, Gwin ran for Congress and was elected. It was the beginning of an elective career that, for a time, would make him one of America's most influential political figures.

When he declined a second term, aspiring to the U.S. Senate but seeing no potentially vacant seat, his chair fell to Jefferson Davis, brother of his business associate. That office launched Jefferson Davis to a place in Franklin Pierce's cabinet as secretary of war, thence to the U.S. Senate, and finally to the calamitous office from which he would never recover, president of the Confederate States of America.

Suddenly in 1849, with the discovery of gold in California, Gwin's ambition took him west. He went not for gold but to create a state, with the intention of being its first senator, an office that had eluded him in Mississippi. The state that would give us such diverse figures as William Knowland, Helen Gahagan Douglas, Earl Warren, Richard Nixon, and Ronald Reagan first gave the nation a Jacksonian Democrat from Mississippi, Dr. William McKendree Gwin, a Holmes County, Mississippi, plantation owner who came riding into the boisterous mining camps of California's gold rush speaking for statehood. With that accomplished, he became California's first U.S. senator. Today his name can be found on every page of that state's early history, though not all commending.

Standing six feet, two inches tall, with a barrel chest and the neck of a stallion, Gwin was an imposing figure. A full shock of slightly wavy hair that salted early accentuated his piercing gray eyes. He had a Roman nose that overshadowed his jutted jaw and small upper lip. His ears seemed out of proportion to his head. Bushy eyebrows drooped over the outside corners of his lids like the fat woolly worms of early fall. He was a handsome man with the physical appearance of an indomitable adversary. Yet his only public physical encounter, a duel with a California congressman held before a cheering picnic crowd with beer and sandwich vendors, turned into a circus and a fiasco with a happier outcome than the duel fought by his brother in Mississippi. Mrs. Gwin, stationed some distance from the scene, had instructed horsemen to keep her informed.

As the first messenger galloped up she heard him shout, "Ma'am, the first shot's over! Nobody hurt."

The next horseman rushed up almost immediately. "Second shot. They're both safe!"

The first rider appeared again with more news. "Third shot's over! Nobody's hurt. They've called it off!"

"That's good," Mrs. Gwin said. A friend with her, impressed by Mary Gwin's conspicuous calm, exclaimed, "Oh, wasn't it wonderful!"

It was reported that with a twinkle in her eyes Mrs. Gwin responded, "Yes, but there's been some mighty poor shootin' today."

One of his many Mississippi kin, Charlton Hutton, seemed to enjoy telling a stranger that prior to the Civil War, Senator Gwin spoke with an eloquence the young lawyer never imagined he would possess in his efforts to prevent the inevitable carnage that war was to cause.

Suspected of being a Confederate sympathizer, which he was by birth and heart, he was twice arrested for that offense, once by General Sumner in New York and once by General Sheridan in Texas. Sheridan held him for eight months in the Fort Jackson stockade in Louisiana, where he was garrisoned by Negro soldiers. It is doubtful he knew at the time that his people in Holmes County, Mississippi, had been similarly humiliated by an expedition of Negro cavalrymen from Grierson's Raiders not far from the first piece of land he purchased in Mississippi, land that would bear his name for more than a hundred years.

President Lincoln pardoned him on the first offense. President Johnson on the second. Probably no other American citizen who has been federal marshal, congressman, and senator has ever in the nation's history been pardoned by two presidents for the same transgression. Whatever suspicions and doubts Sheridan might have had about the senator he chose to imprison, the indelible mark he left on American history continues to influence the national scene. Who dares aspire to the presidency without an eye to the electoral votes of California and Texas? It was Gwin who worked most zealously to bring California in as a state. And as a go-between of Jackson and Sam Houston for annexation of Texas, his influence in that campaign is indisputable. The two states now come with seventy-six electoral votes, more than a fourth of the total needed for election to the nation's highest office.

Gwin was the first person to negotiate the sale of Alaska to the United States. In 1854 he learned that Russia, embroiled in the Crimean War, would like to sell Alaska for as little as a quarter of a million dollars. Gwin saw it as a bargain and urged that it be bought. He failed on that occasion but tucked the idea away for another day. And it was he who urged the acquisition of the Sandwich Islands, now the state of Hawaii.

Largely by his advocacy, railroads to the Pacific were built and the Pony Express founded. As a senator he had urged Congress to "bind these Pacific possessions to the rest of the Union with hooks and steel, regardless of the cost." In the Senate he engineered the one vote needed for the laying of the first Atlantic cable. With railways, Pony Express, presidential go-between, and transoceanic cable on his ledger, perhaps it should have been he, more than a transplant to California who went on to be governor and president more than a hundred years later, who should have been known as the Great Communicator.

Despite his duel arrests and confinement, Gwin's disloyalty to the United States was never brought to open court. Just as many today feel an unaccountable heart tug when something still called "The South" is mentioned, Gwin's heart was Confederate, his head Federal.

Because he was suspect in both North and South, a native Southerner who opposed secession, he spent most of the war years after Lincoln's pardon in France, where he conspired with Napoleon III to establish a colony for Confederate refugees in Sonora, Mexico. Included in the intrigue was that Gwin would be appointed mining governor of Sonora and Chihuahua, a plan foiled by the newly crowned Prince Maximilian.

As Chief Pushmataha had died of pneumonia in Washington, far from the bones of his ancestors, William McKendree Gwin died of the same ailment on a gray September Thursday in 1885 in a New York hotel, far from his birthplace in Tennessee, his plantation home in Mississippi, still farther from the vast western land he had midwifed into statehood, and with no blood kin at his bedside. The wild, tempestuous spirit who had been a major force in shaping the nation for good and for ill, friend of kings, princes, and presidents, who had lived a life of romantic excitement and enjoyed the accolades of thousands on two continents, was swept from the stormy banks of this world to meet his maker in a sea of loneliness.

Buried on a hillside in California, his soul moves like a swift chariot through the pages of America's past.

He was as controversial in his day as Dr. David Minter and A. Eugene Cox had been in theirs. He was perhaps all the things his critics claimed, and doubtless deserving of the praise of his admirers. Many found him dubious of character and looked upon him with disdain. Many were drawn by his gifted and magnetic persona and adored him. I have found no record of anyone finding him boring, and the history of Section Thirteen is richer for his trod upon it.

At his death one of his most vicious California detractors, the journalist and historian Hubert Howe Bancroft, damned him one last time as "avaricious, heartless, and devoted to his own aggrandizement." Yet as the pen wrote on, probably knowing nothing at all of Gwin's early possession of acres called Providence in distant Holmes County, Mississippi, Bancroft eulogized him as

"Gwin . . . the almighty *providence* of California."

Had I been around in his day, I am certain I would have opposed him at many junctures. But should I ever edit an encyclopedia called "Characters," his name will come high on the list. For the dearth of "characters" in our homogenized and technological society drains us of drama, that great gift of the gods.

One of Gwin's partners in a land company following Choctaw removal was Joseph Davis, brother of Jefferson Davis. Whether he had an interest in Section Thirteen, I could not document with certainty. My guess is he did not because the deed to the land was in the name of Gwin alone, not the land company. I present him here because of his close association with Gwin and the history of the period.

Joseph Davis came to personally own a large plantation that experienced even more theater over the years than Providence. He became a Confederate, but his views and behavior were vastly different from his brother Jefferson. When a newly acquired young slave ran away, instead of the usual punishment, Joseph asked him why he did not wish to stay. The young man, Benjamin Montgomery, began to enumerate the evils of the slave system itself. Joseph Davis asked how he would feel if none of those things were the case. He saw the potential of the youthful African and they became friends. Davis, a voracious reader, shared his books with the young slave, and when each had finished a book they sat in the cool of summer evenings or by flickering firelight in the library in wintertime and discussed it. Poetry, history, philosophy, literature, mathematics. Their interests knew no bounds. In time neither did their friendship. Except one owned the other. That, too, would eventually be remedied.

Within today's code only the most blatant racist or a romantic, chauvinistic white Southerner would claim that a slave and his master could have been best friends. The fair and logical question would be asked, why didn't Davis simply set him free? But within the context of their situation, free to do what? Freedom then, as now, was an elusive and illusive thing. Living in the last decade of the twentieth century, it is easy for us to answer: *free to do anything*! But Benjamin Montgomery, as a skilled mathematician, was bookkeeper for the plantation and then became plantation manager. Not a black overseer on horseback, driving his brothers and sisters in the cotton fields with whip in hand, but running the plantation—deciding what, where, and how much to plant; which market to ship the cotton to; when to sell and at what price; which seeds and equipment to buy and from whom; which investments to make. All the decisions corporate managers would make today. This was not a story of Uncle Rastus weeping and clinging to Massa's carriage when the Emancipation Proclamation was read. Nor of Aunt Mandy refusing to leave Ole Missus because she had been so good to her. And certainly not the story of the many thousands of freedmen who stayed on in sheer desperation because they had no other place to go when the war ended. Rather, it is the story of two remarkable men who loved and trusted each other, one choosing to remain technically a slave on a plantation he would soon own. The other blood brother to the president of a fleeting nation called the Confederate States of America.

The plantation at Davis Bend, at a location essential to the control of the river and the key to the capture of Vicksburg in the Civil War, was occupied for two years by Union troops. There are heroic stories from this period of what Benjamin Montgomery tried to do for his people and for his friend Joseph Davis, stories not pertinent to the tale of Providence.

When the war ended, it was the desire of Joseph Davis that Benjamin Montgomery should own Davis Bend. For two years the Freedmen's Bureau operated Davis Bend as what they intended to be a utopian community for former slaves. It failed. In 1867 Joseph Davis, by now an old man, sold Davis Bend Plantation to Benjamin Montgomery for a sum considered far beneath its market value. Because the Black Code of Mississippi forbade the selling of land to a freedman outside a town limit, it was first called a lease and was a secret between the two men. When the Montgomery family openly owned it, living in splendor in the plantation mansion, Benjamin Montgomery was for one year the third largest producer of cotton in the nation.

The story does not end there. Benjamin's sons, Isaiah and Thornton Montgomery, were instrumental in the establishment of the historic all-black town of Mound Bayou. It succeeded and still survives. Perhaps in part because, by then, it had become apparent to free people of color that if they were to be free indeed, it would not be through intervention of government, nor well-meaning whites whose utopian ideas had given them little of lasting value, but at their own hands.

Joseph Davis, who had been a delegate at the constitutional convention in 1817, which made the western part of Mississippi a state, an apocalyptic salvo to the Choctaws because from then on it was open season on them, is not a candidate for sainthood. But the cleavage between the blood brothers, Joseph and Jefferson, and the bond between Joseph and his spiritual brother Benjamin are chronicles that should not be early shelved.

Romance and controversy seemed to stalk and haunt Section Thirteen. A contemporary of William McKendree Gwin was William Pinchback, a man who left a line as distinguished as his neighbor. A line drawn across racial proscriptions that remains in the memory and dower of Providence and Township Sixteen. An identifiable community and lake still bear his name nearby. Pinchback owned Section Eleven, a part of what was later to be Providence Plantation.

Like Gwin, Pinchback was the owner of much land and many slaves. Toward the end of his life he executed a remarkable contract with one of his neighbors. He sold him five slaves for a hundred dollars. The market price would have been a thousand dollars apiece. The document stipulated "at some appropriate time or at the request of said slaves they are to be taken to one of the new slave states and there set free." Perhaps knowing he would not live much longer or perhaps feeling the hot breath of war that was already blowing across the Cotton Kingdom in the late 1840s, Major Pinchback had already accomplished what he called upon his neighbor to do in this document. He had taken Eliza Stewart, a slave woman, and the children she had borne him to Philadelphia where they were legally manumitted. They came to his plantation in Holmes County where they lived in peace. Perhaps he had executed the second document as further insurance that the woman he loved and their children would not be reenslaved in Mississippi upon his death.

When William Pinchback died, his executor immediately sent Eliza Stewart and her children to Cincinnati so white relatives could not disinherit and reenslave them. He failed in his first endeavor but succeeded in the second. The family of Major William Pinchback was denied their inheritance but remained free. But freedom in poverty.

A respectable and successful planter could alter bloodlines

with impunity in the nineteenth century, with no recriminations nor expulsion from the community because of his interracial family. A hundred years later, issue of those tolerant neighbors would drive from camp a little band of Christian missionaries whose offense was civility to the fruit of Eliza Stewart's womb.

One of the children of William Pinchback and Eliza Stewart, P. B. S. Pinchback, would become an important figure in the realm of American politics.

P. B. S. Pinchback, in his day, was referred to as Percy Bysshe Shelley but called Pinkey in his father's document setting him free and P.B.S. by his biographers. His first name was actually Pinckney, perhaps for a South Carolina senator. Still it is curious his white father gave his mulatto son initials insuring that his friends would be reminded of the obstreperous poet. Why? Did the major, a man of letters, sit in the quiet of the evening and read poetry to his young family? Perhaps so, for the children, in the manner of the aristocrats of the period, were educated at home, and at a private school in Cincinnati. Did he look upon the chubby cheeks and strong hands of the newborn babe and fancy Shelley's "Adonais"? Or was he reminded of "Adonai," the ineffable name of God, knowing the very existence of the mixed-blood manchild he cuddled was as unspeakable to many as was the name of God to the ancient Hebrews? Did the callous warrior turn soft with fondness as he sat by the birthbed of his woman, bought but not owned, the ebony beauty exhausted from the aftermath of his desire and Eve's curse, and tenderly recite from Shelley:

> From my wings are shaken the dews that waken
> The sweet buds every one,
> When rocked to rest on their mother's breast,
> As she dances about the sun.

Or did some wretching premonition whisper that this little pink bundle with his mixed ancestry was foredoomed to the same rejection and expulsion as the poet whose name many would ascribe to him? Perhaps, hoping years to come would smile with favor upon his composite child, he then remembered some other words of the poet:

> . . . 'til the future dares for-

get the past,
his fate and fame shall
be an echo and the light
until eternity.

In any case it was an apt nickname—Percy Bysshe Shelley. It fit him well. Shelley's thirty-one articles in "Declaration of Rights" could have been written, for the most part, by the young Pinchback, social activist. They were, in many ways, an abstract of his years. And he must have known the concluding line of Shelley's "A Defense of Poetry": "Poets are the unacknowledged legislators of the world," for, though he aspired to high office as a man, when defeat came the words of Shelley seemed to be his view. This is one of the times when we wish we knew the rest of the story, but this is all we know of the lad's name.

Stranded in Cincinnati, the family of William Pinchback was free but destitute. P.B.S., at the age of twelve, became a cabin boy and worked the Miami canal from Cincinnati to Toledo, Ohio. By the time of the Civil War, he had reached the position of steward, the top position allowed a colored man, and was steamboating on the Red, Missouri, and Mississippi rivers. Early in the war he left the steamer *Alonzo Childs* in Yazoo City, Mississippi, ran the Confederate blockade, and made his way to New Orleans. As soon as that city was in Union hands, he enlisted in the First Louisiana Volunteer Infantry. General Benjamin F. Butler had issued his famous order No. 62, urging free men of color to assist in defending the Union.

Pinchback was assigned to recruit black soldiers, and within two weeks, operating from an office on the corner of Bienville and Vilere streets, he had a company ready for muster. Pinchback found fault with the manner in which his company was assigned in the regiment, and muster was delayed for several weeks. He raised another company and had it ready for combat in six weeks. Now Captain Pinchback, smartly uniformed with the markings of a conscientious soldier, found discriminatory treatment of his men intolerable. Whatever the intention of General Butler in calling for the service of free blacks might have been, the army insisted upon second-class pay and duty for those Captain Pinchback had enrolled. Though his fair skin would have qualified him for any white position, he resigned in protest. Still he did not give up in his efforts to contribute personally to the war's outcome. After a brief rest, he persuaded General N. P. Banks to authorize him to raise a company of colored cavalry. Again he was rebuffed when the general declined to approve Pinchback's commission, insisting he had no authority to use persons of color for anything except privates and noncommissioned officers.

Standing for the dignity of his people was a principle Pinchback would honor for the rest of his life. An early civil rights worker, though not always in the mode of Dr. Martin Luther King, Jr., he organized blockades of streetcars in New Orleans to protest discrimination against his people. He would have been proud when, a century later, black people in his native Holmes County claimed their freedom by endangering their lives for the ballot. He would have been proud when Eddie Noel, a black man living a few miles from the spot of Pinchback's boyhood home, who, according to local legend, shot matches from his wife's teeth with his rifle, used that same weapon to stop a mob, killing three white men in defense of his home, and managed to go free. But he would be prouder still of Robert Clark, another Holmes County black man, who in 1967 became the first of his race in the state legislature since Reconstruction. And of Mike Espy, a man of African ancestry from nearby Yazoo City, who was elected to the U.S. Congress in 1986 to represent Holmes County and all or part of twenty-one others. P. B. S. Pinchback would applaud, for it was in utilizing the ballot that he, like William McKendree Gwin before him, made his most memorable contribution to his country. Like Gwin, Pinchback became a lawyer and was appointed inspector of customs at the port of New Orleans, operating from a building constructed by Gwin before he left for California. And he was later appointed as register of the Land Office at New Orleans by President Grant, an office given to Samuel Gwin in Mississippi by President Jackson. He moved speedily up the political ladder. As versatile as the Gwin neighbors of his youth, he always kept various enterprises as a financial base, from owning and publishing a newspaper in New Orleans to serving as superintendent of schools in that city.

In the state senate he was elected lieutenant governor, and when Governor Henry Clay Warmoth, a carpetbagger from Illinois, was impeached in late 1872, Pinchback became governor of Louisiana for forty days. That forty days was said to be as stormy as the forty days of Noah, but the governor is recorded as displaying administrative skills to match any the state had ever known.

When his term as governor expired in January of 1873, the state legislature elected him to a seat in the U.S. Senate. Through backroom maneuvering and chicanery, the Senate did not vote on seating him for two years. When the matter reached the Senate floor, Senator Oliver P. Morton of Indiana introduced a resolution: "Resolved, that P. B. S. Pinchback be admitted as a Senator from the state of Louisiana. . . ." Two years later, the matter still not resolved, Senator George Franklin Edmunds of Vermont moved an amendment to Senator Morton's resolution. His amendment was to insert the word "not" before "admitted." Another year later the amended resolution passed. The handsome son of Holmes County, now an astute politician with the recognizable traits of a statesman, would not be a U.S. senator. Several stories circulated as to why he was denied his place in the Senate: he was a man of dubious character; the senatorial wives told their husbands that they would not associate with his wife; those already seated, some in their dotage with young wives, feared that Pinchback's charm and "Brazilian" good looks would be a temptation to the fleshly yearnings of their wives. Somehow, after nearly seventy years of observing and being a part of the nature of the males of the species, I find it easier to believe the latter version.

Whatever the reason, "Little Pinky," another illustrious son of Providence who added mightily to its legacy, never enjoyed the ripe fruit of his labor in Louisiana politics. Still, he had his say, as he stood on the Senate floor and declared:

> Sirs, I demand simple justice. I am not here as a beggar. I do not care so far as I am personally concerned whether you give me my seat or not. I will go back to my people and come here again; but I tell you to preserve your consistency. Do not make fish of me while you make flesh of everybody else. . . . several Southern Senators think me a very bad man. If this be true I fear my case is hopeless, for I am a bad man in the eyes of Democrats and weak-kneed Republicans. . . . I am bad because I have dared on several important occasions to have an independent opinion. I am bad because I have dared at all times to advocate and insist on exact and equal justice for all mankind. I am bad because having black blood in my veins I have dared to aspire to the United States Senate. . . . Friends, I have been

> *told that if I dared utter such sentiments as these in public
> that I certainly would be kept out. . . . all I have to say in
> answer to this is that if I cannot enter the Senate except
> with bated breath and on bended knees, I prefer not to enter
> at all.*

Though he would not have served with Senator Gwin, they doubtless encountered each other on many occasions. Each was too important in national affairs for it to have been otherwise.

With all P. B. S. Pinchback's fierce loyalty to racial selfhood, one who came after him was just as vehement in denying his lineage. One of his grandsons, Jean Toomer, author of the critically acclaimed novel *Cane*, despite the fact that he was one of the icons of the Harlem Renaissance movement, adamantly refused to acknowledge his black genes, declined to have any of his works included in Negro anthologies of literature, and maintained that his grandfather claimed to be a Negro only for political advantage in the Reconstruction period.

From Choctaw red to Gwin and William Pinchback white, from Eliza Stewart black to P.B.S. yellow—no matter the pigmentation, those who traversed the environs of Section Thirteen wrote out their messages on the slate of time. They too would pass, pushed aside by the same cold and fickle progression of civilization's hubris as had been those who came before them. But in the while, they would have their day in the sun.

CHAPTER 7

During the two decades following the removal of the Choctaws, the chancery court records of Section Thirteen, and all of the land ceded by the Treaty of Dancing Rabbit Creek, read like Old Testament chronicling. Brief reigns abounded. It was not unusual for parcels of land to change hands two and three times in one year. Land companies, attorneys, bankers, white settlers, and planters circled each other like matadors, each awaiting an opening for a thrust with his fiscal sword. The Choctaws who had been awarded sections of land by Article 14 of the treaty were prime targets for swindle by grasping men from far away and near at hand. Lawyers, and sometimes speculators pretending to be lawyers, feigned sympathy with Choctaws trying to establish claims under terms of the treaty. For half interest in the disputed lands, they would take the claims through the courts. William McKendree Gwin was among those who plied the scheme with vigor, which led at first to vast holdings and then to near disaster when it was challenged.

The influx predicted by Robert Walker at the celebration of the treaty was understated. In the decade of the 1830s, the population of the state grew by 175 percent, the largest growth of any decade in the state's history. Daily wagon trains and riverboats brought droves of new settlers and land speculators from all over the country, all in search of quick fortunes. The coronation of King Cotton was effected in dozens of florid ballrooms in Natchez, Vicksburg, and Clinton. Grand hotels for speculators, gamblers, traders, and visiting dignitaries sprang up in villages and new towns like toadstools that followed the warm summer rains. The rapid rise of stately mansions, slave quarters, and modest houses of ordinary folk reached for timber into the regal forests of virgin cypress and longleaf pines. Seamless rugs of the Orient, costly furniture and costumes from Paris came directly to plantations overland and by riverboats. Railroads with names like Natchez & Hamburg, Vicksburg & Clinton, or Mississippi Springs Railroad Company were being chartered and built to connect the cotton fields to the markets. Many of the railroads were also lumber companies and would soon have banking privileges, adding to the copious quantities of cash and easy access to it for buyers of land. Roads that had been virtually nonexistent on the frontier began fanning out from the Natchez Trace and Robinson Road like sunrays, reaching deeper and deeper into the bowels of the old Choctaw Nation.

Standing in the wings with both envy and awe, watching the prosperous few alter forever the world they had known, were the early white settlers who had eked out a meager existence on ground they often claimed by impinging extralegally upon Indian territory but which the newcomers, interlopers to these simple and hardworking folk, were quick to point out they did not own and probably never would. Yet they stayed on. To become the tools of the newly arrived aristocracy. To serve as plantation overseers on horseback, supervising the black slavedrivers who prodded their fellow slaves to greater productivity with bullwhips. Stayed on to become their "white trash," disregarded in matters of government, education, and commerce until they would be needed to fight a war in which they had no stake at all. It would be they who would swell the ranks of the Confederate army, would, for the first time, be needed and thus evangelized by the learned chaplains of the patricians who would convince them theirs was a holy war, and that, incidentally, there were human beings—black people—to whom they were superior. Down the road lay a revolt of these whom the carriage trade callously referred to as "rednecks," but for now, in this formative period of the Cotton Kingdom, they were not needed. Slaves made up more than half the population. Why then should unlettered whites be paid to do work that one's own property was doing? So their simple structures, the pioneer log cabins and dogtrot houses, built to turn back the heat of summer and stifle the chill of deep winter, houses they had built with pride, now became symbols of humiliation and defeat as they watched the elegant homes of well-bred gentlemen from New England, Virginia or Tennessee dwarf their abodes, the quick successes of the aristocracy negating the ambitions and dreams the plebeians had for themselves and their young.

White Mississippi society in the 1830s was constructed like a pyramid, rising from a broad base of the poor to a sharp peak of the very rich. At the bottom were the "rednecks," "river rats," or "ridge runners." Slightly above them were the yeoman farmers, working alongside their few slaves. Many more owned no slaves at all, the family doing all the work. The next level of the pyramid was formed by small planters, merchants, or managers for the large plantations whose owners lived in town or sat in a special room of the plantation mansion. Sitting at the apex were planters with fifty or more slaves, along with those of equal rank in the cities and towns—lawyers, political leaders, and men who had reached the top in their professions.

Despite the romantic stereotypes of Greek Revival mansions, gangs of slaves numbering in the hundreds working plantations of thousands of acres, the number at the top was exceedingly small. Fewer than 6 percent of Mississippians owned more than fifty slaves; the vast majority owned none.

Outside the pyramid was still another group, the slaves. Although they existed primarily for those at the peak, they undergirded the system as a whole, supporting the gentry financially but also serving emotional needs of the yeomanry by giving them someone to look down to. Completely outside were the banished Choctaws.

Those few planters who were at the summit saw their ascendancy as approaching divine right. Many of them had the view that the right to rule inhered naturally in them because they were best. The more cultured believed that alongside that right was a responsibility to behave decently toward those they ruled. Not because their charges were worthy in themselves but because to behave otherwise was to defile that inner fortress that they saw as their true self. Others saw the slaves, and even poor whites, as a subspecies and felt no obligation to treat them as anything but objects.

Such was the world into which the geography recently christened Section Thirteen, Township Sixteen, North Range of Holmes County, Mississippi, began its march across the pages of time.

William McKendree Gwin was one of the few on the pinnacle.
What was called Jacksonian democracy was hardly democratic for
the masses. Such a hierarchy could not prevail for long. The
bitter fruit it bore is well known and was destined to scramble the
pyramid.

In 1837 came the inevitable crash. The bank crisis would be the
first erosion of the system. Fratricidal war would be necessary to
raze it completely, but the financial crash of '37 should have been
seen as prophetic caveat. Confusion had reigned as newly chartered banks competed with each other, railroad companies
became banks, and gold watches or nonexistent property became
collateral for large sums of money. Planters, doctors, and lawyers
routinely signed notes for each other to buy more land and more
slaves. Within five years—1833 to 1838—the land offices sold
seven million acres, more than a third of it in one year. The
problem was not that people were speculating but that they were
doing it on credit, usually with little of value to back it up.

The crisis was explained to me on one of my many trips to
Holmes County. At the suggestion of Lee McCarty, a Delta potter
who seems to know everyone in Mississippi, I stopped by the
Holmes County Bank, where I was warmly greeted by Billy Ellis,
chairman of the board of the bank. Billy Ellis, in addition to being
a third-generation banker, is also a writer, voracious reader, and
internationally known big-game hunter. His spacious office is
testimony to his skill as a hunter and to the craft of taxidermy. The
walls are lined with mounted trophies: heads of pronghorn,
buffalo, cougar, mule deer, grizzly bear, and mountain goat
among them. Standing by the door, as if waiting for an opportunity
to bolt from it, is an enormous musk ox, mounted in its entirety.
With its thick, blackish gray wool, springy to the touch, it has every
appearance of life. Across the room, as if pausing in mid-leap, is
a ten-point whitetail deer, its enchanting eyes canvassing the
room like a security guard. In a corner, tusks framing a vicious
snarl, is a grown javelina, appearing anxious to race to the beech
mast and acorns of the Chicopa Creek swamps. I had to ask what
it was. Billy explained the javelina is the only native North
American member of the swine family and reminded me that
razorbacks are relics of De Soto's days amongst us. Drawing on
both his trade and avocation, he spoke of the javelina, or peccary,
as a dangerous animal. "They are a lot like FDIC bank examiners,"
he laughed. "They usually run in packs, they have sharp teeth

which can inflict severe retribution if provoked, and they are basically argumentative in nature."

The animals were taken by Billy Ellis with a bow. There is a story, an adventure, with each one. Hundreds of other mementoes fill the large room. The bows of hunting greats Fred Bear and Glen St. Charles hang behind Billy's desk. I have to be told that Glen St. Charles founded the Pope and Young Club. In beveled glass cases are memorabilia of other hunters and other days: Ellis's great-grandfather, who fought with Lee's army in Virginia; his grandfather, who taught him to hunt; Teddy Roosevelt, who hunted black bear with Wade Hampton not far from where we sat. Billy Ellis, the historian, told me Wade Hampton once owned ten thousand Delta acres.

I had never met Billy Ellis before. But immediately it was obvious this urbane, exquisitely groomed and tailored man of books and high finance seated behind the work-worn mahogany desk knew also of cat-head biscuits, tin-can coffee, and thick-slab bacon sizzling over a campfire.

But I was not there to hear stories of hunting wild sheep in the MacKenzie Mountains or stalking grizzlies in the Yukon. "Tell me about the bank failures of 1837," I said when he took a breath between tales of hunts and expeditions.

He reached into one of the glass display cases and pulled out a twenty-dollar bill. "I can't tell you much about it, but here's what caused it," he answered. The bill had the printing and coloring of a twenty-dollar bill in circulation today. But instead of being inscribed "Federal Reserve Note, United States of America," it read "Post Note, Bank of Lexington." And instead of bearing the signature of the secretary of treasury, it was signed by the cashier and president of the Bank of Lexington, Lexington, Mississippi. Dated April 1831, it promised interest of 5 percent per annum. "We call it broken-bank currency," he added. "The new banks issued their own money. When they needed more, they had it printed. Lots of it. It was a formula for disaster. And it wasn't long in coming. Within ten years it was worth no more than Confederate money was worth in 1866."

William McKendree Gwin was one of the victims, though it did not defeat him as it did many others. The policy also influenced the history of Section Thirteen for half a century.

Although Gwin owned Section Thirteen, he did not live on it. Nor did Wiley Davis, who had somehow wrested ownership of it from Turner Brashears. Davis lived nearby, but Gwin's base plantation was in the vicinity of Vicksburg. Gwin did, however, have a farming operation at what was to become, or was already named, Providence Plantation. I spent many days and hours trying to establish when, by whom, and why the plantation came by the name Providence. And who placed the white and blue lettering on the stile at the end of the walk where the old plantation house stood. In the beginning I assumed it had been put there when the property belonged to William McKendree Gwin. Then I discovered such lettering did not become fashionable until around the turn of the century. I located many examples of the same pattern in front of fashionable Jackson homes built about that time. It was during that search that I first came across the name "Providence" referring to Section Thirteen and the surrounding area. It had to do with a famous outlaw band of the 1820s–40s known as the Murrell Gang. Operating out of a cave near Tchula, they carried on a slave- and horse-stealing traffic and were notorious for their violence. Often victims were robbed and then murdered along the Natchez Trace. Slaves and horses were stolen under cover of darkness and hidden in the swamps of the Big Black River until they could be taken to a distant market, where they were sold. I had heard the stories of how Murrell was captured by a farm woman and her husband named Nevels. In a bicentennial edition of the Durant, Mississippi, *Plaindealer,* published in 1976, I found a story that described the capture of John Murrell, leader of the gang. Having assigned his highwaymen and thieves to other chores, Murrell was in the Delta region alone. In early morning he stopped at the Nevels's home and demanded that Mrs. Nevels fix him breakfast. Pretending to go to the smokehouse for meat, she alerted her husband of Murrell's presence. The husband waited until Murrell sat down to eat, then, seeing the outlaw's gun carelessly leaned against an outside door, Nevels grabbed the gun, captured Murrell with no resistance, and took him to Vicksburg for trial. The article stated, "Tradition holds that Murrell was captured at Providence Plantation near Tchula at the home of the Nevels family." Although there was a sizeable reward offered for Murrell's capture, Nevels declined to accept it, insisting he had only done his civic duty.

According to the National Postal History and Philatelic Museum of the Smithsonian Institution, a U.S. Post Office was established at Section Thirteen on April 29, 1847, and named Providence. Charles C. Campbell was appointed postmaster. Correspondence between him and William McKendree Gwin suggests the remote community got a post office through the prestige of Gwin, although he did not own Section Thirteen at the time. James Knox Polk was the Democratic president, Gwin had been a congressman, and his influence was ample to command the patronage. The tenure of the post office was unstable. It remained open during the war years but was discontinued in early 1867. The next year it was reestablished only to be closed for good four months later. Since the community was already known as Providence at the time of the Murrell incident, the post office must have taken its name from the plantation.

Little not open to question can be established about the development of Section Thirteen and the adjacent land between 1836 and 1855. The growing pains of flush times receded into depression and panic. Banks that had extended credit with the casual air of the saloon keepers serving drinks found themselves holding title to vast acres. Planters' Bank, opened in 1831 to discourage those wanting to acquire a branch of the U.S. Bank for Mississippi, and to forestall the efforts of Jacksonian Democrats to have a banking monopoly in the new state, suffered mightily from the bursting of the bubble. In 1840 Section Thirteen, along with many other sections, passed from the hands of William McKendree Gwin to Planters' Bank. But before that, Gwin had already sold it, only to buy it back at a considerable profit.

A deed bearing the date of February 1, 1837, on record in the chancery court of Holmes County shows William McKendree Gwin sold Section Thirteen and other lands, a total of 3,500 acres, to Samuel Thompson McAllister for $195,000. Gwin had paid Wiley Davis $40,000 dollars for the land the year before. With a few minor variations, such as Section Eleven owned by William Pinchback at the time, the legal description of the land was the same as the description as that sold by T. C. Parrish to the Providence Cooperative Farm 101 years later. By then the price was considerably nearer the original $1.25 paid for patented land at the time of Dancing Rabbit Creek than it was to either McAllister's or Gwin's selling prices.

The deed given to Samuel T. McAllister by William McKendree Gwin, in addition to describing the land, also states that included in the sale were all the stock of the plantation.

> *Horses and mules, all the farming implements and utensils*
> *with all the oxen, cattle and hogs, provisions and proven-*
> *der now on said plantation or in any wise attached thereto*
> *on the first day of February one thousand eight hundred*
> *and thirty seven, also the negroes exhibited by schedule to*
> *W. T. Hunt by James M. Gwin being fifty eight in number*
> *at the day of sale and also with their increase.*

The lengthy title, in beautiful script, legible in every detail although including some grammatical errors by today's usage, lists the slaves by name: Bill, Old Bill, Silas, Panama, Aaron, Hannah, Dorcas, Esther, and fifty others, most with names from the Bible. Apparently W. T. Hunt was the administrator viewing and inspecting the slaves for McAllister when they were shown by James Gwin, brother of William McKendree Gwin.

It was an ambitious start for the young planter, Samuel Thompson McAllister, along with "his heirs, executors and administrators forever." But it was a short forever. Four months later, June 7, 1837, he sold Section Thirteen, along with the other lands, to William McKendree Gwin for $143,594. A tidy profit for a physician in Mississippi too timid to be a barrister in Tennessee.

I was not able to ascertain what happened to McAllister. Both transactions took place the year the banks were in trouble. I assume he paid Gwin fifty thousand dollars as down payment with a promise from Planters' Bank for the remainder. When the bank could not fulfill its promise, he had no choice but to sell the property back to Gwin. Apparently the bank did not want it, or had no legal claim on it. Already they were faced with so many repossessions and foreclosures that they had notice-of-foreclosure forms printed in quires. They had only to fill in the blanks.

Gwins are still prevalent in Holmes County. Only one McAllister remains, and he originally from Webster County, claiming no kin to the brief owner of Section Thirteen.

Perhaps McAllister went to Texas, as many indebted planters were doing. A common sight was to see a plantation at dusk with everything in order—cows milked and fed, hogs grunting contentedly in their sties, chickens at roost, horses stalled and fed, children ready for bed, slaves in their quarters for the night. Early morning found the hogs complaining from hunger, chickens cackling to escape the henhouse, cows lowing to be milked and put to pasture. Stillness reigned in the slave cabins, the plantation house quiet. When the sheriff arrived to serve notice from the bank, everything was exactly as it had been when darkness came. But there were no horses and no people. During the night horses had been saddled to carry the master and his family. Slaves were led on foot through the dark swamps. By daybreak they were safely across the river, on their way to Texas, where neither federal nor state government had jurisdiction. There to start again.

McAllister, by the blessing of tenure, was spared that. Whatever his personal fate, William McKendree Gwin was once more the owner of the land.

Though never in his name for long periods, the land would remain in his lineage for nearly a century.

Mildly daunted by the currency problems, Gwin was not defeated. He set about combining assets and working fervidly to secure the success of Andrew Jackson's legacy in Mississippi.

Two others held brief title, but it would be more than a decade before the land where Luther Cashdollar and Jesse Furver reached manhood would reach its own majority under white domination, murmuring and complaining all the while, as if resisting, hesitating, throwing chocks and boulders in the path of any who deemed it theirs.

The year 1855 began a new era for Section Thirteen. A man named Richard Davis came. Although not a direct descendent of William McKendree, by marriage he was part of the Gwin dynasty. And it would be he who, half a century later, would put Section Thirteen back into Gwin hands.

I had pursued the history of Providence for more than two years. From the rotting plantation commissary—later the Providence Cooperative Store—to the county's surviving gentry. From the humble homes of aging offspring of slaves to parlors of Jackson's rich. My search had taken me to libraries ranging from Nashville's Vanderbilt to California's Pepperdine, the Smithsonian, University of Oklahoma, and many in between. I had reams of notes and correspondence, dozens of taped interviews. I had visited with former governors, former sharecroppers, and anyone I could find who might tell me even the shortest story about the past of a place called Providence. Still there was something I did not know and could not find. There seemed to be a secret somewhere, something outrunning me. The missing pieces seemed to hide in some dark and secret place, as if my young friend Luther Cashdollar had let them sink with him in the Arkansas cypress swamp where he died. Elusive fragments fled me down arduous days and sleepless nights. My perplexity flirted with despair; just give up. But through it all something impelled me, would not let go, as if the land itself cried out to tell the story entire.

Then, like some long-awaited yet unexpected epiphany, it came. I felt it more of an encroachment at first. Like something was saying, "You know enough. You know all to which you are entitled. Perhaps more. There are things about all of us to which another has no right. Privacy. Yes, in death also. Isaac Backus. John Leland. Your antecedents. Why are you prying? You are chasing secrets, dissecting skeletons, lusting after the flesh of those who trod these acres. The fate of the land is your sole business, not the glands of its inhabitants. Let their human frailties be interred with their bones. Gwins, Wyatts, McAllisters, Davises; humans all. And a human is a human, and a saint's mighty hard to come by. Let it be. Write of the land."

I was sitting in the living room of a ninety-eight-year-old woman in Tchula. Her sixty-eight-year-old son, archetype of Old South nobility, had driven me there from Jackson. Kenneth Foose. Erudite, fruitful in business, halcyon of spirit but acquainted with grief. I had not known him long but I liked him. He was of this place, knew its strength and weakness. Any notion of white Holmes countians as mean-spirited bigots faded in his presence. "Everyone calls my mother Miss Pet," he told me. "Her name is Ida but 'Miss Pet' is what she's always been called."

He showed me what remains of the town of Tchula before going to visit his mother. A rambling two-story house, one block from the center of town, had been their home. "A black family owns it now," he told me, with no inkling of resentment. He pointed to other houses along the street, old but still substantial. "All black owned," he said, calling historic names of whites who had raised their families in them, sometimes for three generations. "Tchula is 95 percent black now."

"Where are the white people?" I asked.

"Gone. Dead. Moved to the cities."

The fears and dreads in 1955 of what would happen if Negroes gained control had not happened. Even my own prediction at the time—that Negroes, being fully human, would behave with comparable power as white power had behaved—had not come to be. If equally good, then equally evil, I had argued. It had not occurred here. Why not? I wondered.

We drove out of town, across Lake Tchula, and saw lush fields of cotton, the lovely white and pink blossoms waving friendly and prosperous in the August sun, a stark contrast to the scene along Dr. Martin Luther King, Jr., Boulevard with its shanties and lean black faces.

As we passed each plantation, he called out a name. "White?" I asked each time.

"White," was the answer.

Perhaps it was the answer to my question. Power? What is power? Where is power? Perhaps only the land is power, for only the land is everlasting. The land was power when the Choctaws had it, so they had to be dealt with. And were. Gwins, Davises, Wyatts, the banks were also dealt with in one fashion or another. And yes, so were the Coxes and Minters. So not until. . . .

"What do these people do?" I asked as we again passed the row of houses once owned by prominent white families. "These houses look rather expensive."

"Not really," he answered. "This isn't Jackson's Eastover or Nashville's Belle Meade. Bricks and boards don't cost that much more than they did a hundred years ago. It's where the houses sit that counts." Yes, and the neighbors. We pay big money for neighbors.

I asked my question again. "What do they do? The blacks?"

"Work for the government, a lot of them. The county, state, federal programs."

Better than it used to be, I thought, remembering the days when college-educated Negroes did menial labor to survive. But not good enough. Blacks have moved from outside the pyramid, as it existed in antebellum days, to be a part of the pyramid. Generally they are not part of the base. The apex has shifted in personnel; pigmentation still the fence.

White folks own the land. Virtually all of the banks, the insurance companies, the manufacturing industries. They are the munitions makers, and engage in the hostile takeovers of each other. And the number at the peak is still small.

Not yet. Not until. . . . If then. If ever. Ah, the curse of Eden!

It was not so much what Miss Pet Foose was able to tell me about the history of Providence that made the pieces come together as the spirit she exuded. At ninety-eight she is a beautiful woman and gracious lady. Her fresh, never forced smile suggests she is at peace with the world. Her hair is thick and in tasteful curls. One imagines her at a sprightly eighteen. The son and daughter in the room deferred to her like doting and respectful children. She made her home with her daughter, but there was nothing to imply she thought of herself as a guest. The room was artfully decorated, and recent books, good books, clearly being read, were lying on a desk.

After coffee she apologized for not remembering more about Providence, then began to call names of others who should be summoned. Her daughter telephoned each one, and soon the room was alive with recollections. Both Gwin and Foose kin had gathered.

Mrs. Foose remembered Richard Davis; the others remembered the stories. "Oh, he was a big man. Very big. Weighed close to five hundred pounds." That was amended a bit as time went by.

I felt I was meeting Richard Davis for the first time. I had been looking but had not really found him before. Like a lifted veil. "He came here from Louisiana," someone said.

"No, no. Wilkinson County, Mississippi," said another. Charlton Hutton had told me earlier Davis had come from Wilkinson County. "We'll go with Charlton," they agreed. I had found a Louisiana census record that showed a Richard Davis at age twenty in 1830. Later, in the Wilkinson County chancery clerk's office in Woodville, I found no record of a Richard Davis as a landholder. Still later, in the National Archives, I learned that Richard Davis was, in fact, born in West Feliciana Parish, Louisiana. By taking one step across the West Feliciana line, one is in Wilkinson County, Mississippi. Everyone was close.

Mr. Hutton had told me Richard Davis's father was Samuel Davis. Samuel Davis was also the father of Jefferson Davis, whose boyhood home, Rosemont, still stands just outside of Woodville, in Wilkinson County. I asked if they were related. Different Samuel Davis was the consensus.

They joked about Richard Davis's size. Someone said he had his casket made and stored at Captain Gwin's Tchula Cooperative long before he died. He was so big he knew he wouldn't fit into an ordinary coffin. I asked about a "cooperative" in Tchula, thinking of the Providence Cooperative Farm. "It was just a store," someone said. "Sold everything from salt meat to mules."

"I remember hearing people say some folks shot craps on top of that casket for years," Ken Foose laughed. "He said he wanted to weigh as much as a bale of cotton. He rode in a wagon wherever he went." I could see an immense Buddha seated in a meditative position on a flat-bed wagon, pulled by two dappled Percheron mares. "Fat, but courtly," someone said. "Yes, Papa said he always dressed for dinner," my ninety-eight-year-old hostess said. "He kept a selection of jackets in a closet and if a guest was without one, he would have a servant fit him before the meal was served." The scene came clear.

They talked of a chair his bookkeeper ordered for him. When he heard about it, he was angry. Said he would never sit in it. Then when it came he wouldn't let anyone else touch it.

"Cap'n Sam was one of ten pallbearers."

"That was Samuel Donnell Gwin?" I asked.

"My granddaddy," Gilliam Gwin said. "He got the place. He and Uncle John."

As we talked on that spring morning I suddenly realized I was no longer angry at the white people of Holmes County for doing what they did to my friends of Providence Cooperative Farm. It wasn't that I approved, just that I understood. Then I was mad at myself for not being angry. Anger is usually easier than understanding. These were real people, not unlike other real people all over the world. I recalled some thoughts I had about white Holmes countians on my first visit to Providence in 1955. And the words I had written about them:

> *I knew that those who had attended the mass meeting in Holmes County, Mississippi, where my new friends had been summarily tried, convicted and sentenced to exile were no different from those from whose loins I had sprung in Amite County, Mississippi. I knew their essential impulses were honorable. I knew it well. But how could eminently decent, spiritually knowing human beings become so quickly devoid of the civility they had taught me?*

I had not learned the answer to my question in my pursuit of Providence. But when I left Mr. Foose in Jackson, I decided to go immediately to Amite County and give it some thought. And take my boxes of notes on Providence and see how what I had found out earlier compared with what I had learned in the presence of a ninety-eight-year-old white Holmes countian.

Daddy was dead by then. Been dead almost a year. I had started this part of my search with him, when he took me to the historical marker commemorating the Fort Adams treaty of 1801.

I had not been back to the old homeplace since our father's death. I had thought of him often while visiting with Mrs. Foose. As I approached his house, the house where I was born and spent the first seventeen years of my life, I slowed down to pull into his driveway. Then drove on by. This is not where I am going, I thought. One of his grandsons lives there now. I drove slowly enough to get a close look. It did not seem the same. The brick chimneys on the east and west sides of the house were gone, the garden that Daddy had not planted for many years was back, there were chickens, goats, cats, and dogs. Daddy never had a goat, was not partial to cats, and seldom had a dog on the place. At first I was dispirited. Then quickly took heart. This is Steve's house now, I thought. My sister's seventh child. It is supposed to evoke Steve. Just as it always evoked Lee Campbell when he was here. Steve's wife left him two years ago. His little daughter comes here on weekends and for a month each summer. She loved this old house when her mother and father lived across the road in a doublewide. Steve held his granddaddy in the highest esteem and is lonely now. It is meet and right that he has the old homeplace. It will be good to him and he will be good to it.

I was glad, for Steve and the homeplace, as I guided the Budget Rent-a-Car—now owned by Sears and Roebuck, which supplied our clothes by catalog and parcel post when we were children here—over the half-mile trail leading to my brother Paul's cabin in the most remote woods of the Lee Campbell place.

The cabin is more than a cabin now. It began as a simple camping shelter when Paul's children were small and he was a rising sales executive in New Orleans. Over the years it evolved into a cottage with all the appliances and conveniences of an urban home.

Only two bits of primitivity remain. There is no telephone, which suited my present purpose. And there is a well with windlass, rope, and pulley, and the long cylinder bucket still in the front yard. I let the bucket ease down the tile curbing, heard it hit the water, then gurgle when the bucket was full and the leather valve snapped closed. I had forgotten how heavy a well bucket full of water is. I strained to bring it up from the sixty-five-foot hole in the ground, wondering if it would be as clear and cold as I remembered it being when I was a boy. I tilted the bucket and drank directly from it. It had no taste at all: pure water never does. I emptied it into a wide-mouth glass jug, thinking as I did that never in my life had I had a toddy with water directly from my father's earth. Remembering too that he never had a drink of whiskey in his entire life, I felt mildly mischievous as I poured brown whiskey into the crystal clear water from Daddy's ground, stirred it briefly, and drank it down. "Daddy, I hope you understand." Knowing where he had been for one whole year, where no judgments are passed, I was sure he did. I hung the well bucket back on the rack, came inside, and went to work.

Where the property line of Daddy's place begins on the western boundary is where the end began for the Choctaws. For this is where they ceded a portion of their land to the white man and gave him permission to build a road through their nation, build trading posts that would sell them goods, where they would incur heavy debts which Mr. Jefferson knew they could not pay, leading to more cession of land until at last there would be no more.

I planted, hoed, and picked cotton on the land where this cabin sits. Sometimes the spring-tooth side harrow or buzzard-wing sweep would unearth the relics of the Choctaws—spear points and arrowheads, bits of pottery, and pieces of metal from their farm tools. Sometimes I picked them up, kept them for a while. Mostly they meant no more to me than finding an eight-track Beatles tape would excite my grandson today. So I plowed on.

What if they had resisted in 1801? Had said, "This is Choctaw land. It is not for sale, cession, or trade. Please get off our land and don't come back." But they didn't. So now I was sitting in an air-conditioned cabin on what we call the Campbell place, writing about them on a Tandy 1400 computer, fed by energy generated by the currents of one of their rivers.

Occasionally a deer, like the ones they knew, darts past the window, making its way to a nearby pond where mud turtles and willowy catfish contend for food in the drouth-shallow water. Rabbits and squirrels play, birds sing, and wild turkeys come by at night to feed on the cracked corn I have scattered on the ground. Coyotes have returned to the piney woods, and their ghostly howls pierce the night. Red foxes prey on rabbits and ground-roosting birds. *Tchula.* Red fox.

No phone rings here. I hear no cars and no airplanes. Things seem much the same as they were when the Choctaws treated with Thomas Jefferson in 1801 because of their friendly nature and a great famine. Except above the droning of the air conditioner I can hear the chugging of an oil-well motor, straining to suck the martial nectar from two miles beneath where both the Choctaws and the Campbells cultivated their corn.

I think of another famine. This one in the 1930s, known as the Great Depression. I hear my daddy treat with another agent of Caesar. This agent also wanted land for a road. Highway 24. I see them standing by the mailbox. The man says it is for our good, for the good of all the people. The road will be hard surfaced with macadam. It will connect Hattiesburg to Baton Rouge, just as the Natchez Trace had opened a route from Natchez to Nashville. Something about a farm-to-market route also. And no more road dust coming through the open doors and windows in the summertime, nor muddy ruts in winter. There is a problem. Our little house, not much bigger than the Choctaw houses of their day, was standing in the middle of where the road would run. The proposed road, straight as an arrow, will have not a single sharp curve from McComb to Liberty.

The man says they will move us. A more merciful kind of move than what Andrew Jackson imposed upon the Choctaws. Or so it seemed, though time would dispute his pledge. Instead of moving us to Oklahoma, they would put the house on wheels, move it back so slowly and so gently that cream would not be broken on the milk in the safe, and the wood fire in the stove could go right on cooking during the move, and fires in fireplaces need not be disturbed. In addition, they would give us five hundred dollars. It seemed a generous treaty, a blessing, an end to the protracted famine. Daddy said we could buy a radio, maybe even a car.

The dust was gone, as the man promised. But instead of four or five vehicles a day groaning in the sandy gravel past our house, soon hundreds, then thousands of speeding cars and eighteen-wheel trucks were roaring past throughout the day and night, their diesel smoke polluting the air we breathed, disturbing sleeping babies and ailing adults. Cattle no longer had open range, for a farmer was liable if a cow, hog, or horse was struck on the highway. Chickens must be penned, cats and dogs carefully watched.

Then one sad Sunday morning the blessing was revoked forever. A car moving at great speed struck my daddy's twelve-year-old grandson, Will Edward, brother of Steve, throwing him through the windshield, slashing his throat. Three mornings later he died.

What if my daddy had said no to the state's agent? But he didn't. And Will Edward is gone, as the Choctaws are gone.

Reminiscing on all that, remembering the time my father recited what was on the marker on the edge of his place commemorating the Fort Adams treaty with the Choctaws, brought me back to Providence and Richard Davis. He must have been one of the early benefactors of that treaty. For somehow he made enough money to buy a huge tract of land in Holmes County, Section Thirteen among it.

Or was it family money? This is another of those times when we can't be sure. We know his half-sister married James Madison Gwin, cousin of William McKendree. Perhaps it was Gwin money, for Richard Davis was just twenty years old at the time. We don't know.

He was known as Colonel Dick Davis; I first thought he was a veteran of the Mexican War, or perhaps being a major planter and owner of many slaves gave him the title. He was a bachelor on November 5, 1855, when he bought four thousand acres of land along Chicopa Creek. Lacking two weeks, it was exactly a hundred years later that several hundred citizens gathered in the Tchula High School and ordered the Coxes and Minters to leave the property Richard Davis had bought.

Large plantations must be named, to more closely identify them for mail delivery. Sometimes towns and cities were more than a hundred miles apart. Areas were not divided into RFD's and zip codes, so farms where large numbers of people were located were given names. Plantation names were generally chosen with the same care as naming children. Sometimes historical, sometimes personal, more often romantic. Laurel-hill, Grange, Magnolia Grove, Anchorage, The Oaks, New Forest.

Someone named this plantation Providence. I still did not know who, or why. I once thought Richard Davis named it, but that could not have been, for it had the name in 1847 when the post office was established. There are legends and oral tradition, but I found nothing of written history. Once I gave an elderly man a ride from near Providence to Tchula. I asked him if he knew where Providence Plantation got its name. He said he had always heard that old Colonel Dick Davis was sickly and prayed that in the providence of God he might be healed. He named his plantation Providence so God would think kindly on him. I remember the man asking me if I believed in prayer. He said he had just prayed that the next car to come by would stop and give him a ride so he could get to Tchula before the store that always cashed his Social Security check closed.

A distant relative of Richard Davis told me she knew it to be a fact that the plantation was so named because he and Miss Marcella didn't have any children, and they thought giving the plantation a Bible name would please God and He would bless them with children. Not possible, for Colonel Davis wasn't married to Marcella O'Reilly when Providence was named.

I asked many people and checked many records. Almost everyone was convinced of a religious connotation. Yet of that one cannot be certain. The word "providence" appears only once in the Bible and then as an accusation against the Apostle Paul by a religious agent addressing an agent of government. Tertullus, an orator for the high priest, toadying before the governor, said to him, "Very worthy deeds are done unto this nation by thy providence." Then he spoke of Paul as a pestilent fellow and a mover of sedition. Providence as foreknowledge, divine intervention, and favors came later, especially with John Calvin, who thought the most trivial occurrences of everyday life are directly decreed by God.

A more interesting exegesis of the word than divine intervention with benevolent intent is the harsh notion that providence has to do with disastrous accidents, catastrophic events, fatalities, regarded as acts of God. When Section Thirteen is considered in terms of the storms that befell it, perhaps some stern Calvinist had this definition in mind.

There are many possibilities. Slave ships were named Providence. Men and women carry the name. And Providence, Rhode Island, was an important city to Mississippi planters at the time, for it was the largest port and purchaser of their cotton.

There was a greater reason, I believe, why Providence, Rhode Island, became important enough for a tiny community in Choctaw country to bear its name. In most conversations the name of Roger Williams came up. "I think it had something to do with Roger Williams," they would say. Some knew that Williams had named his own plantation Providence when he was driven into exile. Some knew he had been the greatest champion of religious liberty and separation of church and state this new nation had known. Or has known since. Some knew he had organized the first Baptist church in America. Many, including Baptists, knew none of that. And no one with whom I spoke knew that it was his defense of the Indians that first got Roger Williams in trouble. His view was "that we have not our land by Pattent [royal decree] from the King, but that the Natives are the true owners of it, and that we ought to repent of such receiving of it by Pattent." He insisted that the Indians were sovereign peoples and not subjects of the king of England. If others wanted the land, he argued, they had to buy it from the natives. That notion was revolutionary enough to have him driven into the wilderness. There he was the constant and trusted friend of the Indians, learning several of their languages in order to mediate between them and the British in an effort to prevent the shedding of blood. And when their lives were threatened if they would not pray to the Christian God, it was he who reminded Governor Winthrop that the English settlers had been a persecuted people also.

This, I believe, is how the name Chicopa was changed to Providence, later lending the name to Providence Plantation and Providence Cooperative Farm. Cyrus Kingsbury, Presbyterian head of Eliot Mission School, where Luther Cashdollar and many other Choctaws were converted and taught, was a graduate of Brown University in Providence, Rhode Island. Brown was still heavily under Williams's influence. Kingsbury, when the Choctaws were being persecuted, would have told his students the stories. When they returned home and heard of the threat to their survival, they remembered. And began calling Chicopa Providence. That is what I believe about the naming of Providence. It is not what I can prove.

Maybe it was fortuitous. Maybe it was providential. In either case, it was fortunate for those of us who would come later to consider the history of a place called Providence.

About that history there are things we do know. We know that by 1855 Section Thirteen and the surrounding acres had changed hands eight times since the Choctaws had been removed. Planters'

Bank had been landlord longer than any individual. We know the land had been cultivated all the while, going far back into Choctaw history. And we know that for the next seventy-five years, though at times grim, it would know its greatest stability and continuity since Luther Cashdollar and Jesse Furver called it home.

Generally, when a working plantation was sold, the slaves were included in the sale price. Some things change slowly. More than once, as a Mississippi boy eighty years after Richard Davis bought Providence, I heard men, when negotiating the price of a farm ask, "Niggers go with the place?"

The slaves went with the place when Richard Davis bought it. Some carried the same names as those on the place when William McKendree Gwin sold it to Samuel McAllister.

> *One Negro man named Six, about 40 yrs.*
> *One Negro man named Randolf, about 13 yrs.*
> *One Negro boy named William, about 16 yrs.*
> *One Negro man named Jacob, unsound, about 31 yrs.*
> *One Negro woman named Petina, about 17, with her*
> *child named Harriet, about 18 mos.*

How were the chattel graded and cataloged? What did "unsound" beside Jacob's name mean? The word followed like a title. Or like a surname. Jacob Unsound. What standard applied to deem Randolf a man at thirteen while William was a boy at sixteen? Was Randolf a product of the selective genetics of one of the Virginia breeding farms and was stronger and bigger at thirteen than William, descending naturally, was at sixteen? Jimmie "the Greek" Snyder, on national television, cited the breeding farms that came into prominence after the Atlantic slave trade was abolished in 1805 to explain the dexterity and strength of black athletes and was consequently thrown in the corporate meat grinder. As evil, as detestable and obscene as it sounds to the tutored ears we use to filter the facts of history and deceive us, it did happen. And it worked. But if the unseemly of our past is ignored long enough, if it isn't discussed on national television, well, it must not have happened at all. Even the denial of the Nazi Holocaust is bordering on getting a scholarly hearing.

Richard Davis wasted no time beginning construction of the plantation house that would stand for almost seventy years. It was not to be a mansion such as those found in the Natchez and Vicksburg area but a huge, sturdy structure built for durability and comfort. While other planters had lumber shipped from distant forests, Davis determined that his own trees would be cut. The timbers and boards would be sawed at the nearest sawmill. Instead of importing foreign architects and artisans as neighbors such as Greenwood Leflore had done, he would design the house himself and it would be erected by his own slaves.

Most of the slaves who went with the place were young. Most planters preferred to buy the young, and doubtless Davis was among them. He did not trust himself to engineer the building of his house and he did not trust the slaves he had. He would buy others.

On three successive Wednesdays he made the trip to the Vicksburg slave market. On his last trip he took Jacob, listed on the roster as "unsound." Perhaps it was his infirmity that won the trust of the master. Davis himself, grossly overweight, was said never to have been in good health, although he outdid the biblically allotted three-score years and ten. I imagined I was with them on the entire trip.

Often a prospective buyer would talk to a slave being displayed for sale before bargaining with the trader. "You do the talking," he said to Jacob. "I'll do the buying."

Jacob didn't talk much and that might have been the source of his unsoundness. "Yassah," was all he said.

"You know what we're looking for?" Richard Davis asked him.

"Virginny," Jacob answered. Davis didn't know if Jacob had come from Virginia and was perhaps thinking he might find a long-lost father, brother, or mother. He didn't ask what he meant.

"We need a carpenter. A builder. Someone who can use a froe, a miter square, a plumb line, read a ruler. Everything."

"Virginny," Jacob said again.

They had not seen the usual posters advertising Negroes for sale as they rode into town, Jacob driving and Richard Davis seated in the middle of the wagon drawn by the big Percheron mares. Richard must have thought it would be another useless trip. But when they reined the horses to the hitching posts, then walked through a wide gate into a narrow courtyard almost totally enclosed by open-fronted sheds, they saw several small groups of Negroes wandering about the sale lot. The usual procedure was for all slaves offered for sale that day to stand in a semicircle, facing the sun, from the oldest to the smallest child, standing like ebony statues, speaking only when spoken to. These were talking among themselves, sometimes laughing, jostling for front position. Slaves generally tried to be bought first. It was a kind of status, meaning they were somehow favored, or they simply wanted to get the ordeal behind them.

There were several dozen. Slaves who had left Virginia or another of the older plantation states in brown rags at the market wore a common uniform: a short, close-fitting jacket called a roundabout, pants of coarse corduroy velvet, strong shoes, a white cotton shirt, and a black fur hat, generally held by the side to make for easier inspection. The market uniform was soon abandoned after sale, for it reminded them they had recently been on the market, a mark of opprobrium.

The women, clean and tidy, wore long, calico skirts, white aprons and capes, and fancy kerchiefs tied as turbans on their heads. They were even more active than the men. They constantly chatted in subdued voices, showing a keener interest in the transactions than the men.

Some of the traders brought the Negroes overland, traveling for weeks and months from places as far away as Missouri on foot, sometimes with wagons for the very old and babies. The more experienced traders had learned such journeys meant lower prices and therefore brought the slaves by boat or railway. This batch, as they were called, was obviously rested and clean, conditioned for quick and profitable sale.

Planters or their agents were moving from one group to another, asking questions, examining teeth, backs, arms, hands, and legs. Occasionally one would tell a woman to grin for him, turn around, or pull her dress above her head. Even this had the apparent air of business.

Jacob stood looking around, not speaking to anyone at first, but listening to what the buyers were asking. Richard Davis was resting on a bench neath the shade of the office building, as if waiting for a word from Jacob.

"You got 'bacca fuh ol' nigger?" a restless older man asked Davis. He didn't answer, just nodded his head in the direction of the slave man he had brought to do his talking. The old man was stooped and moved now at a shuffling gait. The few front teeth he had were worn and jagged, like a shark's teeth. The white man's nod seemed to confuse him at first, but he soon moved to where Jacob was standing.

"You got 'bacca fuh ol' nigger?" he asked, whispering the words, glancing furtively about, as if demeaned by begging from one of his own rank.

They stood facing each other directly. I fancied I saw a look of compassion on the thirty-one-year-old Jacob's face as he looked into the tired, sad eyes of this man twice his age. I saw him fetch a brown rag from his pocket, unwrap a small piece of chewing tobacco, pull it in half with his fingers, and hand it to the old man. Other men in the group moved closer, their hands extended for a similar favor. Jacob ignored them. The old man did not thank Jacob, did not say anything at all, as if to be openly grateful to another slave would heighten the humiliation. He had been bought and sold before. That he was about to be again did not appear to concern him, except he clearly wanted to be sold first. Still he seemed curious as to the role of Jacob in the present case.

Jacob had not spoken a word to him. The other men formed a circle around them and watched as the gaze of each seemed to intensify to a language beyond speech.

"Virginny?" Jacob said finally.

At first the old man did not answer and his face showed no expression at all. When he did respond it was not with words but with a broad smile of recognition and approbation and affirmation of what the younger man was about.

"Virginny?" Jacob asked again, more insistent than before. As if he had to be convinced totally before continuing.

"Ah yessuh. Ole Wirginny. Bone and bred in ole Wirginny. Mammy too. Way back. Ole Wirginny. Ole Tobit full-blood Wirginny. Yessuh. Yessuh." Jacob, unsound, probably had never been called sir in front of white folks before. He seemed to draw back, though the white folks were about their own concerns. Except Richard Davis, who had raised his mighty frame from where he sat and was watching.

Jacob moved closer to Tobit and they talked in hushed tones for several minutes, the old man gesturing wildly, nodding his head up and down, glancing often at the enormous man who would soon be his new owner. The whites could not hear what the two were saying, and only a few of the slaves, those closest to African birth, would have understood if they could have heard.

Jacob guided the man through the milling crowd to where Richard Davis was waiting. "Dis bees duh one," Jacob said.

Davis did not question him and did not inspect the aging slave. A tall, gaunt man dressed in white linen and carrying a riding crop approached them. "You want to buy this boy?" he asked Davis, seeming surprised.

"How much?"

"Well now, he's not a prize. I bought him right off a wagon in New Orleans. I'll tell you what, though. I've got six young and hardy ones to sell too. Strong girls and as fine a bucks as you'll ever see. I don't lie to folks. I'll tell you the truth. One of the boys broke bad back in Virginia. I got him cheap. But he's all right now. I worked him myself and you won't find a single scar from the adjustment." The slave merchant winked and made a gurgling laugh deep in his throat, an obvious boast that he had mastered the art of administering severe whippings without leaving lasting marks. "You take the lot and if you're not satisfied in three months, I'll take that one back. If you buy the lot, I'll throw the old one in for nothing. Reckon he's pretty well spent, but you must know what you're doing. He might make you a good house nigger for a few years yet."

The old man moved to the side of the two men, listening.

"I didn't come here for presents," Davis said, heaving from the burden of standing. "Let's agree on this one and then we'll talk about the others."

The old man looked at Jacob and smiled, perhaps pleased he would be sold, not given away as a bonus. And to him would come the distinction of being sold first that day.

"Give me a hundred dollar bill and he's yours," the trader said. Seeing accord, he quickly added, "Providing you're serious about the others."

"Never mind the others," Richard Davis said. "How much for this one?"

"You're a strange one," the trader said, shaking his head. "You strike a hard bargain. All right. A hundred and fifty and you got yourself a good old nigger. I guarantee him. And my word is my bond."

The two men moved toward the office, saying nothing now. Tobit changed abruptly. His shuffling gait became a steady stride. His carriage was nearly erect as he moved quickly through the crowd of Negroes waiting to be sold, encouraging them as he moved. "You be next," he said as he passed each one. "You shore lucky, Tobit. To be so quick sol'," one of the younger men said. "Neber you min'," Tobit said. "You be sold soon. Good place too. You be next."

He still had not put the tobacco Jacob had given him in his mouth. Now he did, and rushed back to the slave market door where Jacob was waiting. There had been a reason for wanting to be bought early.

"You buy ol' nigger's woman, please. Fuh Massa. Good wife fuh me. Good fuh Massa's great hus. Cook. Sew. Iron. Nurse. Bes' woman ol' nigger evuh have." He pointed to a frail, light-skinned woman of about forty, standing alone. "Cora. Ol' nigger's woman name Cora. Das her dare. Das Cora. Ol' nigger's wife. Sho nuf 'preciate you buy'er fuh Massa." The woman saw them looking and turned away.

"Virginny?" Jacob asked.

"Wirginny! Yessuh! Wirginny. Care'lina afoe dat. Den Wirginny. Massa brung her from Care'lina. Please buy ol' nigger's woman."

"You jump duh broom?" Jacob asked. Marriage was not taken seriously on most plantations, even as late as 1855. Often when a couple asked to be married, the master or overseer would have them jump over a broom, knee high, or some other ceremonial silliness, and tell them they were married. Others allowed parties, rituals, and celebrations.

"Aw nawsuh. Marred. Me and her real marred. Big party at Massa's house. Jes' afoe he died. Cakes. Pies. Julep too. Real weddin'. She a good woman. Bes' dis ol' nigger evuh have." He was pleading with Jacob, squeezing his arm and moving as he moved. Jacob did not promise. Instead he talked quietly with the other slaves wearing the same trader's tag.

Before noon Jacob, unsound, had skillfully maneuvered Richard Davis into buying all the slaves the trader had brought. Davis did not know he had bought an entire family, including the wife of the old man he was offered free. He paid the trader, arranged for the slaves to be delivered, then led the procession toward Providence.

Tobit was not the obsequious buffoon he had presented himself as being. He had, indeed, come from Virginia. But instead of being a worn-out ignorant slave with bad teeth, he was a man of considerable learning. He had not learned in the way Benjamin Montgomery had learned from Joseph Davis. Nor was he as scholarly and refined. But he had learned when subservience had been the intent of his Virginia master. He had been sent as a body servant for his master's son when the young man went to the College of William and Mary. Just as many wealthy young Confederates took slaves with them to war, servants were taken to boarding schools to meet the personal needs of the sons of wealthy planters. He was groomsman, valet, and general helper. When the student went to class, the servant followed along, carrying books, supplies, or sometimes simply serving as a mark of rank and affluence. While their young masters were attending lectures, they would lie on the floor in the back of the lecture halls or in the corridors, in much the same fashion as a faithful dog would do, sleeping if they wished, or just waiting obediently.

Not all the servants slept. Some listened, learned, absorbed, at times more than their masters who were often inclined to riotous living. Tobit had been one who didn't sleep through class. In addition to what he learned from the lectures, when his master was at play he observed the groundskeepers, maintenance men, engineers, shopkeepers, and those who built libraries, lecture halls, and dormitories.

He had told Jacob none of that. Nor had Jacob asked. Evidently he felt that Marse Davis's best chance of buying a slave who knew how to build a house was one from Virginia, where big houses abounded, and one with the experience only age could afford those in bondage.

It was not that Richard Davis took completely the judgment and recommendation of the unsound vassal. No doubt he asked Tobit many questions, gave him many tests, before deciding he was the one to superintend the building of the big house of Providence.

From all I could learn, that's the way it happened.

CHAPTER 8

There was, of course, no good slavery. To be human is to be free. Slavery, by definition, was evil. It denied, and sought to negate, one's humanness.

There were, however, variations in the treatment of slaves, whether out of stoic accountableness to one's own selfhood or pragmatic utility of property. As there is diversity today among those who own work animals, land, houses, or tools. I have known people to tie mules to trees and beat them with chains when they didn't behave as they wished. I have known others who coddle, cajole, and reward toward the same end. Some abuse their land through neglect and overuse. Others try to preserve it. Some shelter their tools and equipment from the weather. Others seem content to let them rust out and buy replacements. And so it was under the system of slavery. Slaves, despite all the revolting thoughts the practice elicits today, were property. Without denying some people are by character and temperament more kind and gentle than others, it is no great credit that some owners of dark-skinned humans wanted to keep them healthy and content. They cost money to replace. For whatever reason, Richard Davis appears to have been a man who chose to take care of all he owned. No one alive can document what did or did not happen during the years Richard Davis owned slaves and operated Providence Plantation. I heard many stories, none of them accounts of slaves severely punished with the lash on Colonel Davis's place. Yet they were property. Many who owned slaves saw the lash as no more of a transgression than dehorning a bull or branding a steer. While not designed to soothe the object possessed, it does enhance him as property.

Turn aside and reflect upon what this nation would be like today if the institution of slavery had never existed. Would the Cotton Kingdom have flourished as it did for half a century, bringing with it all its curses and blessings, curses and blessings generally indistinguishable in detached and conscienceless history because the alleged blessing of one so often resulted from the curse of another? Would there ever have been that particular and peculiar region wearing both the mark of Cain and the bartered birthright of Esau called forever "The South"?

"The South." With its romance, stories, legends, myths, mystique, separate history. Of what would we have written, expounded upon, defended? Who would we have cursed if not "The Yankees"?

Surely we would not have had "The War." At least not the one that put in escrow the stories, romance, myths, legends, and history that keep flowing from the pens of the thousands called Southern writers, but that has also kept the nation less than whole for 130 years.

No *Mind of the South* for W. J. Cash to leave the world as his legacy. No Southern Festival of Books held each October in Nashville. No Center for the Study of Southern Culture in Oxford. No stupendous *Encyclopedia of Southern Culture* on our library shelves. How sad, to be without any of those.

There would have been no Providence Cooperative Farm, and A. Eugene Cox would have spent his life as a bookkeeper in west Texas and Dave Minter a doctor far from the Loess Bluffs of Holmes County, Mississippi, and I would never have known the bonds of their friendship. No *Brown v. Board of Education*, and May 17, 1954, would not be remembered as a day of infamy by some and a time of jubilation by others. Who remembers that also on that day the U.S. Supreme Court ruled on a case called *The United States of America v. The Borden Company*?

No Big Jim for Mark Twain and no Dilcey for William Faulkner? No Uncle Remus? No Sojourner Truth, W. E. B. DuBois, Jackie Robinson, Mary McCloud Bethune, Ralph Bunche, Langston Hughes, Alice Walker, Thurgood Marshall, James Baldwin, Barbara Jordan, Andrew Young? Who would want to extract them from the glory of our past and present?

Without slavery, and all it held by way of promise that the new country would develop into a rich and important land, would we even have bothered to have a revolution? Would we now be watching the Lord High Chancellor on our, or their, CSPAN as he bows to the queen, she reading his prepared speech he hands her about drugs in the colonies, a bit about education in Wales, and something of the prisons in the territory of Mississippi where there is talk of mutiny, a new bill about to be introduced to further curb terrorism in Northern Ireland and violence in New York, then the House of Commons rising for the queen, bowing low as she passes, wigs in place, no blacks among them? Maybe. Still it is a poor argument. Assuredly the presence of Africans has culturally enriched this new country. So have those from Europe, Asia, Australia, South America. Only the Africans came in chains. For them to have come in the same fashion as the rest of us would not have taken from their cultural enrichment of the melting pot.

But will "The War" ever end? Perhaps it is because I am afflicted with that incurable skin disease called whiteness, or because I am of the South, that I believe to be true what J. F. H. Claiborne, a white Mississippian who believed slavery to be a sin and a crime and who was not sympathetic to secession, wrote not many years after the guns of "The War" ceased to sound: "Slavery was forced upon the South by the French, the English and the speculators of New England." Or perhaps I believe it because one day in Springfield, Massachusetts, a day when I had just come from a bloody racial confrontation in Birmingham, the pastor of a church located on what at the time was reputed to be one of the richest street in America, old money, made from the sale of slaves and rum, told me his most pressing liturgical problem was that one of the Sunday morning ushers refused to wear the traditional cutaway coat, and minutes later, with patronizing hand on my shoulder, asked if I thought the white churches of the South would ever give leadership to the racial crisis.

Claiborne continued:

> *If slavery was a crime—and this is not denied—what part of the*
> *responsibility should they bear who introduced it in the South,*
> *and did not hesitate to appropriate as many of its benefits as they*
> *could lay their hands on? Their merchants made colossal*
> *fortunes by the importation and sale of slaves, and then by*
> *handling the rice, tobacco, cotton and sugar they produced. They*

*placed their capital in all the ports of the South to deal in slave
labor products, and to supply the luxuries to be paid for by the
sweat of the Negro. Their very churches were built, their foreign
missions were supported, by contributions from Southern slave
holders.*

*They ingrafted it in the federal constitution, thus nationaliz-
ing its character and guaranteeing its stability. They made more
money out of it than the South made. And they only discovered
the sin, when to secure political supremacy for their section, it
became necessary to emancipate the slaves. (J. F. H. Claiborne,*
Mississippi, as a Province, Territory and State, *Jackson,
Power & Barksdale, 1880, reprinted by Louisiana State
University Press, 1964, p. 146)*

Claiborne was a wealthy and powerful man in the political
affairs of Mississippi, before and after the war. He was the first
elected congressman from Mississippi following the first Democratic state convention in 1835. He, and his family before him,
had been large slaveholders. If those were his sentiments, why
assess blame, as correct as his assessment might have been? Why
did not those on both sides of that tragic and savage conflict try
to heal the wounds? A few did, Claiborne among them. But their
numbers were too few to quell the whirlwind of racism that still
blows mightily across the land, a storm that carries no promise of
a day of calm to come.

Why are we still North and South? Was it not the prophet Amos
who gave us the answer a long time ago? Hearts can become so
hardened that even repentance is impossible. But it was not the
war of which we could not repent. That was a barbarous error that
could have been so easily avoided, though many still revere it. It
is, I believe, the event of slavery that continues to stalk and haunt
the land, and bear the bitter fruit of which all of us, black and
white, North and South, East and West, continue to partake in
ever-escalating portions. Is it because we who are white just don't
seem to be able to forgive people for being black? Hear the
evening news from Los Angeles, New York City, Chicago, Jackson.
Witness the prisons we go on building as quick-fix solutions, a
rate so high that unless it is reversed, in fifty years half the
population will be in them, the other half, I assume, guards and
wardens. Is there no other way? Is the warning of Amos, the name
of whose God we inscribe on our coins and recite in our pledge,

of no account? His warning was that transgressions can be so great that hearts become so hardened, by God himself, that we cannot repent even if we want to. It is a bleak prospect. Yet there was hope at the end of his story. Hope having to do with justice for the oppressed. He excoriated the privileged of his day for "selling the righteous for silver, the poor for a pair of shoes." He shouted to them that the soul of religion had taken leave of the houses in which they practiced it, their exaggerated and lavish religiosity empty of morality. Surely, then, he has something to say to our own rich and full religious edifices—fuller prisonhouses, teeming primarily with the poor. Surely we must hear his sardonic laughter as the poor are required by the mighty to repay the billions they have stolen in their banking and savings and loans schemes, attention diverted from this by a president calling in his high priests to bless him on the eve of carnage of the innocents in the Persian Gulf.

But never mind all that. The question was, "What if slavery had never existed?" And it is moot. Slavery did exist. And on a late winter day of 1855, a year when the subject controlled the passions of politics North and South, and Mississippi had just completed the most emotionally surcharged election it had ever known as Know-Nothings battled Democrats for ascendancy, Richard Davis and his servant Jacob were on their way from Vicksburg to Section Thirteen with seven of those caught in its web, as war clouds were gathering that would liberate them de jure but not de facto.

For months crosscut saws and broadaxes sounded along the banks of Chicopa Creek where the largest cypress trees stood. Winter was coming and the rains would drive the cutters to higher ground: the bluffs, where oaks, ash, and cedar trees were plentiful. Cypress would be for joists, sills, and rafters. These would be hewn to size by hand, the heaving, sweating big black men swinging the sharp broadaxes with rhythmic might from sunup till sundown.

Some of the women dragged the slabs aside as fast as they fell free, stacking them in piles to be cut into short pieces later for firewood.

Other women cooked over open fires camp style. Two meals were served. In the morning it was flapjacks—flat cakes made of flour and milk, or water when milk was short. These were served with molasses and salt pork thickly sliced and fried. In mid-afternoon a meal of boiled beans or peas, seasoned heavily with hunks of the same kind of fatback fried in the mornings, potatoes, fall greens, and cornbread made by mixing meal, salt, and water, patting it into thick cakes, and dropping it into bubbling lard. Sometimes there was rabbit or squirrel meat, fried in the fashion of the pork.

Older children made huge brush heaps of the limbs as they were cut from the felled trees, to be burned as soon as they were dry. Younger children brought buckets of water from an ever-flowing spring for drinking and cooking.

Tobit, rejuvenated in his new dispensation, moved spryly about the work area, ruler in hand, indicating the length to cut each log, the width and breadth of the timbers to be hewn. Occasionally Colonel Davis would ride slowly among them on his wagon. Work neither slowed down nor speeded up when he appeared. Tobit, late of Virginia, who never again after reaching Providence referred to himself as "ol' nigger," nor mentioned chewing tobacco, was clearly the one to mind. And if he resented Jacob spending his days in the colonel's house with his Cora, there is no record of it. Perhaps his gratitude at not being separated from her at the slave market knew no bounds. Or perhaps he had discovered the real reason Jacob was listed as "unsound" and felt no threat to his own ebbing manhood. We can't know. Jacob's "unsoundness" remains as mysterious as the "thorn in the flesh" to which St. Paul so often alluded when speaking of himself.

When enough of the long cypress logs had been fashioned into joists, sills, and rafters, they were loaded onto iron-wheeled wagons and pulled by oxen to a high-roofed shed and stacked into ricks to be cured by the sun and air.

When the crews moved to the bluffs, Tobit taught some of the men how to split red cedar into roofing shingles with the razor-sharp froe. Others went about dropping giant oaks and ash, cutting them into sixteen-foot sections that were hauled to a sawmill on the edge of Lake Tchula, sawed into one-inch boards for siding, some as wide as three feet. The durable ash was sawed into narrow strips to batten the cracks of the vertical siding when it was in place. Oak was also milled for flooring. All of it was returned to the kiln shed where it would remain until crops were harvested the following year and the building began.

It would be two years before the plantation house of Providence was completed. The production of cotton was the main agenda; building was done in off-season.

The preserved perception of Mississippi plantation houses is that of tall colonnades, festooned by Spanish moss waving sleepily from overhanging oak branches, its noble, charcoal slate roof accentuating with its dullness the colors of artistic draperies showing through broad, crystal windows, all of it extending cordial welcome to the carriage approaching up a mile-long avenue of majestic magnolias.

Such existed. But more often they were of the style of Providence, completed by the slaves of Richard Davis just before Christmas in 1857. Expansive but not showy. Designed for its utility and comfort. Built high off the ground, high enough for a man to walk unbended beneath the massive porch that extended the length of the front and wrapped the entire right side. A lattice railing, three feet high, edged the high porch and trailed down the steps to the ground. Two windows, glassed and shuttered, on either side of double doors, reached from the floor to the ceiling. The doors, similar to French doors but of heavier construction, were made of solid oak, intricately carved with outlines of birds, fish, and animals, reminiscent of early Choctaw writing. The posts supporting the roof, which respectably might be referred to as columns, though not colonnades, were cypress logs hewn square and sanded smooth.

A smaller, second half-story, centered in the middle of the first story and with a pitched roof meeting in a sharp gable, formed a modified pyramid. A small balcony reached out between two small windows. The roof was made of red cedar shingles, all carefully split and cut to be six inches wide and two feet long, overlapping in symmetric harmony. There was the usual hallway separating the house and leading to a thin passageway connecting the kitchen to the main house.

Nothing was painted. Sun and rain would supply their own decor over the years, thinning the cedar red to stylish brown, deepening the cypress beige to warm gray, leaving lumbered whorls, grains, and burls to make their own aesthetic statements.

There were no ornamental shrubs or anything of luxury to mar the natural landscape, which consisted of giant oak, hackberry, beech, sycamore, and sweetgum trees, not lining a graveled avenue but growing in no particular order, wherever the mated acorn, ball, or berry fell to the earth and took roots, all serving as bastion to a house named Providence. A house that would know lonely nights; Miss Marcella O'Reilly would not come for more than a decade.

Cotton was what it was about. Cotton and Negroes were the constant theme. And land. Projected profits were as exact as today's most skilled actuary with all his computing tools. A planter has fifty slaves. Each slave would make seven or eight bales of cotton. Each acre yields one or two bales. The average bale is four hundred pounds, bringing twelve to fifteen cents a pound. At the bottom figure, the planter has made more than twenty thousand dollars. If his land and slaves are paid for, he buys more of each. If not, they soon will be paid for and then he buys more. A wilderness blossoming like a rose.

It was simple arithmetic. An arithmetic that fed the mania that brought thousands into the Yazoo Valley as soon as it was cleared of the Choctaws. They came until the last acre was appropriated and every acre waved with the snow-white fiber.

But manias are irrational. The exponent of the equation failed to warn them of certain variables. Their mathematical formula did not tell them that every turn of a furrow in this rich loamy soil was a potential bayou. The loose, friable texture of the land could not long stand the annual plowings, followed quickly by heavy rains, and could not long remain the place where, with a little luck, any industrious investor could be rich by simply following the formula. The loam that formed the soil of Section Thirteen was slight of depth, and even the picturesque undulating ground of the Delta portion was prey for the floods to come.

But the always impalpable future seemed so clear, so simple and bright to Richard Davis as the Christmas celebration christening Providence Plantation's new house drew scores of the Yazoo Basin's elite.

Nor did the arithmetic reckon with an epidemic of cholera and a war that would begin in three years.

With the house completed, Tobit, under his master's watchful eye, turned to building the plantation commissary, the only one of the original buildings still standing on Section Thirteen. It was built with the same solid timbers as the great house, though not with the exacting attention paid to style of architecture. All one long room, it was designed like a general store, which it was. A place for everything needed on a plantation. From sacks of salt, barrels of flour and sugar, to surcingles, plows, axes, hoes, ropes, and clevis; cloth and thread for making summer and winter clothes to leather, cobbler's nails and lasts for making shoes and harness. All the things Gene Cox would stock in this same building a century later when it was the Providence Cooperative Store.

From the house to the commissary, which also served as the plantation office, Richard Davis had a row of cement pillars, fifty feet apart and three feet high. I was told the extremely overweight planter could not walk from the house to the commissary without stopping to rest.

Mississippi plantations existed to raise cotton. Although some also produced grain for livestock feed, hogs and chickens for meat, others found it more economical to buy those things and put every acre under cotton cultivation. Richard Davis chose to produce everything the plantation needed. Not only were there a large garden, flocks of geese, ducks, and chickens, swine and a herd of cattle for meat, butter and milk that belonged to the plantation, but also slave families were allowed to have their own individual plots. What they did not use they were free to sell to others. Most slave owners frowned at this because there were increasing numbers of slaves who saved enough to buy their own freedom. There were not many free men and women of color in Mississippi, less than a hundred by 1860, but the dream was alive. Others encouraged the efforts. Slaves were, after all, a commodity to be owned, bought, and sold for a profit. If an individual slave could pay a thousand dollars for himself or a member of his family, when he would bring much less at the slave market, the advantage to the owner was obvious.

Tobit was one who tried. His idea was to buy Cora, his wife, send her to freedom in Natchez, Vicksburg, or New Orleans where, as a domestic servant for a wealthy merchant who owned no slaves, she could soon earn enough to pay for his own freedom. He knew his master would not let him go for the pittance he had paid for him. He had proved his worth by overseeing the building of the house and was caught in his earlier maneuver. But the house was completed, and he had been relegated to picayune chores a child could do. He knew the master's yen for turning a profit.

He designed a lightweight hoe that a small woman or child could use for chopping cotton. Grass and weeds were a constant threat to a good yield in rainy weather. Two and three times in a season it had to be hoed. No chemicals or machines existed to do the job. The average hoe was made of heavy metal and was six inches wide and five inches deep. With a goose neck, which added to the weight, this was attached to a five-foot hickory or ash handle. It was a grown man's tool. The one Tobit perfected was of a very light alloy used for cotton-planter hoppers and housing for the cotton gin. A two-inch blade was as effective as the five-inch one. And instead of being six inches wide this one was four inches. It was attached directly to the handle with a short straight neck. The handle was made of lathed sassafras, the very lightest wood.

His project had hazards. He knew the master would want them made first for his own use. Tobit could do that in a few days. And the colonel might also simply assign him to the blacksmith shop and market them himself. Also, raising cotton was a competitive business. No one wished to give another an advantage. It was a gamble. But he could not sneak and sell them to others when he was on pass, the term used when a slave had permission to be absent during his off-time. Decency triumphed. Tobit quietly made a dozen or so, leaving them in the tool shed without comment. Richard Davis said nothing, just had more hands in the fields. Tobit peddled them when he could for half a dollar, burying the money in a bucket underneath his quarters. Mr. Lincoln intervened before Tobit had saved enough to make Colonel Davis an offer. But the day the proclamation was read to them, Cora and Tobit had a secret. And a choice.

The big spring that gushed thousands of gallons of cold clear water every day from far beneath the surface of the bluffs was not more than fifty yards from the plantation house. It had a life and history of its own. Luther Cashdollar and Jesse Furver drank of its purity. When all other sources dried up in summer drouths, it was where cattle and work animals were watered. Its flow was sufficient to supply power for the cotton gin Richard Davis had built, which, though primitive by today's computer-operated standards, was enough to meet the needs of Providence and three neighboring plantations besides. Perhaps the spring's greatest accomplishment was that Providence had running water, hot and cold, the year round. Water flowed by gravity from the spring to the house. In winter a large reservoir constructed above a Franklin furnace caught and heated enough water for bathing and washing clothes so the wash did not have to be done outside with washboard and water heated in an open iron washpot. A smaller tank attached to the wood-burning kitchen stove was sufficient for dishes and kitchen utensils.

Providence was doing well when the nation was plunged into civil war and everything it was or ever had been was threatened. Providence Plantation was not typical because there was no mistress to be served and no children to require nurses. Even so, the same rank and station among his slaves existed as on the others. There was a gardener, coachman, cook, seamstress, and housemaid. The masses were field hands. While more formal and fashionable households would number among personal servants, footmen, hostler, and chambermaids, the more practical Davis felt no need for them and if, on special or ceremonial occasions, they should be needed, he had someone from other services who could perform those duties. Because of his lack of physical dexterity, and probably declining health, Richard Davis did have a trusted body servant who remained with him constantly, and even had a room in his house. At first the war seemed far away from Providence and Holmes County, a matter that would be settled in Virginia, Pennsylvania, or the Carolinas. Yet loyalty to the Confederacy ran high, and soon a patriotic fervor swept the state touching the poorest subsistence farmer in the hills, who had only a visceral stake in the outcome, and the most powerful of the gentry. It seemed closer when word came in late 1861 that Union troops had occupied Ship Island in the gulf, from which Confederate forces had withdrawn. Richard Davis knew there was a war on if New Orleans was in hostile hands.

That war made its mark on Section Thirteen and Providence Plantation as it did on every part of the nation. Much has been written of it, and my purpose here is not to add more to that vast body of history. Holmes County, its western flank protected by miles of alligators, moccasins, bears, and quagmires, the still largely undeveloped Delta no one wanted to cross, was not a major battleground. Some things, though, brought the war to the doorsteps of Providence Plantation.

Samuel Donnell Gwin, a favored nephew of Richard Davis, was a student at the University of Mississippi when the war began. Richard Davis intended to bring him into his growing farming operation as soon as the nephew finished school and for the plantation some day to be his. However, he raised no objection when in March of 1862 Gwin's class was declared graduated and marched from the Ole Miss campus to take their places in the bloody conflict.

Gwin's record shows he enlisted as an independent and served with the Virginia forces at Leesburg and Bull Run. In the "Remarks" column it also states, "Received bounty." Although common in the Union, it was the exception in the Confederate states for a soldier to be given money for his enlistment. For whatever reason, Gwin was one who was.

When his one-year enlistment ended, he returned to Mississippi and assisted W. L. Kiern, a planter and physician whose niece Samuel Gwin would marry, in organizing a company for the Thirty-eighth Mississippi Infantry Regiment. Within a year the name was changed to Thirty-eighth Mississippi Mounted Infantry and by the end of the war was known as the Thirty-eighth Mississippi Cavalry.

Samuel Gwin was a sergeant in the new company but was soon promoted to lieutenant. Apparently he was an exemplary soldier, passionate in his Rebel stand. The history of the Thirty-eighth Cavalry reeks with carnage at Harrisburg, Iuka, Corinth, and Vicksburg during the years of the bitter struggle.

Richard Davis sat on his porches, or one of the cement rest pillars stationed between the house and the commissary, and followed the war with absorbed concern. Almost every day he sent his body servant to Tchula for newspapers from Memphis, Jackson, Natchez, Vicksburg—or from wherever papers had not become war casualties. He knew the location of even the most minor engagement, followed troop deployment and tactics, outlined his own strategy with the devotion of a general. Although the news in the papers might be days or weeks old, full of propaganda and mistakes, there were few days when he did not think he knew the exact whereabouts of his beloved nephew. When a battle in which Gwin was a participant ended, Richard Davis would predict where Company A would next be sent, generally with uncanny exactness.

As the wages of war came ever closer, King Cotton was imperiled with each passing day and every battle fought. Field scenes were unchanged, the same slaves doing the same things. Men followed horse-drawn planters in the spring and cultivators, side harrows, turning plows, and buzzard-wing sweeps in the summer till laying-by time; then the scores of men, women, and children, bent over or crawling on their knees, dragged the ten-foot-long canvas sacks as they picked the cotton, their doleful songs mingling with the mood of war and economic disaster. It was when the harvest was over that there was a difference. It was felt from the kitchens of Section Thirteen to the looms of Lancashire as blockades kept thousands of cotton bales stacked on loading docks or lying impotent outside the ginhouse, cut off from New Orleans, Memphis, Vicksburg.

Only occasionally did the reality of shooting come to Holmes County. Although fifteen hundred men from the county went to war, little of the fighting was done there. Soldiers from Grant's Army, scouting for another route to Vicksburg, were not uncommon, and once a party from Grierson's Raiders, on their second swath through Mississippi destroying railroads, made a brief but humiliating appearance.

Billy Ellis sat in his bank office, a spacious room that looks more like a wild-game preserve than the place where the fiscal fate of his clients is decided, and talked about Grierson's visit like a seasoned classroom lecturer. He often used the plural, first-person pronoun for both sides. "We" might be Grierson and his raiders in one sentence, Confederate in the next. If he felt ambivalent in a setting, "we" became "they."

"It was Christmastime 1864," he began. "Colonel Benjamin H. Grierson, who had come down in 1863, tearing up tracks and raising hell, was now a brigadier general. Major General Napoleon J. T. Dana had been ordered to destroy the Mobile & Ohio Railroad so Hood's Army could not be supplied by that route. It was a job for Grierson's guys." Billy Ellis paused, motioned to a nearby shelf of books and said he had learned everything he knew about the raids from Edwin Bearss, a friend and major writer of Civil War history.

Billy Ellis the banker, now professor, magically rode us out of Memphis on December 19, 1864, in a heavy rain. Trying to cross the Wolf River at Raleigh, all ammunition was ruined and the brigade turned back. On the twenty-first we left again, taking a different route. Christmas Eve found us at Ripley, where Grierson sent out two patrols to wreck the Mobile & Ohio tracks. On Christmas morning we heard the sound of "Boots and Saddles" near Tupelo and moved out. Verona, Harrisburg, Shannon, Okalona, Egypt. Fighting, burning, destroying. Tracks, engines, depots, flatcars, bridges. Nothing was spared and nothing was sacred that Christmas.

As the raiders turned west, in the direction of Grenada, I noticed Billy Ellis changing his pronouns to third person more often. The objective lecturer was fading, deferring his bias less and less. I knew that by the time the column reached Holmes County he would be a full-fledged Confederate.

Not far from Grenada, Union troops bivouacked on the site of the old Eliot Mission School, where Luther Cashdollar had studied, was baptized, and received his Christian name under Cyrus Kingsbury.

Billy Ellis took us through Duck Hill with the Union cavalrymen. I stopped him long enough to tell him a story. Seventy years later two black men, Roosevelt Townes and "Bootjack" McDaniels, accused of murdering a white man, were abducted in clear daylight by twelve men, driven to Duck Hill, and chained to two pine trees and there burned alive with blowtorches. Their bodies were left hanging by the chains until a white preacher convinced the undertaker to place them in a single pine box and let him conduct a funeral in a storeroom. Buck Kester, chaplain of Providence Cooperative Farm though never a full-time resident, had investigated the duel lynching for the NAACP and had narrowly escaped with his own life, crossing the Tennessee state line minutes ahead of the vigilantes, the cyanide pellet given to him at Tuskegee Institute by George Washington Carver in the ready position. Kester testified to the U.S. Congress on the celebrated case, and an antilynching bill was passed in the House in 1938, only to die in the Senate following the longest filibuster in that body's history. Billy thanked me perfunctorily and continued.

I had asked him to bring the war to Providence Plantation. Now he was getting close. At Duck Hill, Elliot (an extra *l* had been added subsequent to Luther Cashdollar's days there), and Grenada, the troops under the command of Colonel John W. Noble destroyed four locomotives and tenders, twenty-one boxcars, fourteen flatcars, a pile driver, two depots, six thousand barrels of wheat, four thousand barrels of corn, two hundred muskets, one hundred bales of cotton, and the Grenada newspaper's printing press.

Billy Ellis, even less the lecturer now, was concentrating on one unit, the Third Iowa Cavalry, a regiment of colored troops, as he brought us across the Carroll County line into Holmes. I asked him about the Third Cavalry Regiment being from Iowa, a state that had no slaves and, according to the 1860 census, just over a thousand free colored, and that counting men, women, and children. "Bounties," he answered. "Hell, in effect they *bought* them. Just like we had bought them in the first place. There were 86,000 colored troops in the Union army. Almost all of them were bounties." I remembered that Samuel Donnell Gwin had also received a bounty for enlistment.

The Third U.S. Colored Cavalry passed through Blackhawk, a few miles east of Providence, intending then to join the main body at Ebenezer. Billy Ellis digressed to remind me that Ebenezer was the home of Robert Clark, the first black state representative in Mississippi since Reconstruction.

Instead of moving on to Ebenezer, the raiders chose the Franklin Pike. Not far off of what is now State Highway 17, between Lexington and Pickens, the Third U.S. Colored Cavalry was fired on by Confederate troops at a small church. "Probably home guardsmen," Billy said. The colored troopers quickly dismounted and fought back.

For the next several minutes the description of the battle might well have come from one of the banker's big-game safaris. First one, then another held the advantage, advancing, falling back, stalking, mounting, and dismounting, the Negro soldiers rushing forward, moving from tree to tree as they fired. The bank chairman had abandoned his professorial bearing totally. He was sitting around a campfire, reporting on episodes of a thrilling day's hunt.

He leaned far back in his chair, laughed heartily, and summed it up. "They kicked some ass that day, friend. I'm telling you now, those colored boys just flat whipped our ass. Right here in the county." He paused long enough for me to catch up on my note taking. He snapped his fingers and touched his forehead, as if to add an important detail or correct something. "You asked where Iowa got enough black troops for a regiment. Most every one of them came from right here in Mississippi." Then he winked, smiled, and added, "Maybe that's why we don't talk much about that battle around here."

He stood up and strolled around the room, touching various trophies as he moved. "You want to know something else those black soldiers did?" I nodded yes. "Of course, all the Bluecoats did this. Steal, I mean. They looked for hams, picked up eggs out of the nests. Did your folks say, 'Go pick up the eggs' when you were little?" I told him they did. "Anyway, the soldiers got everything they could carry. Then they found the molasses. Well, a bucket of sugar cane syrup is heavy. Hard to carry many of those on horseback. So they poured the molasses on all the floors, then ripped the feather pillows and mattresses and scattered feathers all over the syrup. What a mess!"

"Now that was just plain meanness," I said, assuming that was the kind of response he wanted.

He turned to the big musk ox standing by the door, as if talking to him. "You think about that," the banker said. "Black soldiers. Some of them just a few months off Mississippi plantations. Slaves. Now free. Just womenfolks and children around. Think about it." He moved back to his big chair behind the desk, leaned forward, and spoke to me directly. "But they didn't." I knew what he meant and was sorry I had mentioned meanness.

Billy Ellis didn't tell me, but some months earlier Samuel Donnell Gwin, who would live to be a bank president in Holmes County himself, was fighting the same raiders at Harrisburg, just west of Tupelo. His unit, Company A, Thirty-eighth Mississippi Cavalry, was attached to Mabry's Brigade in that battle. His captain, J. S. Hoskins, was wounded that day. Captain Hoskins had replaced Captain Kiern, who became lieutenant colonel of the regiment but retired from duty when his right hand was shattered by a bullet, his sword drawn.

The encounter with Grierson's Raiders that morning was one of many battles Company A, Thirty-eighth Mississippi Cavalry, fought in Mississippi. In addition to Harrisburg, they were at Iuka, Corinth, and the Vicksburg Siege. Harrisburg was the most ferocious. Of the 279 rank and file who entered the battle, only forty-four escaped being killed or wounded. At the dedication of the Confederate Monument in Lexington, it was reported this regiment had the largest percent of loss in a single battle of any in the Confederate army.

At Chickamauga, Samuel Donnell Gwin commanded a detachment of his company, sustaining heavy losses. With him was D. N. Foose, grandfather of the man who spoke a word of kindness on behalf of Dr. David Minter ninety years later.

In May of 1865, Company A surrendered at Citronelle, Alabama, a full month after General Lee's surrender at Appomattox. Gwin's service record lists him as a prisoner of war for eight days. It states he was paroled at Gainesville, Alabama, on May 12, 1865.

Three years and two months earlier he had marched proudly and bravely from the University of Mississippi to a war from which he expected to emerge the victor, for the war was going well for the Confederacy at the time. When he visited his Uncle Dick Davis at Providence defeat was discernible; the pride undiminished. He was a Gwin.

Thirteen days after he was paroled in Alabama, Samuel Donnell Gwin married Martha Rosalind Durden. They moved to Wicklow Plantation, named by his mother, Susanah Van Houten Davis Gwin, out of love for the oppressed people of the Emerald Isle. The groom was assured by his mother's brother that Providence would one day be his.

Richard Davis did what most planters did whose plantations were intact when the war ended. Lincoln's Emancipation Proclamation went into effect January 1, 1863. But it spoke only of the slaves in states then in rebellion, not to slave states that had not seceded. Thus it was an order from an enemy and meant nothing. With defeat, the slaves free, Richard Davis told his body servant to summon every Negro man, woman, and child by ringing the plantation bell. When they were all assembled, Davis, sitting on one of the resting pillars mid-way between the house and commissary, as if removing himself as far as possible from the two symbols of bygone ascendancy, unfolded a faded and rumpled copy of the Chicago *Times*, a paper once raided and closed by General Ambrose Burnside for "repeated expression of disloyalty and incendiary statements," and began to read aloud. Holding with steady hands the paper his nephew had found on a battlefield, hoary locks falling over his forehead and partially blocking eyes already bedimmed by his poor health, he read Lincoln's proclamation in its entirety. While many similar scenes reported wild jubilation, with whole families racing from slave quarters, carrying nothing but the rags on their backs, exulting as they ran at hearing the word "free" from the lips of the master, there was only silence here. Doubtless many did not understand what they heard, though all knew the war and slavery were over.

Richard Davis sat staring at the ground, adding nothing to what he had read. There was only a scant stirring in the ranks of those gathered, no longer owned, as helpless in their freedom as the hapless Choctaws had been in their captivity and trek west.

It had been but thirty years since the *Brandywine* weighed anchor in Vicksburg harbor taking the last of the Choctaws, leaving the cheering throng certain of quick wealth and a kingdom that would last forever. Thirty years. From desolation to abundance to destruction. Section Thirteen had not been the same since the days of Luther Cashdollar and Jesse Furver. And now, again, it would not be the same. Ever.

> *How are the mighty fallen,*
> *and the weapons of war perished!*

The whips of scorpions had begun. The spoils of Dancing Rabbit would be grist for the receivers of tribute who would soon be coming, like the floods of Chicopa, with not even their satchels made of cotton—but carpet.

Both William McKendree Gwin, the father of Providence, and Abraham Lincoln had dreamed of a union preserved without the elimination of the institution of slavery. Their fantasy was short-lived. Lincoln was dead. Gwin, recently freed from prison in Louisiana, was back in Mexico trying to salvage the empire he fancied he could build there. Jefferson Davis, the man who had taken Gwin's seat in Congress, starting him on the speedy trek to the presidency of the lost cause, was in prison, arrested, it was believed, trying to flee his defeated confederacy.

Richard Davis's heavy thighs were draped over the edges of the cement pillar like a nesting swan, his hands folded over his floating belly. There still had been no response to his reading of the fallen president's words. They must have known their shackles had been but slightly loosened by the terms of Appomattox. And Richard Davis must have known his life as landlord or employer would be no different from a life of alleged ownership, that the unfettering of the chains of history that inextricably held himself and the pitiful souls standing or hunkering nearby was a long way off.

I, of course, do not know exactly what happened that day. What I have said of the day's events is not of one cloth but are bits and pieces of folk history, remnants gleaned from the elders of Holmes who have kindly shared the stories they heard from others who, in turn, heard them from yet others. I like to imagine it was Tobit the builder who spoke first. "What we gon' do, Massa?"

If that's the way it happened, it was a question of great profundity and magnitude. It was the appropriate question, the only question, a question of understood, intuited community and mutuality: What *we* gon' do? The question that should be directed at every house of government by every heir of Jacob Unsound, every issue of Jesse Furver and Luther Cashdollar, every ghetto dweller and street person, and then, as an echo, asked by every agent of government and society of those who asked: What we gon' do?

I want to believe what I was told Richard Davis said in response. If so, it was honest and inspired. Shifting his mighty weight, struggling to stand and walk, he replied, "I don't know. But we'll do something."

The first evidence I found of either party doing "something" was a document in the National Archives entitled "AGREEMENT WITH FREEDMEN."

> *This agreement made this . . . . . **19th** . . . . . day of . . . . .*
> ***August** . . . . . A.D. 1865, by and between . . . . . **Richard Davis***
> *. . . . . of the . . . . . **County of** . . . . . **Holmes** and state of*
> *Mississippi, of the first part, and the person hereinafter named*
> *and undersigned, Freedman of the same place, part hereto of the*
> *second part.*
>
> *. . . . .*
>
> *WITNESSETH. That for the purpose of cultivating the planta-*
> *tion known as the . . . . . **Providence Plantation** . . . . . in the*
> *. . . . . **county and state** aforesaid, during the year commencing*
> *on the . . . . . **19th** . . . . . day of **August** A.D. 1865, and*
> *terminating on the 1st day of January, 1866. The said . . . . .*
> ***Richard Davis** . . . . . party of the first part, in consideration of*
> *the promises and conditions hereinafter mentioned on the part of*
> *the second part, agrees to furnish to said laborers and those*
> *rightfully dependent upon them, free of charge, clothing and food*
> *of good quality and sufficient quantity; good and sufficient*
> *quarters; medical attendance when necessary, and kind and*
> *humane treatment; to exact only one half of a day labor on*
> *Saturdays, and none whatever on Sunday.*

The contract further stated that if either party did not meet the terms, legal recourse was left to the parties aggrieved, and the offending party would also "be punished in such manner as the Provost Marshal of Freedmen shall deem proper." Grievous words for both parties, for a principle forced to turn to the sanction of law bespeaks its failure.

There was no mention of wages in the contract. Although some small stipend was assumed, except for a signed agreement with the U.S. government calling for humane treatment, the Freedmen's Bureau contract was no different from slavery. Still there was that melodic ring to the magic and long-dreamed word: *freedom.*

> *Ooooo Freedom,*
> *Ooooo Freedom,*
> *Ooooo Freedom over me, over me.*

> *Before I'll be a slave*
> *I'll be buried in my grave,*
> *And go home to my Lord,*
> *And be free.*

Surely those huddled around Richard Davis that day did not foresee that a hundred years later those words would echo from the steps of the liberator's monument to the banks of Chicopa Creek where they were gathered, still in quest of the dream deferred. The document Richard Davis had read said they were free that very day.

Although the creeping tendrils of subjugation had penetrated every acre of Southern ground, Providence was more fortunate than those plantations caught in the burning and ravening of advancing armies. At least the fertility of the fields had not retired, their barns were standing, their stock alive; they could somehow go on. Money was what Richard Davis's crippled empire lacked. If the Freedmen's Bureau required payment of cash to the laborers—cash impossible to borrow, for their land was worthless on the market, Confederate currency good only for papering the freedmen's shanties to partially meet the pre-scribed "good and sufficient quarters"—the landowners were stymied.

A different arrangement, one in which each party would assume both risk and responsibility, with cash at a minimum, was needed.

Sharecropping had begun. In that system, one party owns the land, and another works it for an agreed-upon portion of the crops. Sharecropping would last in various forms until the middle of the twentieth century. It could have been a benign system, a propitiation for the cruelty of slavery. In some cases it was. In *Lanterns on the Levee*, William Alexander Percy gave a summary of what the system intended when he quoted the words of his grandfather to the former Percy slaves on a plantation not far from Providence:

> *I have land which you need, and you have muscles which I need; let's put what we've got in the same pot and call it ours. I'll give you all the land you can work, a house to live in, a garden plot and room to raise chickens, hogs, and cows if you can come by them, and all the wood you can cut for fuel. I'll direct and oversee you. I'll get you a doctor when you are sick. Until the crop comes in I'll try to keep you from going hungry or naked insofar as I am able. I'll pay the taxes and I'll furnish the mules and plows and gear and whatever else is necessary to make a crop. This is what I promise to do. You will plant and cultivate and gather this crop as I direct. This is what you will promise to do. When the crop is picked, half of it will be mine and half yours. If I have supplied you with money or food or clothing or anything else during the year, I will charge it against your half of the crop. I shall handle the selling of the cotton and cottonseed because I know more than you do about their value. But the corn you may sell or eat or use for seed as you like. If the price of cotton is good, we shall both make something. If it is bad, neither of us will make anything, but I shall probably lose the place and you will lose nothing because you have nothing to lose. It's a hard contract in these hard times for both of us, but it's just and self-respecting and if we both do our part and have a little luck we can both prosper under it.*

Two equally honest and sincere men, each seeing the other as his equal in every regard, sitting on the levee discussing their common plight, could not have improved on such a covenant. It seemed, from the former slave's seat, a better deal than the freedmen's work contract, which promised him nothing except continued existence on land belonging to another. But like most economic systems, it did nothing to harness the inherent perversion of humankind. Percy represented the most benevolent among Southern planters and meant to keep his end of the bargain. For the system to work fairly, let alone profitably, for the freed slaves, the owner had to be upright in all his dealing. This proved to be the exception, and the bitter fruit the system bore would be harvested for many decades, with one of its abuses giving rise to the advent of Providence Cooperative Farm seventy-three years later. That abuse, in the days of Henry Wallace as secretary of agriculture under Franklin Roosevelt, both men sympathetic to the plight of the poor, reached its peak when planters were paid by the U.S. government to plow under thousands of acres of cotton, then subsidized not to plant those acres in the years that followed, reducing the need for sharecroppers or farm labor. A lumber company "farming" seventeen thousand acres of cotton could reduce the planted acreage so that half the families were of no use so they were simply removed. When tenants and sharecroppers tried to organize themselves as the Southern Tenant Farmers Union, the evictions became commonplace. When chemicals and machines began doing most of the work, the situation was compounded. The lord of the land was lord of its increase. From deceitful scales to Smith and Wessons at settlement time to appropriating government programs to their own coffers, landowners could always see to it that the one who hoed the corn need not be the one who ate the corn.

But all that lay in the future on the day in 1865 when Richard Davis gathered those he had owned and told them they were free to leave.

I do not know how many of the ex-slaves left Providence Plantation. I found contracts for thirty-one adults and eleven dependents. There were far more than that number when the war began. Perhaps some had been sold when the blockades made raising cotton unprofitable. Maybe some had run away, joined Grant's scouting patrols or the Third Colored Regiment when it came through. Or perhaps there were other labor contracts I did not find. It is also conceivable that Richard Davis chose to contract with just those he needed or wanted. Apparently the old way of ranking workers was retained. Among the labor contracts there were two eleven year olds and two eight year olds. On the "dependents" roster there was a twelve year old, one eleven, and two eight year olds listed. I searched in vain for the names of Jacob Unsound, Tobit, and Cora. Possibly they took the money Tobit had made selling his lightweight hoe and left. I don't know. I especially wanted to know what last names they would have taken. Only four adults listed Davis as their surname.

Richard Davis was thirty-five years old when the war ended, and he decided to continue Providence Plantation with labor contracted with the government so recently an enemy. I knew he had sworn allegiance to the Confederacy and did not fit the conditions of general amnesty announced by President Andrew Johnson. Under those provisions, Confederate leaders and those whose property exceeded $20,000 were required to ask the president individually for forgiveness and restoration of citizenship. Richard Davis was not a Confederate leader, but his holdings were worth far more than $20,000. He must petition the president directly. I needed to know more.

I talked by phone with a man named Mike Music of the Military Records Center of the National Archives. Somehow so delightful a name seemed incongruous with so martial sounding a job. He was courteous and accommodating, promising to call back as soon as he found anything on Colonel Richard Davis's military career. In less than an hour he called. He laughed and said, "If your 'Colonel' Davis was in fact a colonel, he must have been one hell of a soldier. His total time in the army was three weeks." I had long suspected he was colonel of the land, not of battle.

Two days later I received Richard Davis's plea for amnesty and pardon.

> *TO HIS EXCELLENCY ANDREW JOHNSON,*
> *PRESIDENT OF THE UNITED STATES OF AMERICA*
>
> *Your petitioner Richard Davis, a citizen and resident of Holmes County and state of Mississippi states that he was born in the parish of West Feliciana in the state of Louisiana, has resided in said county of Holmes about thirty one years & is thirty five years old. He believes that his property is worth something over twenty thousand dollars. He further states that he was during the late war between the United States & the so-called Confederate or Southern states liable to military service under the Confederate government as a conscript, and, as such, was sworn in as a soldier, recommended for light duty but was in a few weeks discharged from the service on account of physical disability. He further states that he is advised he is excepted from amnesty and pardon in consequence of his property being worth twenty thousand dollars, by the first exception of your proclamation of and on the 29th day of April 1865. He further states that*

he has taken and subscribed the amnesty oath set forth in said
proclamation, and intends to observe & keep the same. He
further states that he desires to see harmony & good feeling
between the two sections restored and will use his influence to
that effect. He further states that he is a planter. He wishes to be
restored to all the rights of citizenship. The premises being
considered he asks your excellency to grant unto him amnesty
and pardon as a participant in the late rebellion, according to
the terms of said proclamation, with the restoration of all rights
of property, except as to slaves.

Sworn to and subscribed
before me this 13th day
of July 1865

Richard Davis

It must have been a harsh elixir, retroactively denouncing the
Confederate Cause; calling it a rebellion, the "so-called Confederate or Southern states."

While awaiting restoration to full citizenship, Richard Davis
went about running Providence Plantation the way he had done
since he came to Section Thirteen in 1855. But now there were
added expenses. An elaborate system of bookkeeping had to be
maintained, for the watchful eye of the Freedmen's Bureau was
never far away. At one point that required two full-time ac-
countants.

When I was growing up, the turbulence of the years following
the Civil War was etched into the consciousness of every white
schoolchild of the South so graphically it could never be forgotten.
I have since wished I could have known how the subject was
handled in the then rigidly segregated black schools or in other
regions. Scalawags, carpetbaggers, and Republicans were words
as odious as Judas. The word "scalloway" was an epithet brought
by our Scots-Irish forebears and meant a filthy cow, sheep, or hog
of the Shetland Islands, applied derisively to anyone considered
to be the lowest form of humanity. In time it was corrupted to
"scalawag," generally used on a personal level with no political
significance until it became synonymous with a native Southerner who joined forces with the Yankees for personal gain.
Carpetbaggers were those of the North who came down by the
tens of thousands following the war, or Union soldiers who

simply remained, and carried all their belongings in one piece of hand luggage, the carpetbag, expecting soon to have it filled with what was left of the South's gold. In time I learned what had been described to us were not portraits but caricatures. The scalawags included men who had been Confederate generals, wartime governors, planters, poor whites, lawyers, clergymen, former Whigs, and businessmen, principled and unprincipled. Some were motivated by greed alone, some by conviction they could best serve their states through an alliance with those they had so recently fought, some out of allegiance to the Union, the dissolution of which they had never approved.

But whether dissolute or upright, behaving out of conviction or opportunism, the words "scalawag" and "carpetbagger" remain loathsome in the Southern vernacular. And no one can dispute that the years 1865–76, from Lincoln's assassination to the close of the Grant administration, were years of intrigue and corruption, a dark era of vindictiveness and calculated political and economic rape from which that region called "The South" has not yet fully recovered. Tobit the Builder had the proper question. *What we gon' do?* But its profound implication of community and mutuality was not heard by either side. Providence Plantation was part of the story. Providence Cooperative Farm tried to be part of the answer. Neither enterprise overcame. Perhaps neither truly wrestled with Tobit's question.

CHAPTER 9

How the Reconstruction period was viewed by the principals of Providence can be seen in some words from a beautifully hand-written journal of Mrs. Samuel Donnell Gwin, words written long after Reconstruction was over, when she was seventy-five years old. They are words of pathos, resistance, and hope:

> *In March 1872 Samuel D. Gwin, Jr. was placed in my arms, only to remain three brief weeks. My one little daughter, Martha Rosalind was deeply grieved that her baby brother must go to heaven without her so she asked to take her dolly to the cemetery and all go to heaven together. Just seven months later this precious little sister joined him. In deepest gloom we consigned her to the tomb. My reason was almost dethroned, but God in His beneficence led me out of the gloom, and in the exercise of faith bright vistas of hope were opened up and we pressed forward determined to rejoin her in the heavenly home.*

That tender account of a distressed young mother grieving for her young turns immediately to the harsh actuality of a family's response to what they saw as tyranny. The very next words of her journal were these:

> *I have lived through three periods of war—the Civil, the Cuban and the World War. Their ravages can hardly compare with the reconstruction period. For in those years the oppression of our Northern enemies became so unbearable Southern indignation*

*was aroused to throw off carpetbag rule in our Southland. For a
time the safety of our beloved protectors was agonizing. I now
rejoice that my heroic husband risked life itself in the successful
issue. On one occasion when ready to leave me for a night of
investigation he bade me good-bye saying, "Here is a double
barreled shot gun, be very brave and use it if necessary. I am
leaving Sam Lee, a trusted Negro of the plantation, on the steps
armed with pistols, and he knows if harm befall you his life will
pay the penalty." He then bent over our sleeping boy (John D.)
with choking voice said, "Good-bye my son. Should I not return
your mother will teach you that I died trying to defend your
rights." He returned a victor at the dawn of a new day. There
never seemed to be a limit to his possibilities, having the stamina
and courage to do the right thing whatever befell, to elevate his
purposes and dignify his plans.*

Such was the heir of Providence. Samuel Donnell Gwin. His
proud widow did not say what the "night of investigation" meant.
Anyone familiar with the way the defeated whites resisted the iron
fist of Reconstruction can fill in the blanks.

Emancipated slaves, for the most part illiterate and unknow-
ing in the world of economic reality, had supposed freedom
would carry with it some measure of security. Emancipation had
taken away the only previous right they had: subsistence. With no
land of their own, they were still at the mercy of those who did.
One of them, who had not belonged to Richard Davis but to a
neighbor, talked about the years following freedom to George
Rawick, a WPA interviewer, in 1936. Elvira Boles was old by then,
as Mrs. Gwin had been old when she wrote:

*I'se a child of the marster. His wife, she told me. Dey tuk us to where
dere was a heap o' white people down by the coaht-house and we's be
there in lots and den de whites 'ud bid for us. Man bought me was
Elihn Boles. I don' know how old I was, but I washed dishes at de
marster's house. Den dey put me in the fields. We don' git a nickel
in slavery. I worked in field and brick yard. Toted brick, six bricks
each load all day. That's the reason I ain't no-count. I'se worked to
death. I had to work evva day. I'd leave my baby cryin' in the yard
and I'd be cryin', but I couldn't stay. Done evvy thing but split rails.
I've cut timber an' ah ploughed. Done evvy thing a man could do.
I couldn't notice the time, but I'd be glad to get back to my baby. My*

oldest child, he a boy by Boles, almost white. Marster was good to slaves. Don't believe in just lashing 'em. He'd not be brutal, but he'd kill 'em dead right on the spot. Ova-seer's git after 'em and whop 'em down. We had to steal away at night to have church on de ditch bank, and crawl home on de belly. Once ova-seers heard us prayin', give us each one hundred lashes. Freedom was declared, but de slaves didn't know it. We'se refugees, young mistress and masta brought us out to keep us from being free. Dey toll us de Yankees would kill us iffen dey found us. We was a dodgin' in and out, runnin' from de Yankees. We was free and didn't know it. Ah lost mah baby; it's buried some where on de road. Dey turn us loose in the world. Not a penny. Oh, dey was awful times. We just woked about from place to place after freedom. Hiahd to white people by month, week, day.

Yes, awful times. Awful for those who didn't know how to be free. And for those who really didn't know how to set them free even when or if they had wanted to, and who couldn't get along without them even when they didn't want them.

More and more Richard Davis turned to Samuel Donnell Gwin, grooming him to take his place. Davis seemed sure he would not live long.

Instead of dying, four years after the war ended, the big man got married. Samuel Donnell Gwin stood nearby as his uncle, friend, and benefactor took the solemn vows.

The ceremony was a quiet and private affair at the O'Reilly plantation, Aruba. At first I didn't understand why the marriage of a patrician planter was not the social event of the year. And legend has it that it did become a festive occasion. When the lord of the manor returned in late afternoon from Yazoo City with his bride, he found the house and grounds teeming with neighbors and relatives. Tables inside and out were laden with food and drink. The servants, told by Mrs. Samuel Donnell Gwin to decorate the house, had hauled all the Christmas decorations from the storeroom and hung them in place. A string band played soft music in the parlor, the violins predominant. Whites and former slaves, Reconstruction anger for the moment shelved, mingled freely in the gaiety, some of them already prey to indulgence.

The courtly Colonel Davis, seeing that his nuptial plans had not remained the secret he had intended, stood on the first step of Providence House, welcomed the cheering crowd, and introduced his wife saying, "I love this lady and I am sure she loves me in return. She will be good to me as I shall be good to her, and this will be a house of happiness. Providence will never again know a lonely evening." Then he gave her a vigorous embrace that she modestly but readily returned.

The celebration lasted far into the night. Inside the center hallway was a long banquet table. Older folk were seated, the young standing or milling around. Glasses were raised in honor of the new Colonel and Mrs. Richard Davis. A former slave proposed a toast that brought laughter but also applause of approval when he became confused and forgot what he intended to say. Meaning to flatter his former master he said, "To Colonel Dick Davis, whose heart is as big as his butt."

Samuel Donnell Gwin told the crowd about the time he and some of his soldier friends, home on furlough, played a trick on the people of Lexington and some Union soldiers. Word had come that a regiment of Federal soldiers was approaching the town. Gwin and his friends hid in some shrubbery, and when they saw the Bluecoats coming fired several shots into the ground directly in front of the startled soldiers, who turned out to be merely a few scouts searching for a better route to Vicksburg for General Grant's Army. When they heard the volley of shots, probably thinking they had encountered a regiment of Confederates, they came charging down the hill, firing, reloading, and firing again as they ran. The mischievous boys watched from a distant hillside as the Yankee soldiers found only women, children, and a few terrified old men as they searched the town.

Richard Davis told of his own experiences as a new and short-lived conscript: the frustrated quartermaster who tried to find a uniform that would fit him, and the desperate sergeant who had been ordered by his captain to find a horse that could carry him. Davis added that neither assignment was found possible. He roared with laughter. "So I came on back to Providence. A colonel in just three weeks."

When the stories had all been told, the final toast lifted, and the last dance over, the guests mounted their steeds and carriages as if to leave. Instead they withdrew to the quiet shadows. As soon as the wedding lights of Providence were dimmed, the traditional shivaree began. Frolicking neighbors returned with their noisy mock serenade. The clamor of banging pots, ringing cowbells, untuned fiddles, off-key singing, and pistols fired in the air filled the night. Their carousal was joined by the noise of chickens roused from their roosts, frightened livestock, and barking dogs. A fidgeting horse stepped on the hem of a woman's hoopskirt, which ripped from her body when she jumped to free herself, leaving her embarrassed and shivering in the light of the January moon. Another horse, making a hasty retreat, threw his rider to the ground, leaving him unhurt but on foot for his trip home.

When the merrymakers were sure the welcome to the estate of matrimony was amply stated, they respectfully retired, leaving the groom and his bride to the sanctity of their nuptial home. As do I.

Learning the name of the colonel's wife was one of the most perplexing chores of my search. Richard Davis, despite his vast wealth, left few tracks. His wife was even more elusive than he.

It began as a simple genealogical question. The Family History Center of the Church of Jesus Christ of Latter Day Saints, a reliable resource because marriage and families are believed to endure throughout eternity, and the keeping of the records is a religious mandate with them, showed that Richard Davis was married to Marcella S. O'Reilly in 1869. I didn't question this until I found Richard Davis's will in the Holmes County Courthouse much later. There were several bequests listed before the statement that the residence and all the land was to go to Samuel Donnell Gwin. One bequest was five thousand dollars and a house to a Marcella D. O'Reilly. He had already directed that he be buried next to his deceased wife and, "if I have not already erected a suitable tombstone or monument over her grave I wish one placed over both of us, the selection of which I leave to the discretion of my Executor hereinafter named."

Who was the other Marcella O'Reilly? Was there an error in the genealogical records and Richard Davis had been married to someone else? The record said the marriage in 1869 was in Yazoo County. But where? A telephone call to the courthouse in Yazoo City yielded no such marriage record. If I was to find the correct name of Richard Davis's wife, I had to find his grave. She would be beside him.

Early one chilly morning in late November, I drove through an archway leading to the Glenwood Cemetery in Yazoo City, Mississippi. This was the last place I knew to look. I had exhausted all other possibilities I could think of. It was a Saturday and I was on my way to Billy Ellis's wild-game preserve in Holmes County. I had told him I still had a number of missing pieces in my search for Providence. He said the time to get information from local folk was after a good hunt when the men, following a big supper, are sitting in front of the fire sipping brandy and telling lies. Billy's hunting lodge is at a place called Indian Bluffs, a few miles from Tchula and Providence. I think of Luther Cashdollar and Jesse Furver when I'm there, sure they once stood on every boulder, explored every cave.

The past two days had been spent looking for the graves of Richard Davis and his wife, whatever her name. The first day I had driven to the community of Ebenezer, in Holmes County, where I knew there were some O'Reillys. No one knew of a Marcella O'Reilly married to Richard Davis. Back in Lexington I talked with Mrs. Sadie Parrish, an elderly Holmes County aristocrat who had helped me with other Providence details. "Colonel Richard Davis died before I was born," she told me. But she was certain he would have been buried at Providence. Or nearby. "You know transportation was a problem in those days," she said. "Oh, he was a big, heavy man. They would have planted him right where he dropped." She told me there was a cemetery on Providence land. "I romped around there one time when my late husband and I were buying some timber on the place." She said there was not a road to it, just a walking trail. I remembered there was an old graveyard there where black people were buried. She said that wasn't the one she was talking about. "No, no. There's another one. I'm sure you'll find him there." Two hours of traipsing about Township Sixteen were futile.

Back to Lexington. The chancery clerk had a directory of every cemetery in Holmes County. In two hours I found many Davises but no Richard. Several Marcellas but no Marcella O'Reilly Davis.

I called Sadie Parrish again. Maybe the burial ground she found near Providence, but which I couldn't find, was in Carroll or Leflore county, she said. A look at the wall map in the courthouse showed that could not be.

Daylight was gone and I was late for a dinner appointment in Jackson, nearly two hours away.

I *have* to find the grave of Richard Davis!

Next morning I called Yazoo City information. The city cemetery had no listing. The police dispatcher and two funeral homes told me they knew of no directory where I would find a listing of everyone buried there. Anyway, there were numerous cemeteries in Yazoo County. And I wasn't sure Richard Davis and his wife lay in any of them. The officer said the main cemetery in Yazoo City was Glenwood, established in 1856, he thought.

I was supposed to meet Billy Ellis at his hunting camp by mid-morning. The quickest route from Jackson is up I-55, not through Yazoo City. I took the longer route. When I reached the Yazoo City line, I glanced at my watch and decided to hurry on to camp.

A few miles out of town I had to stop for a train from the Mississippi Chemical Corporation crossing Highway 49. It was a long and slow train. I turned the motor off and sat watching the bright yellow smoke from the stacks of the chemical plant swirling in the wind. Owen Cooper built all this, I remember thinking. He was president of the Southern Baptist Convention in 1973 and 1974, nominated in Philadelphia by Jerry Clower, the Grand Ole Opry humorist, who began his nominating speech to the thousands of Southern Baptists gathered in Pennsylvania by saying, "Y'all can look at him and tell he didn't ride into town on no watermelon truck."

A hodgepodge of something that could not be described as thinking churned inside my head: Crematorium/Dachau/Baptist/Death. Just some crazy disjointed and abstract twaddle, meaning nothing. Something about the ominous-looking smoke from the tall chimneys perhaps. (Maybe the twaddle meant more than I thought.) When the train was gone, I continued to sit, fixed in my reverie, until the horns of those behind me moved me on.

A few miles up the road, still somehow absorbed, I turned around on the shoulder and headed back south.

A young clerk in a convenience market told me how to find the Glenwood Cemetery. She shrugged and giggled when I told her I was looking for Miss Marcella and Mr. Richard. "Good luck," she said. "It's a big ole graveyard though." I knew about the size. The officer at the police station told me he thought there were about ten thousand people buried there. I took my pen and pad and figured that if I read one tombstone per minute it would take me twenty-seven eight-hour days to check every one. I didn't have the time.

I drove into the cemetery a few hundred yards and stopped. I got out of the car, with no notion as to why I had stopped at that particular spot. Nothing but tombstones and scattered trees as far as I could see. About fifty feet from where I stood was a big juniper, the bluish gray berries shedding from its massive branches reminding me of gin. And my dinner partner of the night before. I took several aimless steps toward the tree.

Marcella. Looming directly in front of me was the name.

In a half circle near the top of a brown-mossed grave marker was the name I had come in search of: Marcella. As the name registered, I was not aware of moving again. Just of being there, tracing the chiseled, concave lettering with my fingers in Braille fashion, making sure I had seen what I thought I had seen.

Marcella?! I called her name as an ecstatic interrogative. Then read aloud the inscription underneath a Latin cross:

> *Marcella M.*
> *wife of*
> *Richard Davis*
> *Died at Her Home*
> *Providence, Miss.*
> *April 30, 1901*
> *Blessed are the pure in heart for they*
> *shall see God.*

> DAVIS

"It's epiphanal," I whispered. "Some thing, some spirit, some one has led me through the cold to this spot." I stood dazed. And a little afraid, thinking of Saint Paul on the road to Damascus.

Beside the tall, slender gravestone was a ponderous, un-dressed granite marker. I imagined it to be the size of the colonel himself. At the very bottom of the stone, almost at ground level, was the lettering:

> *R. Davis*

That was all. No Latin cross to suggest he was a believer. No boasting beatitude to imply his goodness. No epitaph. No date of birth nor death. Not even a full name. Just R. Davis. From the instruction of his will, I assumed he had placed the stone himself.

There is a thin line between arrogance and humility. Which it was in this case I cannot say. Either the usual elegiac niceties violated his humble estimate of himself, or his arrogance told him that his first initial and surname were enough to remind the world he had been here. Possible also that no one ever bothered to inscribe the vital statistics in the polished rectangular area left above his name for that purpose. Whatever, that was all. R. Davis.

I walked around the area. Within a few feet of their graves were tombs of priests, a monsignor, and nuns. I realized I was in the Catholic area of the cemetery. I had heard that Richard Davis married a Catholic. This confirmed it.

I ghoulishly envisioned what was underneath where I stood. Maybe nothing but two straight rows of shroud buttons. He had willed his wife's gold chain to a relative. It would not have been buried with her. Maybe two little gold bands, rings that bound them together in life, the covenant unbroken. What else after all these years? A few bones not yet turned to dust? Teeth maybe? The casket the big man had contracted and stored at Tchula Cooperative, where men rolled dice and children played upon, would be long gone. What else is there? Fifty-eight tiny mother-of-pearl beads, each one lying separate now in a pattern like an infinity symbol, would be there. Beads that had once been on a string attached to a small crucifix—Miss Marcella's rosary. It would have been wound round her hands before she was put in the ground. If the corpus on the cross was made of metal, it might have withstood the years. What else? Is that all that is left when the earth reclaims its own? Marcella O'Reilly Davis with her rosary thought differently. Maybe now the colonel knows differently too.

I was strangely with these two. I felt a closeness to them I had not known before. It was not just that for the first time I knew for sure the colonel had married Marcella O'Reilly (Marcella M., not Marcella S.). Something deeper.

I had learned a great deal about Richard Davis in the past three years. There was still much to learn about his wife. How old was she when she married Richard Davis? A distant relative told me she was quite young, fourteen, he thought. Somehow that didn't fit my perception of the big colonel. What was her story entire? Even part of it? I had not found a Marcella O'Reilly listed in the Mississippi 1850 census. There was one listed in the census of 1860. If this should prove to be the same one, then she had to have been between nine and eighteen years old when she married in 1869. Of her I must learn more. Something didn't fit.

I stood there talking to them. I asked Richard Davis about

Tobit. And what had made Jacob unsound. I asked Marcella about life in the big Providence house, about her Irish ancestry, why she never had children as most other Irish Catholic women did, and if she had yearned to do so. How she felt when neighbors made jokes about her piety. "Aunt Marcy is off counting her beads." I had heard the stories.

"What were you thinking and feeling that day, Colonel, when you sat on the stile between the plantation house and the commissary and read Lincoln's words to the freed slaves?

"Although you had no children, you had other relatives. Why was Samuel Donnell Gwin so special that you gave him your house and all of Providence land?

"Tell me more about William McKendree Gwin, who owned Providence not many years before you?

"What would you do differently about slavery? About share-cropping?

"Did you consider dividing the plantation land equally among the slaves at the time of emancipation? Is that what you would know to do now?"

We talked for a long time. And then I left them.

I wandered through different parts of the big graveyard, looking for nothing in particular now. A man stopped his old-model car nearby. A three-year-old child sat close beside him. "I'm just riding my little granddaughter around," he said, as if he needed to explain to me. "She likes to ride around in here. I got three grown boys past thirty and this is the only grandchild. She's grandpa's little girl," he said. The little girl smiled and climbed in his lap. "A lot of big people buried out here," he said. I told him I knew it. "John Hancock's got two grandsons right over there," he said, pointing to the crest of the hill. "You know which one I'm talking about." I told him I thought so. I wondered what John Hancock's grandsons were doing in Yazoo City when they died. So far from Boston. When the man and his granddaughter rode away, I found the Hancock graves. A solid marble slab covered them. The epitaphs, in flowing script reminiscent of the defiant and immodest signature appearing on the nation's most famous document, read:

Sacred to the memory of George M. Hancock, Born in Frederick Co. Va., Sept. 30, 1806, Died in Yazoo City, Oct. 28, 1853, Aged 47 yrs, 28 days. An honest man, a dear brother.

And,

*Sacred to the Memory of John H. Hancock, Born in Fairfax Co., Va.,
Dec. 8, 1796, Died March 6, 1854.*

Here lie the Grandsons of John Hancock, first signer of the Constitution.

The historical error reminded me to check the genealogical
assertion when I returned to the archives in Jackson. That inquiry
told me the John Hancock who signed the Declaration of Independence left no male children to perpetuate his name or inherit
his fortune. His only son died at nine, a daughter in infancy.
Another source said John Hancock's personal papers were purchased for a thousand dollars and "suppressed." One is left to
wonder about the Hancock brothers lying in the lonely graves in
Glenwood Cemetery, placed there a century and a half ago when
Yazoo City was a new hamlet on the Yazoo River so far from the
Boston of the grandfather they claimed. In these times of journalistic dissection of the personal lives of political figures, one is
also left to wonder if the suppressed papers might have revealed
something the two brothers knew but the historians didn't. I
don't know.

In another area of the cemetery, not far from Richard and
Marcella, I saw a plot about half the size of a tennis court. The
marker said six to eight hundred unknown Confederate soldiers
who were killed defending Yazoo City were buried there. Where
is the mass grave of the Union soldiers? I wondered.

I have to get out of here.

Learning more of the bride of Colonel Richard Davis was more
difficult than I had feared. I drove into Yazoo City, just driving.
I saw a sign in front of what had once been a school, long
abandoned by the decree of Chief Justice Warren's Court. YAZOO
CITY MUSEUM AND ARCHIVES. Inside I found the museum door
locked. A woman seated at a desk in a room marked ADULT
LEARNING CENTER told me she would call the archivist who
worked in the library next door. In a few minutes an attractive
black woman arrived and unlocked the door. The archives and
museum were in one large room. I told the woman I was looking
for birth, baptismal, or marriage records of Marcella M.
O'Reilly, wife of Richard Davis, that I was trying to establish her

age. The diminutive black woman, dressed in fatigue jeans and gingham blouse, who told me she had moved to Yazoo County, Mississippi, from Chicago so her daughter could go to school in a healthier environment, busied herself in a room filled with musty plantation and Cotton Kingdom memorabilia. "My daughter did just fine. Never got into drugs. She's in the Navy now." *Up from slavery. In the Yazoo basin. Not the land of Lincoln.*

While she looked, I found a card file containing partial Glenwood Cemetery records. The cemetery was divided into sections. Richard Davis and Marcella M. O'Reilly Davis were buried in Section Thirteen. The day's discoveries and revelations were beginning to overwhelm me. Still no age though. Revelations are never *fait accompli.* "Through a glass, darkly."

"Maybe you'll find something here," the woman told me, handing me a manuscript-style document. It was titled "History of the Catholic Church in Yazoo County." I hurriedly browsed through the pages. When I reached the account of the building of St. Clara's School and Convent, my eyes stopped on the first paragraph. "In 1871 Father LeCorre designated Mrs. P. M. Doherty, the former Miss Mary O'Reilly, who received her education in Nazareth, Kentucky, and her sister, Mrs. Richard Davis, to visit Nazareth to see if a colony of Sisters could be induced to take this mission." Richard Davis had not only married a Catholic, he had married a Catholic of stature. I had known of St. Clara's School. During the hundred years it existed, it educated numerous church leaders. Among them was Father Frank Twellmeyer, instrumental in building Loyola University in New Orleans and later its president. Others taught at Spring Hill College, the noted Jesuit school in Mobile. Another was a leader at St. Joseph Abbey in Covington, Louisiana, where the novelist Walker Percy was an oblate and where he is buried.

The document I was reading said the beginning of the school was shaky. In 1875, three years after the school opened, Father LeCorre died of pneumonia, caught while returning in the rain from a country wedding. Three of the nuns recruited by Mrs. Richard Davis and her sister, Mary Doherty, died during the yellow fever epidemic of 1878. Father John Batiste Mouton, another French priest sent to replace Father LeCorre, died of yellow fever in the same epidemic. All interesting information, obliquely related to the history of Providence Plantation, but it told me little of the persona of the young woman Richard Davis had brought to Providence in 1869 as his bride. Or at least I was assuming she was young. I would plow on. The next week I called a friend, Tommy Mayfield, a prosecuting attorney for Hinds and Yazoo counties. I told him I had established that my Richard Davis had married a woman named Marcella M. O'Reilly, but the clerk in Yazoo City had not found a record of the marriage and I wanted to know how old she was. "I 'spect they'll find it for me," he chuckled. A prosecuting attorney for the county? "Yes, I 'spect they will," I said. Next day he called to say he had a copy of the marriage license and surety bond.

"Surety bond? For what?"

"Yeah. I never heard of that before but he had to post a two hundred dollar surety bond." I asked if the bond might have had something to do with her age, that I had heard the bride was fourteen. Tommy said the license didn't give her age or date of birth, that he supposed that was possible. It showed the marriage was performed by Father LeCorre on January 17, 1869. Marcella and Richard were buried a few feet from Father LeCorre's grave.

I called the mother house of the Sisters of Charity in Nazareth, Kentucky. The genial nun who was the archivist said there had been several O'Reilly girls at the convent during the middle 1800s. I told her I was looking for information on Mary O'Reilly, who had been a student at Nazareth and who returned in 1871 at the behest of Father LeCorre of Mississippi to recruit Sisters to begin a school there. She said her records showed that a Mary O'Reilly, daughter of James O'Reilly, had entered Nazareth in 1865. She was a Catholic and was twelve years old. She was not certain how long she stayed. She offered to help in any way but needed more definite information.

"I'm about to the end of the trail," I sighed, remembering the census records in Mississippi had shown that James O'Reilly also had a daughter named Marcella two years younger than Mary. If Mary was twelve in 1865, she would have been eighteen when Father LeCorre sent her and her sister on the recruiting mission. Marcella would have been sixteen when she and Mary boarded the train in Vaughn, Mississippi, the preface for an illustrious Catholic academy in Mississippi. In 1871 she had been married two years.

According to this, Marcella M. O'Reilly was fourteen years old when she came to preside over the big house of Providence on January 17, 1869. It was what I had been told more than a year earlier. Why had I questioned it? It was not unusual in 1869 for a teenaged girl to marry an older man. Still I was bothered. The Richard Davis I had come to know didn't seem likely to have waited until he was forty to find a fourteen-year-old bride. The trail had turned cold again.

A closer look seemed indicated. Tom T. Hall, the novelist, songwriter, and entertainer, said he would go with me to the convent in Kentucky to check further. He offered to have his driver take us. He had been interested in the research from the beginning. The thought of riding into Nazareth in a long black Cadillac limousine with a uniformed chauffeur struck a sporting chord of contrast. Since I began the research on Providence, I had covered the miles in airplanes, cars, buses, and on foot. I thought this might be the final leg of the journey. "Might as well do it in style," Tom T. said. "We'll go in the limo." Even if I didn't gain any new information on Mrs. Richard Davis, it was sure to be a memorable addendum to the search.

We were surprised but pleased by the reception at the convent. The arrival of the shiny limousine caused little more stir than a fine chariot moving through the Nazareth for which this one was named might have caused two thousand years ago. The major surprise was, there were no rules at their archives. I had become accustomed to archives having lots of them: Check your briefcase in the locker room. State exact reason for your inquiry. Use only lead pencils when making notes. Submit to a search of all papers when leaving. Give your research card number when you sign in or out. Unfortunately, inconsiderate researchers over the years have made the rules necessary. I understand. But there were no rules in the archives of the Sisters of Charity. Instead, an air of innocence permeated the place, an openness seldom seen in institutional settings anymore, a trust at once intimidating and refreshing. "How do they know our business isn't researching a segment for 'Sixty Minutes'?" Tom T. whispered as we were ushered inside. I supposed they didn't care. Nothing to hide.

The Sisters immediately recognized Tom T. as being a famous television personality. "We watch you on TNN," one of them said, as if a house exhaling the refined odor of piety should explain their familiarity with one not of their world. His music was praised in an earnest but not effusive fashion. After that, except for asking him to visit a ninety-year-old woman in a nearby building who was a country music devotee, he was pleased to be treated like any other researcher.

"Yes, of course," Sister Mary Collette, the archivist, told me. "We have lots of material on St. Clara's School." Soon the table was spread with books, reports, pictures, and mementos. And soon I knew that the two women Father LeCorre had sent to Nazareth in 1871 to ask the Sisters of Charity to establish a school in Yazoo City, Mississippi, were Mary Ann O'Reilly Doherty and Marcella M. O'Reilly Davis, daughters of Mr. and Mrs. Phillip O'Reilly of Yazoo County, Mississippi. Both had been students at the convent. Mary Ann was nine years old and Marcella was eleven when they enrolled together on March 4, 1847.

Who were the other O'Reillys also named Mary and Marcella? Another file showed them to have been Mary Elizabeth, daughter of James O'Reilly, also of Mississippi, and Marcella O'Reilly, a Protestant girl from Alabama who entered Nazareth twenty years later. That was the fourteen-year-old girl I had assumed married Colonel Richard Davis.

"Finally I know for sure," I said, louder than one generally speaks in archives and libraries. "Richard Davis did not marry a teenager. He was a forty-year-old bachelor who married a thirty-five-year-old spinster."

I had followed the elusive Marcella a long way. When I found her for certain, I was strangely glad she was not a frightened fourteen-year-old child brought to a strange place by a sick man three times her age. She was a mature and sophisticated woman, secure in the environs of the manor.

Sister Mary Collette, who told us she was a native of Memphis, kept bringing more material, keeping no account of the number of pages or the exact documents I duplicated. "Just tell me about how many when you are through," she told me. "Or just forget about it. It's only a nickel a copy. We're not here to make money." How quaint.

"Have you seen this?" she asked, handing me several pages marked "Sister Emerentia's Account of Early Happenings at Saint Clara's." Sister Emerentia was one of the first teachers when the school was established and was mother superior for thirty-seven years. She wrote of the two Mississippi women who returned to their alma mater in 1871 to beg for a school for their area. She described Mary Ann as being spirited, Marcella as somewhat shy and retiring and very bright. Sister Emerentia, detailing the meeting in which Father LeCorre's emissaries made their proposal, wrote:

Mother Columba replied that she did not think that it was
possible. But Mrs. Doherty was not to be rebuffed, and in her
characteristic impulsiveness, exclaimed, "It must be, Mother.
Nazareth owes too much to the South to refuse this call in behalf
of Souls. Louisiana, Mississippi, and Alabama have helped to
make Nazareth what she is today." Mother answered, "Well,
Dollie," (a name by which she was known at Nazareth) "we shall
do what is in our power, and later we shall make a trip to
Yazoo."

"Dollie?" I laughed, thinking of the tough Mississippi women in a formal audience with one who ranked so high above them.

"Sure," one of the Sisters chuckled. "Can't you see those two children getting off the train, clutching their little dollies, afraid and so far from home, the Sisters there waiting for them? Mary Ann was only nine. I imagine one of the Sisters exclaimed, 'Oh, she looks like a little doll.'"

Apparently Mother Columba was convinced. According to the notes of Sister Denise, another of the early teachers, before the year 1871 ended, six nuns from Nazareth were teaching the following subjects to the Yazoo basin children: botany; natural history; mythology; higher mathematics; higher algebra; music; astronomy; mental philosophy; rhetoric; history of England; the French, German, and Spanish languages; and Greek, Roman, and Jewish antiquities.

How much of the funds of Providence went into that rigorous curriculum I cannot say. Another Sister I talked with thought it considerable, for, she said, "The Church was very poor. This convent was very poor. There had to be some Mississippi angels." Doubtless Providence was one of the angels. Sister Emerentia's notes said the original property, costing fifty-two hundred dollars, was paid for by subscription. Many Protestant and Jewish names appeared on the list.

I was sure the colonel had chosen the beatitude on Marcella's tomb with care. "Blessed are the pure in heart. . . ." What made her pure? A forty-year-old man, terribly overweight and believed to have been dropsical and diabetic, married an Irish Catholic woman quite within the perimeter of childbearing. Yet she never had children. Why? Why had she waited far beyond the usual age to be married? There were the years of intensive schooling and religious training at the convent. Had she desired, but was for some reason denied, a religious vocation for herself? Richard Davis, by all accounts I could find, was a gentleman. Was Providence Marcella's convent, where the nun's vows were held inviolate? "... For they shall see God." Her help in the beginning of St. Clara's School and Convent was not her only involvement in religious activities and good works. Others would follow until the day she died and was placed beside the Sisters she helped recruit in Nazareth, Kentucky, and the French priest who married her to Colonel Richard Davis. I asked one of the Sisters of Charity of Nazareth if she thought it possible that Marcella looked upon Providence as her cloister, considering the circumstances of the marriage. "It was not uncommon in those days," she replied. "There were many devout young Catholic women on the frontier who yearned for a religious vocation. Convents were small, poor, and few. There weren't enough places for all of them. They needed an institutional base for their good works. Such a marriage was sometimes their answer." We talked of whether this detracted from the Davises' standing as male and female. "In my view it helped define the true meaning of womanhood," she said. "And what it meant to be a man." Then she told me about Sister Scholastica O'Conner, a widow and a convert who in 1814 brought a dowry of three thousand dollars that enabled the Sisters to purchase the farm on which they established themselves. "Ah, Sister Scholastica," she said, smiling and crossing herself. Then, looking out over the vast expanse the widow and convert had made possible, she crossed herself again and I heard her whisper, "And Sister Marcella." She turned back to me, surmising I had heard her I supposed, coughed a gentle laugh, and said, "Who's to say?" She sat for a moment with her hands folded underneath her chin, a combination of a child at prayer and a chess player studying a likely checkmate, and added, "Only the Lord knows who's a Sister of Charity."

"Yes ma'am," I said.

Marcella O'Reilly made few changes in the routine of Providence when she came. Although her husband was, by the standards of the day, a rich man, the number of household servants was reduced following the war. There were no slaves to be assigned arbitrarily to chores of whim. By the time of their marriage, the labor contracts of the Freedmen's Bureau had been abandoned for the sharecropping system. Each family had an allotted acreage and every member of the family was needed in the fields. Domestic servants expected to be paid, and even for large landowners like Richard Davis, cash was in short supply. In addition, under protection of Federal troops and the Freedmen's Bureau, former slaves were being elected to public office. Holmes County had a black sheriff, state senator and representative, county supervisor, tax assessor, circuit clerk, and coroner. Other offices were filled by northern carpetbaggers. Schools were being established for black children. The fact that the convent at Nazareth had a program for educating colored children suggests that Marcella might have encouraged it. I found no evidence of support but none of opposition. I did find that black Providence children attended a formerly all-white school taken over by a Catholic-educated mulatto man named R. A. Simmons. Who recruited a Catholic educator in this almost exclusively Protestant county? The children joined him in a march through town in a demonstration of black power and pride, something that would not happen again until the civil rights movement came to Holmes County a century later.

Black and carpetbag control was in time put down, but in its heyday the newly freed women found it demeaning to be in the kitchen of white folks. Even so, the proud, mannerly, and fastidious colonel would not have his lady doing her own cooking and housecleaning, nor deprived of her vocation of good works. The chary formality of the household and ritual of mealtime would continue. Servants would prepare and serve the table comforts, discreetly offering dinner jackets to underclad guests.

The planter class did not intend to be permanently dislodged from the chair of privilege. No opportunity was missed to subvert the reign of freedmen, carpetbaggers, and scalawags. Much of the opposition was in the form of corporal exertion, seen as the only appropriate response to the violence of their antagonists. How active Richard Davis was in such organizations as the Red Shirts, an organization that did by day what the flourishing Ku Klux Klan did by night, I was not able to determine. The picture Mrs. Samuel Donnell Gwin painted of the doughty Samuel Gwin's "night of investigation," and how he "returned a victor at the dawn of a new day," suggests the captain's role in the resistance was more than marginal. That he was a man of influence at the state level is demonstrated in his efforts on behalf of a neighbor, Dr. Tully Gibson. Mrs. Gwin's journal described Gibson as a man of sterling character who wished to put down lawlessness among the races. He was reported to Governor Ames as a disturber. Governor Adelbert Ames, a radical leader and military governor in Mississippi, would not have been expected to be sympathetic toward the two former Confederate captains, Gwin and Dr. Gibson. Gibson had feared for his life and took his family to the homes of different neighbors each night. When Gwin reported this to Governor Ames, he was assured that Dr. Gibson would be safe in his own home. Mrs. Gwin described what followed: "The happiness of his family was restored for only two short days when a troop of fifteen cavalry men demanded entrance to his home. He tried to defend himself, wounding three. The odds were too great and while prone upon the floor with a bullet in his brain they robbed him of his watch and turned his pockets for small coins in the presence of his grief-stricken wife."

The names of Gwin, Davis, and Kiern were now etched firmly in the Bluffs and Delta of Holmes County. Colonel Richard Davis, his title bestowed by three weeks of duty as a conscript and ownership of more than four thousand acres of land, continued to operate Providence Plantation. Samuel Donnell Gwin, wearing the proud rank of captain, attained by three years of ferocious combat, went about the task of becoming a wealthy and powerful man in banking, commerce, and farming. Walter L. Kiern, who preferred to be warrior rather than physician in battle, that option leaving him minus his right hand, ran his family plantation.

Human nature being what it is, by the time the war ended it was impossible for the defeated white Southerners to accept the penalties with anything but extreme rancor. Although most all whites were poor, blacks were poorer. Just as happens today, many of the blacks saw the military as a preferable option to remaining in the cotton fields. There was a garrison of thirteen thousand soldiers in occupied Mississippi. Virtually all the enlisted men were former slaves. Trouble was inherent. Whites would find a way. The way they found was no more salutary than our thinking today that the problem of black urban poverty and crime can be solved by building more prisons.

Seventy-eight thousand white Mississippians went into battle in the 1860s. Twenty-seven thousand didn't come back. Of the total white-male population, that represented approximately one-fourth. Of those who did return, an estimated one-third to one-half were badly maimed. In 1866 Mississippi appropriated one-fifth of its revenue for artificial limbs for Confederate veterans. Scars are healed sores, sometimes concealing underneath seething cauldrons of infection, poisoning the entire body. The abscesses of secession and Reconstruction have not, even to this day, become benign scars. In a conversation with William Winter, governor of Mississippi, in the early 1980s, I was reminded that the sores still fester. "They are," he said, "the economic, psychological, and social debts brought on by the dreadful moral and political errors we, South and North, made a long time ago." The time it takes for nations and states to recover from war, one would think, would give pause to those who have the power to prevent or start them. It does not seem to be the case. Governor Winter told me that as late as 1932 Mississippi was spending more money on pensions and benefits for Confederate veterans and their widows than on all the colleges and universities in the state combined.

Richard Davis and his Gwin nephews were more fortunate than most. They were alive and industrious. In addition, Colonel Davis had remained at Providence throughout the war and his plantation was in better condition than those whose owners had been away. The state had lost 60 percent of its livestock in the war. Cattle and work animals of Providence were spared, giving Richard Davis another advantage over other planters in the state, many of whom had lost everything, including their ravished land. Also, Davis must have felt fortunate that William Louis Sharkey, a jurist and fellow planter from Warren County, though a Whig and perennial Unionist, was provisional governor. His friend and neighbor, Dr. W. L. Kiern, was elected to the constitutional convention of 1865 that was to try to bring some order out of the chaos of war and the virtual mob rule of the early months of Reconstruction. Kiern had been in the legislature before the war and was the youngest delegate to the cession convention that brought Mississippi out of the Union. Surely Davis felt the interest of the planter class would be protected under such leadership.

Still the prospects were bleak. Colonel Davis had in his possession more than a thousand bales of cotton that he had not been able to ship because of the wartime blockades. This would be sufficient capital to pay for needed equipment, supplies, repairs, and the wages for freed slaves under the Freedmen's Bureau labor contracts. This was not to be. Officials of the U.S. Treasury were authorized to seize cotton that had belonged to the Confederacy. That government had foreclosed on many planters, seizing their ginned cotton for nonpayment of debts. In other cases the cotton had been bought by the Confederate government for military use. In the confusion following surrender, it was not easy to determine exactly who owned what. Misapplication of the order spelled dire consequences for many. Richard Davis was among them. Shortly before Christmas in 1865, he contracted with John Edgar Gwin and Samuel Donnell Gwin to transport half his cotton to Tchula where it was to be barged to New Orleans. His plan was to keep the remainder in hope of a stronger market. Before final arrangements could be made, more than a third of his cotton was confiscated as being property the Confederate government had bought during the war. Richard Davis had written his appeal for amnesty on July 25 of that year. His appeal was not honored by President Johnson until sometime in 1867, long after the seizing of his cotton. His right of citizenship denied, it could not be used in any legal redress. Nor do I know if any effort was made. Probably not, for the conditions of disloyalty were so broad few could escape them. Residing in the Confederate lines by choice, voting for secession candidates, holding civil or military office under the Confederacy, furnishing it supplies, arming or equipping any person for its service, selling cotton or other produce to the Confederate authorities, or doing anything whatsoever to aid the Confederate cause were considered acts of disloyalty. Richard Davis would have been guilty of infidelity to the Union by virtue of having voted for Kiern, and even his acts of friendliness to his nephew, Samuel Donnell Gwin. If that did not disqualify him for relief, the allegation itself—that he had sold cotton to the Confederate government—made it a no-win situation for him. He had also lived in a Confederate state by choice. I found no account of adjudication. The army and Freedmen's Bureau had control in matters of "rebellious activities and race." The desperate master of Providence would have been fearful of losing the land itself.

With little cash to purchase supplies, and more especially to pay the labor contracts, there was the real danger of losing the land anyway. In the social and political upheaval of the day, there were widespread rumors of insurrection of blacks to simply seize land to accomplish the fabled "forty acres and a mule" of which they had heard so much but witnessed no evidence of the promise. This did not happen on Section Thirteen. Somehow they worked things out. A frequently heard story is that Captain Samuel Donnell Gwin made regular trips to New Orleans for black-eyed peas, which, along with the goodwill of cows and chickens and the supreme sacrifice of swine and wild game, sustained the freedmen until spring gardens could yield a more lavish fare. The story is used to explain the prolonged and profuse weeping of nearly a hundred black men and women, many of them former slaves, as they joined the cortege that followed the captain to his final resting place forty-three years later. Whether from noblesse oblige, self-interest, or the milk of human kindness, the vicious rhetoric of negrophobia was contained. And the night missions of Captain Gwin became even more convoluted.

In 1878 the scourge of yellow fever swept through the Yazoo basin and throughout Mississippi. With no one knowing how it was transmitted and only symptomatic treatment practiced, entire populations of towns and cities were terrified. Many fled to the country. Others established shotgun roadblocks to keep refugees out. Trains going north were crowded with those fleeing the stricken areas. Outside Jackson there were reports of Negroes being shot crossing open fields. Such was the panic.

The "yellow jack," as the quarantine flag was called, flew over all of Holmes County. In violation of the quarantine, many homes and plantations were opened to relatives and others from Yazoo City, Vicksburg, Jackson, and Natchez. In some cases the residence and appurtenant buildings were like resort hotels, where guests enjoyed the offerings of their hosts in good health. The atmosphere was almost carnival, guests sitting on the veranda or playing croquet on the spacious lawn by day, sipping juleps and dancing the stately Virginia reel in the evenings.

When illness struck, the afflicted one was moved to the next level of care, resembling a hospital. The symptoms were sudden and unmistakable. Headaches, backaches, chills, nausea, followed by fever of 103 degrees or higher, were the cues that a guest had yellow fever. Yellowing skin, bright red tongue, swollen lips, inflamed eyes, flushed face, and intense restlessness confirmed the diagnosis. The houseguest had become a patient. Treatment was haphazard and guesswork, the science of virology unheard of. Purging with calomel or jalap, a dried rootstock of a Mexican plant, followed by tea made from cinchona bark that contained quinine, was standard, though probably useless. Cold-water enemas and cold baths were sometimes used. Patients able to often clutched and sniffed a vinaigrette. The sick, young and old, male and female, were sequestered in one part of the house, only those caring for them allowed nearby. Not for another twenty-five years would it be determined that the disease was not spread in the air, and isolation, burning the bedding of the sick, and hasty burial of the dead accomplished nothing.

That first stage generally lasted three or four days, followed by remarkable but often deceptive improvement. Patients felt better, fever gone. Often that was the end of it. When it was not, the fever returned, the signal the person should be removed to another house or plantation equipped as much as possible for the dying. Providence was such a facility, a primordial hospice. The third and final stage of the mysterious ailment was brief. What the caretakers saw were the markings of the returned fever—deep dusky complexion and black vomit. What they did not see was blood from the stomach walls that caused the thick black fluid, the virulent virus intoxicating the body, the rapidly deteriorating liver. Finally, on the sixth or seventh day, they saw a corpse.

Marcella O'Reilly Davis, who might have aspired to the cloistered life, went about her Nightingale chores with compassion and vigor, bathing, praying, feeding, burning sulphur believed to ward off germs in the air, seeing that the dead were buried within an hour—antecedent of Nurse Lindsey Hail Cox, who would minister to the sick and dying on this slope seventy years later.

St. Clara's School was especially hard hit. The Sisters declined to close the school until a quarantine officer positively required it. Even then Sister Emerentia fudged a bit. Entering one classroom she announced, "Children, go home and don't come back until Monday." It was Friday and the children expected to be back Monday anyway. To another class she said, "Children go home. All the Sisters are sick." In the third room her instructions were, "Children, go home and stay until Father tells you to come back." Then, according to Sister Denise's notes, she sat down and burst out crying. The nuns were told to leave the city. Convent notes indicate two of them, who had been recruited by Marcella O'Reilly Davis, went to Holmes County, presumably to Providence Plantation, where they died. If that be so, Marcella Davis fudged also, violating the edict that the dead be buried within an hour. The bodies of the two Sisters were returned to Yazoo City where they were buried near the spot where Marcella and her husband would later lie, and where Marcella's pastor, Father Mouton, was buried already, also a victim of yellow fever.

It was not the last time Providence Plantation would play a role in the dreadful and recurring epidemics of yellow fever. A turning point was in the epidemic of 1898. By then Richard and Marcella Davis were approaching the end of their own lives, and the plantation was not the hospice it had been twenty years earlier when Marcella O'Reilly Davis cared for the dying victims. However, it is believed to have been a factor. Dr. Henry Carter, a quarantine officer for the U.S. Public Health Service, came to Mississippi and did a statistical study of the spread of yellow fever within certain neighborhoods and families. The Providence community was probably one of the places surveyed, although the records are inconclusive.

Carter was the first to note an intrinsic incubation period between cases. He concluded the disease brooded some place in the environment. He had no idea where. Filth had long been suspected, but Dr. Carter wondered why outbreaks seemed even more prevalent in clean areas.

Before he had reached any conclusions, he was transferred to Havana to work with the U.S. Army Yellow Fever Board, a research team established by the now-celebrated Dr. Walter Reed. Carter shared his Mississippi research with Dr. Reed, pointing out that there was a time lag between the first appearance and second wave of yellow fever. Reed reasoned there must be an insect host. Though still a long and arduous struggle, the end was in sight. The *Aedes aegypti* mosquito was the culprit. Yellow fever was on its way to being eradicated.

"The Gwins always thought they were better than everyone else," a native of Holmes County told me in a moment of candor. I thought of the many Gwins I had come to know. William McKendree. Samuel Donnell. John Durden. And many of their issue. "All of them?" I asked. "Every last one of them."

When I repeated the assertion to a long-removed Gwin descendent, that person thought for several seconds, then said, "There was a reason for that. We were."

I offer no judgment on the harshness or immodesty of the two views. There can be no question, however, that since Dr. William McKendree Gwin came to the Yazoo basin in 1828 at the behest of Andrew Jackson, the Gwin name has been one of energy, ambition, romance, and intrigue. And none can gainsay its weight in the unfolding drama of Providence.

Next to William McKendree Gwin, Samuel Donnell Gwin was the most colorful and influential of the Gwin dynasty to own the land. When Richard Davis died in 1904, Samuel Donnell Gwin was the heir. This Gwin was a complex man who spun a web that still glistens on the overhanging rocks of the Loess Bluffs and the Delta flatlands beneath. Soldier, planter, banker, merchant, husband, progenitor of an unending medley.

Not a churchman. His mother, Susanah Van Houten Davis, half-sister to Richard Davis, was a devout Presbyterian. But Samuel Donnell never joined, was often critical of the superficial piety he saw the steeples embracing, and would not contribute to the institutional church. And when he died, though his funeral was conducted by the distinguished Reverend James B. Hutton, his son-in-law, the service was in the plantation home, not in a church. His slight of the structures did not, however, keep some of his resources from reaching the spires and towers of Christendom through innocent evasions and ingenuous maneuvers. On a trip to Memphis, he took his wife into a costly jewelry store and gave her a choice of two diamond rings. One was a solitaire, the other a cluster of five. By then five of their children had died in infancy or early childhood. Mrs. Gwin knew the solitaire would attract the most attention. She chose the cluster because, she told her husband, "They seem to represent our five shining little ones in the heavenly home." For many years she cherished the gift as surrogate for her dead babies. But the winsome belle who at fifteen had met and staked her claim upon the handsome Ole Miss boy, soon to be a soldier, became a woman of balance. When the Methodist church in which she had been organist, and from which her departed children were carried forth, was raising funds for a new building and Captain Gwin would not contribute, although one account says he gave the land, the diamond cluster was her offering. There are stories that she also gave all the family silver and jewels, but I could not confirm that.

On another occasion her children furnished a room in a Brazilian Mission School in their mother's name. Perhaps her husband objected to the offerings, but they were made nonetheless.

Nor did his rejection of creed reflect negatively on his character. He is remembered by most as a good man. Tough enough to close his bank, combine his assets, and pay off all his creditors when he was convinced the boll weevil was going to wipe out the Cotton Kingdom forever and he did not want the guilt of unpaid debts on his shoulders. Tender enough to twice move with his wife to the house of another to care for motherless children. When he asked the mother of Martha Rosalind Durden for the daughter's hand in marriage and Mrs. Durden's only hesitation was the frailty of her daughter, the young soldier replied, "It will be my constant joy and privilege to care for her." That frail bride bore him eleven children and survived him by thirteen years.

So esteemed by his children that his oldest son, John Durden, last Gwin owner of Providence Plantation, said to his mother, "I would be willing to have my limbs severed from my body if I could see Papa face to face and show him how I have made good."

Cherished by neighbors. His friend, kinsman, and comrade-in-arms who had recruited him for his Confederate company, Dr. Walter L. Kiern, sought to convert the unchurched Samuel when Kiern was dying. "Come closer Sam. I want to put my arms around you. Our souls have been knit together as David's and Jonathan's. There has never been a time in my life when I would not have given my last drop of blood for you. I leave you my wife and children. My friend, I want you to be a Christian." Caring enough to embrace and hear his friend. Confident enough to resist his zeal, to go on believing one does not have to be on some steeple's roster to be fair in business, loyal husband, devoted father, gracious neighbor, stout in his regard for the land that was Providence. And when he died the eulogy included these words: "In religious matters he was broad minded, liberal and tolerant to the opinions of others." He continued the dynasty.

When at last he lay down his burden in 1908 it was not before he had passed the land of Providence to his elder son, John Durden, in the English tradition of primogeniture. Although he legally owned Providence for only four years, having inherited it at Richard Davis's death in 1904, Samuel Donnell Gwin influenced life there for nearly four decades.

There were deficiencies. Let them remain where he lies.

CHAPTER 10

Nearly half a century after Samuel Donnell Gwin died, when the Coxes and Minters were forced to leave Providence, the major activities fell to Mrs. Fannye Booker, and later Mr. Odell Hampton and his wife, Annie. On one of my many visits to Holmes County researching the history of Providence, I decided to visit these three again to refresh my memory of what had happened there after 1955, and to talk again of the way things were when Section Thirteen was still part of Providence Plantation.

It was the last day of July when I made the sharp right turn at the house where Mr. Otto Morgan, the sawmill operator, had lived when the cooperative was active. It is called Providence Road, though there is no sign. On other visits I had always turned left there, down the sandy, always wet road that went to the old community schoolhouse, the store, and the clinic.

I remembered the road to where the Hamptons lived as being almost impassable in earlier years. Now it was neatly graded with well-kept ditches and sturdy culverts. I smiled as I recalled that the Hampton's second son, Odell, Jr., had been on the Board of County Supervisors for twelve years, an elected office that placed him in charge of the county roads in his district, in addition to other county business matters. I had seen numerous yard and roadside campaign signs in and around Tchula announcing his candidacy for reelection. So now the black people decide whose road gets worked first, I thought, driving easily along, remembering the shabby washboard roads in 1955 when I first came here. And Providence Road is getting its fair share of attention.

Mrs. Hampton was standing on the edge of a field picking purple hull peas as I pulled into the yard of healthy, multicolored zinnias and a profusion of red crepe myrtles, the logo of every country home when I was a boy. Now they seemed somewhat anachronistic as they waved a friendly greeting, bordering a large mobile home. Mrs. Hampton hurried toward me, smiling and motioning for me to drive closer to the house. The place she moved from was three or four acres of smartly cultivated corn of various varieties, squash, peas, beans, okra, tomatoes, and a long row of watermelons. It was what, in rural Mississippi, is still called a truck patch—too big to be called a garden, too small for a field. I thought this field must have looked much the same when Luther Cashdollar and Jesse Furver were here. The same crops, grown much the same way. Around the edges were white sheets stretched between poles to full length, banging tin pie plates hanging on tree limbs, and an assortment of scarecrows. They told me later they had to change the ghostly figures almost daily to keep deer away.

"Been expecting you," she said. "But I didn't know what day you was coming. All I got ready to cook is chicken wings. You don't feed chicken wings to company."

We shook hands and she led me up the solid concrete steps. Her husband sat in the living room in a black Naugahyde recliner chair. The room flowed into the kitchen and dining area, all of it spotlessly clean and everything in its place. It had been a long time since I had seen Mr. Hampton, and at first I thought he was too feeble to stand up. Instead, when he saw his wife was not alone, he moved from the chair with the poise and agility of a man half his years. "Ann called us and said you was coming. And here you are. Sit down, sit down." I had called Ann Cox Belk and asked her if she thought the Hamptons would mind talking with me. I apologized for not letting them know when I would be there. I had not realized their telephone was listed in the Lexington directory, not Tchula. "That's all right. That's all right," he said. "Annie's gonna fix us some dinner." I apologized again and insisted I hadn't come to eat. It was past one o'clock.

"You have to eat dinner with us," Mrs. Hampton said. "I have to keep my promise. I told Ann I was going to fix you something to eat when you got here." She had already started stirring batter for corn bread. "You like butter beans?" I told her I did. "Preacher, you ought to go to the store and get some more chicken," she said to her husband. "Ought not to feed wings to company." I told her I was partial to wings, that when I was a boy I didn't know a chicken had anything except wings and a neck. She laughed and went about her work, never moving so far she couldn't be part of the conversation. I knew that Mr. Hampton was known as Preacher but was surprised to hear his wife call him that.

"Me and Annie was gonna sit down and write out everything we remember about Providence. After Ann told us what you're doing. We didn't know what day it would be. She said it would be next week sometime."

I asked if either one minded if I turned on a tape recorder, that I didn't write very fast. Without answering the question directly, Mr. Hampton indicated he had rather I didn't. Mrs. Hampton stood looking at him as he said, "We're gonna tell you everything we remember, but some things we tell you we might not want you telling everybody else." He laughed, comfortable with his response. "Some folks will tell you everything they know and then there's folks who won't tell you a single thing." I told him I would leave the recorder in the car and try to keep up with my pen and notebook. He didn't seem to mind my furious writing, seeming to know he could challenge anything I wrote down but couldn't if it should be recorded.

"I'll go back as far as I remember. I was born in 1919. Lived around here all my life. Not always at Providence though. I can tell you what I do remember though. It was when old man Champ Taylor had Providence. I was six years old. It was 1924."

"That was W. C. Taylor?" I asked.

"Champ Taylor's all I know. Everybody called him Mr. Champ. All the colored people, I mean. Like I say, it was 1924." He seemed mildly vexed I had interrupted. He tilted his chair to its most upright position. His wife stood grinning, nodding her head, seeming to know what he was about to tell me and seeming to approve. "The reason I remember it so well is my daddy had just bought a brand-new car. Model T car. We'd had a good crop year and my daddy had bought this brand-new car."

The story he told was one that would certainly make a deep impression on the mind of a six year old in 1924. More so, I thought, than riding in a new automobile.

What he wanted to tell me first was of a flood that he vividly remembered. Wishing often that he had agreed to the tape recorder, I wrote down what I could. The account I wrote, and here offer, was gleaned from conversations with him and his wife and with several other older citizens of the area. When there were contradictions, I chose the version that seemed most likely, sometimes the one I liked best.

In mid-March of 1924, the rain began. For two days and nights it was no more than a mist. Then it stopped and the moon and stars shined brightly on the third night. Champ Taylor, who had bought Providence from John Durden Gwin in 1918, primarily, I was told, because he thought he could get rich mining gravel off the bluffs, always had the mules and workers in the gravel pit at daybreak. Despite the threatening weather, this morning was no exception. He had an order for thirty carloads of the red rocks for a company in Mobile. He had never made a shipment that far before. His light dummyline engine would pull the cars, three at a time, to Tchula, where, because his tracks were narrow gauge, the gravel would have to be reloaded onto the larger Illinois Central cars. Late morning brought more clouds and a steady drizzle, which continued throughout the day. Though there was no wind, the leaves hung trembling over the rocky bed of Chicopa Creek. Ground animals seemed beset with fears they expressed by frantic scurrying, making their own sounds of panic, aware of the impending vandalism of their lairs, their young destined to death. The mist and drizzle had dampened and softened the crumbly clods, soaking the dirt around the roots of every sprig and plant, easing the chore of the angry torrents waiting their turn to fall.

During Richard Davis's years, the terrace rows and vulnerable wash areas were sodded with Bermuda grass, a tenacious, bluish green grass that sends rhizomes scouring beneath the ground, matting, holding the soil in place with its sturdy network, the stringy, jointed stems clinging stubbornly to the surface above, allowing a harmless runoff for mischief-minded water. As further precaution Richard Davis, and later John Gwin, had built a network of levees and drainage ditches to direct more serious water into the main channel of Chicopa Creek.

In his quest of quick wealth, W. C. Taylor had neglected the Bermuda, or "wire grass" as it was called, and failed to refurbish the levees as they eroded. The railroad bed leading to the gravel pit had left yawning chasms that widened and deepened with each new rain. Too many trees had been cut from the slopes, and erosion was already far ranging.

In Tchula, John Gwin watched the clouds and worried. It had been six years since he sold Providence to Champ Taylor, but his heart still fretted. For his heart was still there. He was proud of the plantation his great-uncle, Colonel Richard Davis, had built. It was only at the insistence of his wife that he moved away. The first three years after he left he would not go back, would not even drive by. He kept hearing things he didn't like but felt no liberty to interfere. Although his father had predicted the demise of cotton when the boll weevils invaded, John still dreamed of the bouquet of white and pink flowers in late June, becoming by fall a parable of a million lambs, waiting to be sheared. Gwins and cotton, he thought, were synonymous. And each a gift to the other. Five acres of Providence property, he was told, formed a deep ravine, the gravel mine. Gravel was the main cash crop now. Locomotives chugged across open fields, powdery clay blowing from the open pit conspiring with black coal dust from the engines, forming on dewy mornings a reddish black crust on the velveted green foliage and chaste open cotton bolls. To John Gwin, it was a despicable violation, an intrusion on the privacy of the earth, an obscenity not covered in his sale. Yet he never spoke openly of it. Nor harshly of Champ Taylor.

What had started as a mist on Monday morning had by Thursday become enormous drops of rain falling straight down, blue as coal, pelting the earth, bruising acre after acre until all of Section Thirteen was in mauled submission, gainsay of the rainbow sign. Champ Taylor sat in sullen silence. Darkness came and the clouds still hung over Section Thirteen and most of the Loess Bluffs. All of the Delta except the eastern edge seemed to be spared. Most of the rain was falling on the Bluffs, making it even more perilous for the lowland.

Fields, lying fallow but already turned for spring planting, appeared as wild seas, the presoaked soil washing to the lowest point. Water from the freshet flowed underneath the high porches of Providence House like a cascade. The frantic engineer and his crew labored to get the last of the open-top gravel cars to higher ground before the tracks were inundated or washed away, train whistle crying out with the soaring birds observing from judicious heights. The snarling rapids, squeezing, mopping, taunting Section Thirteen, would not cease their meanness. Pat Barrett, today the eighty-two-year-old county attorney, remembers riding from Greenwood with his father, the

Ford roadster trying to outrun the approaching deluge, which he watched as it appeared to chase them, wondering if they would both be drowned.

The gravel pit, now a giant reservoir, was ready to spill over. Champ Taylor still sat, maybe now regretting his long neglect of the levees, and wondering too if the tower of water from the gravel mine, when it came, would sweep away the underpinnings of Providence House and send him catapulting to an ignominious end.

His fear was ill-founded. When the dam gave way, the bulk of the raging waters missed the house entirely, hitting instead a tool shed, the chicken house, and the pigsty, sweeping them away like stick men. What remained of the abandoned and fallen-down slave quarters were demolished too, flushed down the drunken cleft, enraged addendum to Mr. Lincoln's proclamation. Bits and pieces of the cabins were swirling round the cement style where Colonel Davis had read the president's words to the slaves gathered, they pleased yet baffled by the ambrosial hum of freedom.

Then the worst was over. On Saturday morning the rain stopped completely. The sun came out to assess the damage. And do what it could to rectify it. Except for the rain, it could not be called a storm at all. There had been no wind as the rain fell. Not one branch was broken. It was solely the opening of the clouds that ravaged the face of Providence that week in March of 1924.

What the sun and the people found when they came out was devastation. For one whole day the rampageous Chicopa Creek ran blood red from the tons of clay-stained water of the gravel mine. As it gradually receded, the brackish water from the silt and loam of the woods and cotton fields was a deep brown, the currents sucking the land of its virility, further impoverishing this already overused parcel of creation. Gullies deeper than the height of a man bespoke the destruction the windows of God's city had set loose. All the chickens and hogs and half the cattle were gone, drowned and swept away in the frenzied flow. The havoc suffered by Champ Taylor's pride, his dummyline railroad, would have been a credit to Grierson's Raiders that had torn up tracks a few miles from Providence sixty years earlier. Half a mile of crossties had been washed from underneath the steel rails, leaving the heavy rails buried in the mud, the crossties gone. Stall doors on the mule barn were fixed shut by massive piles of silt, so high it took three men half a day to shovel them open and get the mules out of the breast-high slime.

The most lasting damage of all was that the main course of Chicopa Creek had shifted. It was a geographic reordering that would be a factor in Providence history for years to come. Chicopa Creek had been a property line since the original survey following the Treaty of Dancing Rabbit Creek. On my first visit with the Coxes and Minters in 1955, I had heard the story of lines being redrawn by that flood. And at the final meeting of the board of Providence Cooperative Farm, as we discussed the future of the land, Gene Cox, in one last, forlorn effort to delay what he knew by then was inevitable, said again, "But we don't really know where the lines are."

The empire of W. C. "Champ" Taylor would never recover. There would be other, more widespread floods to come. In 1927 and again ten years later, the entire Delta would be threatened with extinction. But it was this one, localized but uncompromising, that would leave its mark on the edge of the Loess Bluffs.

Taylor repaired the tracks and the gravel mine, this time leaving an escape route for heavy rainfall. But crop land was so badly eroded that farming was negligible for more than a decade, until the land could heal itself.

Mrs. Hampton had finished the chicken and invited us to the table. Neither of them expressed any great sympathy for Champ Taylor. "You know, he killed a man in Cruger," one of them said. "So I been told."

I vaguely remembered reading about a massacre in nearby Carrollton. I asked if they could tell me about it. "That was before either one of us was born," Mrs. Hampton said.

"Yeah. But we know about it," her husband said. "Killed twenty-odd people at one time."

Later I checked my notes from the WPA files and found the complete story. It had happened more than a hundred years earlier, in 1886, but was still fresh in the consciousness of black Mississippians, including the two at whose table I sat eating chicken wings and butter beans. A black man, Ed Brown, part Choctaw, had filed charges against a white man, Jim Liddell, for a civil offense. Feelings had run high in the community, still smarting under Reconstruction rule. On the day of the trial, a swarm of whites appeared to take Brown. When the blacks, some of them part of the court, resisted, a melee occurred in which thirteen black men were killed outright and ten others wounded so badly they soon died. I found this quotation from an observer who was interviewed by the WPA writer:

> *The twenty-three were all buried by the county in a plat near the old Oak Grove Cemetery. The result of this riot was instantaneous on the colored folks. They were no longer the recalcitrant, unmanageable race that felt so greatly their importance since emancipation, but a very tractable, meek set of Negroes willing and eager to do the white man's bidding, which as any Carroll countian can tell you, is always for the Negroes' ultimate good.*

Mrs. Hampton finished setting the table while we talked of the butchery at Carrollton. Mr. Hampton seemed tired as he folded his hands, bowed his head, and prayed for a long time. I couldn't make out all of his words but could tell it was not a routine table grace he recited every day. It was an impromptu prayer. I heard the names of the Coxes, my own name, family members. As we ate we continued to talk about the Providence they remembered. And who might know more of its early days. Mr. Hampton talked candidly about the people he knew who had lived at Providence, his tone of voice often reminding me, "some things we tell you we might not want you telling everybody else." On those occasions I conspicuously left the pen idle. Several times he said, "Folks had their freedom. . . ." Each time his wife would finish the sentence, "and nothing else."

Mrs. Hampton had worked with Mrs. Fannye Booker in the Head Start program. I asked if she had been a teacher. "Oh, no," she said, laughing lightly, "I was the cook. I cooked for the children." Then she added, "Of course, when you're with little children, everyone's a teacher." She knew. She had raised twelve of her own.

Mr. Hampton seemed especially proud of his flourishing watermelon patch. "You come back in two weeks and I'll give you a big Dixie Queen to take home with you. Sweet as sugar." I thought of many of my black friends who won't eat watermelon because of the racial stereotype, then pictured the airport security inspector as I rolled a watermelon down the electronic sensor belt. "Might be dope in that thing," they would probably think. I told them about the time I took a suitcase full of cedar whittling sticks to Toronto during the Vietnam War, when I was taking dodgers and deserters to Canada. The expatriates liked to watch me whittle when I visited, so once on quick trip, I took several dozen cedar sticks to leave with them, a touch of home. Mr. Hampton laughed as I told him how the customs agent examined, x-rayed, and tried to twist open each stick, sure no one would enter the country with nothing but sticks for baggage.

"Me and you about the same age, ain't we?" he said as we were finishing eating. "In the same war. World War II." I told him I supposed we were. He quickly added, "Everybody calls me Preacher." I knew what he was saying. I had been assiduously formal with courtesy titles. He had called me Will. I had noticed but could not bring myself to address a seventy-year-old black man as "Preacher." Something going way back. A dignified old man hobbles inside a bus he has flagged down and the driver says, "Where you going, Preacher?" as the passenger moves to the back of the bus. Or 'Fessor, maybe Uncle. But never Mister. I shifted in the chair and hedged. "Why do they call you Preacher?"

He grinned and answered. "The night I was born, I've always been told, my grandma took one look at me and called me Preacher. And from then on everybody's called me Preacher." Here was a man comfortable with watermelons, comfortable in discussing the evils of white people with a white man, intimidated not at all by political correctness, as I thought I wasn't, reaching out, not to be my equal but to help me be his equal.

"Let's ride around," he said, getting up from the table and getting a baseball cap with ODELL, SR. on the front. The one who gave him that cap didn't call him "Preacher," I thought, then remembered his son, important in county politics, was Odell, Jr. Not Preacher, Jr.

He told me that when the Minters left, he, his wife, and their twelve children had moved into the Camp House where the Minters had lived. I had not known why it had always been called the Camp House. He explained that when Champ Taylor had the gravel pit and had a dummyline coming to ship the gravel to distant places, the men who worked on the railroad had stayed in two shotgun houses called the Camp. When the Minters came, they built more rooms between the two houses and it was called the Camp House. He told me the house had burned down in 1985. "You think somebody burned you out?" I asked. "Oh no. No, it was an accident. But we're better off. All the children were grown by then. Where we live now is easier for Annie to keep up."

I asked him what his job had been after everyone else had moved away from Providence. "Just look after it. Keep folks from stealing the timber. Keep 'em from burning off the woods. Look out after the hunters when they come. Whatever Mr. Cox wants me to do. Mr. Cox, Lord, he loves this place. Every tree and every blade of grass." I said I knew he did. "And now he's provided it so as me and Annie will have a home as long we live. He's a good man." I recalled their welfare had always been a major item when we talked of closing Providence. "What would become of them?" Gene would ask. "There are enough people on the streets. They would have no place to go."

"Let's stop here," Mr. Hampton said, motioning me to a house near the road. "Hat might know something about the old days."

A short, jovial, very black-skinned woman greeted us on an enclosed porch. She was Mrs. Hattie Granderson. "Annie called and said y'all were coming. Preacher, how you been? I saw you at George's funeral but there was so many folks there I didn't get to speak to you. How you been?" They gave each other a modest embrace as he introduced us.

Mrs. Granderson didn't wait for questions. She knew why we were there and talked fast and somewhat loudly. She had worked in the Providence store, and also for Reverend Sam Franklin and his wife in the early days of the cooperative. "Aw, Child, they was good to me. They treated me just like I was a white girl. Course I left to go north before they left." I asked where she went. "Chicago. We all went to Chicago. Everybody that left went to Chicago. Only place we knowed to go, I reckon. That place gone crazy now though. Lots rather be in my little house down here. Right here in Holmes County. Lots rather."

As Mr. Hampton called off names, she commented on what she remembered of each one.

"Champ Taylor."

"Oh, he kind of believed in slavery. Been a sheriff in Greenwood. And a bad one too. Killed a man in Cruger. So they said."

I called James Henderson's name. Henderson had been one of the white sharecroppers who moved from Rochdale to Providence. "Wife name Shirley. Yeah, I remember them. Knew his daddy too. Daddy was common. Poor? What you talking 'bout? They was some kind of poor. I think he kind of believed in slavery too." I remembered there had been complaints from some of the white sharecroppers when the farm was trying to make it as a cooperative system. Some did not want whites and blacks worshiping, eating together. I assumed Mrs. Granderson never forgot. "James was all right though. I mean, nice enough. He'd be real nice and friendly with me when he came in the store. But soon as somebody else come around, he'd hush right up. Real quiet. Preacher, I don't think you was at Providence when him and Shirley killed that big rattlesnake. Lord, that was the biggest snake I ever saw. Scared the life out of me."

"Sam Checkver." Mrs. Granderson laughed out loud when I said his name.

"You remember him? Now he was a strange one. Good little feller though. Jew. A red-headed Jew. Never saw another one. They told me he was poor too. Raised up in New York. Real poor. Went to school though. Harvard? Yeah. Harvard. Made a lawyer. He ran the store. A Harvard lawyer running that lil' ole store. When he could of made big money being a lawyer somewhere. I worked for him. I used to hear him talking to folks. Sometimes he didn't think much of Reverend Franklin. Thought he had too much power. I heard Reverend Franklin tell him the only power he had was what the trustees give him. That red-headed Jew wanted us all to be the same. Equal. Good to colored folks."

Mrs. Granderson slapped her knee and laughed hard, almost losing her breath. Mr. Hampton laughed along with her. Like he knew what she was about to tell. "You remember that time . . . no, you must not of been at Providence then. Anyhow, he told somebody he'd milk their cow while they was gone. That little feller didn't know nothing 'bout milking no cow. Well, it commenced to rain and some way or nother he got that ole brindle cow up on the porch out of the rain." Mrs. Granderson began to shake with laughter again. This time I laughed along with them, picturing what the porch looked like when the Harvard-educated lawyer finished the milking chore. "But he managed to milk her. Right there on that front porch."

She grew more serious than she had been since we arrived. "But you know what? They put that feller in the penitentiary. Sent him off to Parchman. He didn't believe in no war. Wouldn't register for the war when all the other boys around here was going. . . . Preacher, you went. I bet this man went too. But that little red-headed Jew wouldn't go. So they sent him off to Parchman." Of course, Sam Checkver wasn't sent to Parchman, the state prison of Mississippi. His was a federal offense. After serving his time for refusing to fight a war in which he believed the poor, whether of the Bronx or Holmes County, Mississippi, had no stake, no one associated with Providence ever heard from him again. Not even his college alumni office has an address for him.

From the eager, effervescent Hat Granderson, we drove a few more miles to talk with Mrs. Pattie Wright, sister of George Jackson who had died three weeks earlier. Mr. Hampton had told me her father, Jack Jackson they called him, was John Gwin's overseer. He was certain she could tell me stories about the Gwins. Instead we found a frail and reluctant witness. The neighbor she greeted as Preacher did his best to coax her, but she volunteered nothing and said little in response to our questions. When she spoke at all there was a sharp whistle in her voice. At first I thought she had an artificial larynx.

"Do you remember the old Gwin Plantation house?" I asked her.

"Yessir."

"Can you describe it for me, tell me what it looked like?"

"George could of tole you all that, but we buried him three weeks ago."

"You don't remember anything about it at all? One story? Two? Was it big?"

"I was off in Chicago so long I don't remember all that."

Mr. Hampton remained gentle but was getting impatient. "Now Pattie, you was right here back in them days. You wouldn in Chicago then. You're older than George and he remembered all that." She didn't answer.

"Do you remember Mr. John Gwin?" I asked. "The man your father worked for when you were growing up?"

"Yessir."

"Can you tell me something about him?"

"Yessir."

"What can you tell me? What kind of man was he?"

"He was a good man. That's 'bout all I remember."

"He was a good man. What made him a good man?"

"He was a good man to his help. I know that."

Mr. Hampton looked at me and smiled, shook his head, as if to say, "This is one of those folks who won't tell you a single thing."

Back at the Hampton's house, he apologized for not being more help. I assured him it had been both pleasant and helpful.

I told him I was going to drive to Lexington and visit Mrs. Fannye Booker. As he firmly grasped my hand, looking me directly in the eyes and asking me to come back to see them, I managed to say, "Preacher, I'm much obliged to you." But it wasn't easy. "Free at last?" Only sometimes.

The two of them stood waving as I drove away. "Tell Fannye hello," I heard them say.

Born in Holmes County in 1906, of a proud family owning their own land from Reconstruction days, Mrs. Fannye Booker had been educated as well as was possible for a Negro female in the early part of the century. She attended Jackson State and Mississippi Industrial College, a school operated by her denomination, the Colored Methodist Episcopal, later Christian Methodist Episcopal, in Holly Springs, Mississippi.

She worked in Providence Farm activities almost from its beginning. She had taught in public schools but a whispering campaign that she was a Communist, because of her association with Providence, cost her the job. Her first full-time job at Providence Farm was as receptionist for the medical clinic in the mornings, then working in the cooperative store in the afternoons and evenings. Later she became involved in the educational programs.

I had not seen her for many years. At eighty-six she presides over her own private museum in Lexington, the county seat of Holmes. She was bubbling with Providence memories and stories. She recalled the times I brought my guitar to Providence and named some of the country songs I sang. She talked of Mrs. Cox's nursing school, a program the self-effacing Lindy describes as "just a way we had of training young black women to do first aid and some basic nursing skills so some of the families would have someone who knew how to take care of sick folks."

But more was accomplished than that modest answer reveals. There were nine Negro students the first year. Mrs. Booker told me all of them lived with her. She taught them math, science, and English. Mrs. Cox taught them clinical nursing. While Lindy saw it as a way of having people in the community who could care for the sick, it also turned out to be college preparatory, for most of them went on to college. None, to Lindy's recollection, went into nursing as a profession.

That led to what they called Camp School. It was an early

experiment in what later became known, more than two decades later, as Upward Bound, one of the more successful programs of President Lyndon Johnson's Great Society War on Poverty. During the summer, students from all over the county, generally from the ranks of those who had not done well in the public school system, came to Providence Farm for eight weeks. The fee was three dollars total. Tuition has gone up, I remember thinking. Choctaw children going from here to the Eliot Mission School in 1825 paid one deerskin each. In addition to the three dollars, each student was told to bring a pound each of cornmeal, flour, cured pork meat, beans, and whatever else they could. The menus were built around what the students brought, along with fruit from Mr. Morgan's orchard and peas Mrs. Booker's husband grew. Three families each put a cow on a wagon and brought them to Providence so the students could have milk and butter. "The boys milked the cows," Mrs. Booker told me. "The girls cleaned up. We had strict rules." The boys slept in the medical clinic, the girls in the schoolhouse, which was also called the community center.

Mrs. Booker told me that Odell Hampton, Jr., had been one of the Camp School students. "Hadn't been for the Camp School, that boy probably wouldn't be a county supervisor today," she said. "How could we do in eight weeks what they couldn't do in eight months at the regular school? a lady from the school superintendent's office asked me. I told her because we had strict rules."

Undoubtedly they did. But Mrs. Booker was a dedicated teacher whose only objective was educating the young. She also had the assistance of teacher interns from Jackson State, Alcorn, Tennessee State, and other colleges to help with the remedial tutelage. Mrs. Booker spoke with pride of Camp School's success. "They all did well," she told me. "One's a computer operator for Bloomingdale. Two of them made dentists. One has her own business in Kansas City selling hairstyling stuff. Another one's a preacher. They didn't know what they were doing when they ran us out of there," she said more with compassionate perception than with rancor.

Lindy and Gene had spoken often of the programs conducted during eight successive summers by the Alpha Kappa Alpha sorority, a social service organization of professional women. The women came and set up programs throughout the county. Into the rural communities they brought dentists to people who had never had their teeth looked at by a dentist. Doctors to people who had never had a physical examination. Dieticians to explain how the food they grew could be better prepared. Home economic teachers to talk of child care and the importance of sanitation in primitive living conditions.

Their task was not an easy one when they went into homes without screens on the windows and sometimes cornshuck brooms to sweep the rough floors. Seminars on family budgeting were ludicrous to a household with no cash wages. Lectures on dental hygiene must have seemed strange to a mother who had never been able to afford a toothbrush for her young. But the sensitivities of the urbane intellectuals from Boston, San Francisco, and New York were fine tuned by the orientation sessions of the Minters, Coxes, and Fannye Thomas Booker, who had invited them there and from whom they learned as much as they taught. Learned to instruct discreetly that too much lye soap in the dishwater could cause ulcers, a little salt or baking soda on the end of a mangled slippery elm twig made a fine toothbrush, hookworms were caught from walking with bare feet in fresh cow manure, hair lice could be killed with kerosene diluted with hot water, and clap was caught the same way babies were made. "The Alpha Kappa Alpha folks did some good work," Mrs. Booker told me. Understatement seems to be routine with Providence dwellers.

She showed me some of the quilts from her quilting classes at Providence after the others were forced to leave, a program she continues. She seemed especially proud of her cotton-boll pattern—hand stitchings of cotton blooms, full-grown bolls, and fully opened cotton bolls, all in an intricate design on alternate squares. "Never thought I'd find a cotton boll pretty after all the cotton I picked as a girl," she told me.

A tour through her museum is a journey through the nation's history. Just inside the door a poster greets you: "When God made man, She was only kidding." Before the tour is over, you know the caption was not there to be frivolous. This eighty-six-year-old black woman has labored hard for her racial and sexual freedom. It would be redundant for her to tell you she's a feminist, so she doesn't. Further down the wall is the inevitable portrait of Sojourner Truth.

A large ox yoke hangs from the ceiling. The sign underneath it says, "1801–1820."

"These all came from Providence," Mrs. Booker says, pointing to various articles on tables made of wide planks and sawhorses. A coffee grinder. "We ground the coffee right there in the store." Several aluminum milk cans. "You know we ran a dairy there for years." And a twenty-gallon crystal clear-glass jug. "That's what whiskey came down the river to New Orleans in. Mr. Cox got that somewhere. Of course, we didn't do any drinking out there. None of us. But Mr. Cox thought the jug was pretty."

Mrs. Booker showed me a cooling board and told the story of a man who had been put on it but was found to be alive when they got to the cemetery. She laughed as she told of the mourners' stormy response.

"And looka here. That's a witch pot. Goes back to slavery days. You know at first the slaves had to slip off in the woods late at night to have services. They would turn this pot a certain way and Massa couldn't hear them praying and singing and shouting. That's what they thought. Who's to say?" Yes, I thought, who's to say? "This here is from slave times too. This little bell. When Missus rang it at the table, my grandma came running." She held the bell for a long time, tingled it gently, and stood there, as if saying, "I don't answer anybody's bell now." "And this is a foot warmer." It was a stone jug, slightly flattened. "Old women would have the slaves put hot water in it and sit with it between their feet."

She showed me chairs handmade by relatives, brass knuckles that had belonged to her uncle, her grandmother's trunk filled with quilts she had made, and a heart-of-pine pie safe with an ornate design of punched holes resembling birds and flowers. She said it was done by her father.

"Now I want you to take a good look at this." It was a framed oil painting of a hog-killing scene. Fields of open cotton were in the background. Children were playing as big hogs were being scalded in big iron pots, the hair scraped off with knives and thrown on long tables to be carved into hams, shoulders, and middlings. I thought of Luther Cashdollar and Jesse Furver. "Notice the black folks doing the hard part. Whites cutting up the meat." She stepped back and admired the colors the painter had chosen as if she had never seen it before. "Saul Haymond, Jr., did that. Lives on a plantation out close to Cruger. My, my. All that black talent and him sitting out there on a tractor. Don't seem right. Wasted. Wasted."

We moved to another room where dozens of other articles

were displayed. She opened a small leather trunk. "This is an old preacher's library." A well-worn Bible, two other books, and a frazzled clerical collar. That was all. "He couldn't read a word of it but he wore that Bible like a glove. He was proud of his library."

Nearby was a tattered and faded poster offering a hundred thousand dollars for the assassins of Abraham Lincoln. She slipped a cylinder into an Edison gramophone, turned the crank, and shook her head at the harsh metallic sounds of a piano coming from the mounted horn. "Better than TV," she laughed. "It didn't poison the children."

Inside her residence, a neat brick house, immaculate inside and out, she displayed several other quilts made by her and her present quilting group. "All already sold to white ladies in Natchez and Vicksburg and Dallas, Texas." She fixed cold drinks for us and talked some more of Providence. "No, they really didn't know what they were doing when they ran us off from there. We meant them only good. All of us."

She repeated a story Lindy Cox had told me before. Some Presbyterian missionaries to a leper colony in Africa had spoken in their church, and the church was raising money to help finance their African mission. Lindy and Gene gave each of their children a dollar and, to teach them the parable of the talents, told them to use it any way they wished to make more. She wasn't sure what they had done with it. "I believe they bought some lemons and sugar and sold lemonade. Made some little pot holders or something like they did in Vacation Bible School in the white churches. Ours too. I'm not really sure." She thought the offering for the African lepers had come to about fifty-six dollars. Mr. J. P. Love, the state legislator who had been one of the leaders at the mass meeting to close Providence Farm, and an elder in the church, had come out to the farm to commend the children and have his picture made with them. She was quiet for a long time, gazing out the window. I thought she was going to cry but she didn't. Tears were a luxury seldom afforded in her long and hard life. Finally she said, "Then two weeks later, there he was, running some other missionaries off. My, my."

She began showing me pictures and scrapbooks of her head-start program at Providence. "Of course, nobody ever heard of Head Start back then. I mean, when we were first doing it. Way back there then.

"Then when the others, I mean the government and them got

into it, under Johnson and Shriver and that bunch, Lord, did they ever mess things up." I recalled some of the controversy in Mississippi over Head Start, following the Mississippi Freedom Summer of 1964 when there had been an intensive voter-registration drive by the Student Nonviolent Coordinating Committee, the Congress of Racial Equality, and small contingents drawn from other civil rights organizations. As hundreds of northern students, white and black, fanned over the state urging poor black citizens to register to vote, it became the most violent period of the civil rights movement in that state. Mrs. Booker and I tried to reconstruct the story of the Head Start program during the middle and late sixties.

"First there was CDGM," Mrs. Booker told me. "Child Development Group of Mississippi." With Sergeant Shriver as head of the Office of Economic Opportunity, the largely indigenous CDGM was funded heavily in 1965 and became the subject of immediate controversy. Elite opposition saw it as a holdover of young militant blacks, inflexible in their determination to change the political climate of the state. CDGM employed many parents, seeing them as positive role models for children who had seen their mothers and fathers only in servile positions. And it created jobs. Attention was given to nutrition, health, emotional support, play, and learning, all the things the Providence Farm Camp School and Alpha Kappa Alpha programs had stressed years before.

"I heard Senators Eastland and Stennis didn't like that much," I said.

Mrs. Booker laughed. "Oh, no! They wouldn't put up with much of that. They brought wrath. Lots of wrath down on them." The senatorial pressure had resulted in CDGM being defunded while a long investigation took place.

Together we recalled that a new organization had been formed, Mississippi Action for Progress. Popularly called MAP, it entered the controversy with some of the leading white and black liberal Democrats as backers and became a sharp competitor with the Child Development Group of Mississippi. Out of that contention came still another endeavor, called Friends of the Children of Mississippi, or FCM, a sort of baby CDGM, which successfully contested Stennis and Eastland's perennial and predictable charge of financial malfeasance.

"Do you think it was the White Citizens Council, the same

crowd that forced y'all off of Providence land, that caused all the trouble?" I asked.

Mrs. Booker appeared to be tiring of talk of politics. She sat fondling the nursery-rhyme characters on a baby quilt she held. Instead of answering my question she said, "Of course, Mr. Cox and I, we never got mixed up in any of that. We just went on doing our little thing ... bringing those little children in, teaching them their ABC's, giving them nourishing meals . . . just loving them, you might say. You know, I never had any children of my own. Yes, we just went on doing our little quiet thing. Right there at Providence."

I had one other thing to ask her. Earlier that day I had visited with Frank Smith, a former congressman of the Delta who had been defeated when it became apparent he could not be trusted to espouse the traditional line on racial segregation, and his district was mostly merged with Jamie Whitten's. Though he and I had differed on the issue of strip-mined coal when he was a director of the Tennessee Valley Authority following his defeat, he was a man I greatly admired for his wisdom and integrity. As he sat in his Jackson bookstore, a remarkable establishment called Choctaw Books, surrounded by thousands of rare and hard-to-find volumes, I asked him to tell me what he knew of Section Thirteen. "It's some poor land that has broke a lot of people," he replied.

His answer supported what I had begun to suspect about a piece of geography I had approached with awe and studied with diligence, that it had been a failure at every turn of its long history. As home for the Choctaws, as speculation for William McKendree Gwin, as a working plantation, and as transient prospect of rescue from the sharecropper system for a few people who soon found themselves back working on shares with some-thing called "The Cooperative" as boss man. I had never thought of Providence as a failure. Thinking about it now I had to concede that, given the goals they had set—their dreams of having a plantation where white and black worked, shared, owned, and profited jointly and equally—they too had fallen far short. Even before the White Citizens Council ran them off, they had given up on such a lofty notion as, one by one, the founders and early residents had followed other dreams. Was Providence as a cooperative and interracial endeavor just one more white-dominated plantation, with a white overseer, albeit with charitable motivation and intent, yet still driving the impoverished blacks for greater production, melding the system to meet their own emotional and moralistic needs? Do not even the publicans the same? Writing about Providence and other utopian communities in 1939, journalist Jonathan Daniels said, "The most dependable cash crop has been the benevolent individuals and foundations who have made possible these courageous experiments in the deep South."

"It's some poor land that has broke a lot of people," Congressman Smith had said. But not all the land was poor. And it was not the deficiency of the land that had broken the Choctaws but the poverty of soul of those who wished to possess it. Was it then somehow jinxed, singled out as surrogate by the Great Spirit of Nanih Waiya to judge and curse the predators who had robbed them of their birthright? Or did it serve, like an infant martyr, as propitiation for the Delta's pelf?

"Do you see the Providence Farm experiment as a failure?" I asked the virtuous lady of whom I was about to take leave.

She stood up, neatly folded the small quilt and placed it in a chest. A trace of a smile showed on her lined but still beautiful face, a summary of her years. She came and stood behind me, gently patted my shoulder and answered, "You'll have to ask the folks who came by."

Somewhat abashed, I moved silently through the door, closing the reporter's notebook I held. She followed, her nearness assuring me she had not meant to be brusque.

I told her I wasn't sure how to get back to the courthouse. "I'll direct you," she said. I expected her to point me in the right direction with her walking cane. Instead she embraced me warmly, saying, "I never did forget you, Reverend Guitar Picker Man, and don't you forget me. I'll see you up there, if not before." She looked toward the heavens, then got in her car, and spryly drove away.

"And ain't she a woman," I whispered to myself as I tried to keep up with her on the narrow curves, remembering the words of Sojourner Truth underneath the picture I had seen inside Mrs. Booker's warehouse of memories and things whose time had gone. And marking her words about the meaning of failure: "You'll have to ask the folks who came by."

When I finished my work at the courthouse, Mrs. Booker's

words were still with me. I thought of some who had "come by" Section Thirteen over the years. Who had failed? Who had succeeded? Reverend Alexander Talley came and preached a gospel of love to Luther Cashdollar's people, with Chief Greenwood Leflore as interpreter. Did that message of love condition the Choctaws to the point of abdicating to the Christ-bearers? Was Tobit, who built the stately mansion that stood for seventy years, a failure? What of William McKendree Gwin, called by a political enemy "the providence of California?" And William Pinchback, sire of a mulatto family he set free long before the compulsion of Caesar, and long before the Coxes and Minters came with their more timid word of interracial cooperation.

Mrs. Booker had talked of healing mind, body, and soul. I thought of Marcella O'Reilly Davis, helping to found an important teaching institution. And nursing yellow fever victims. She had been a forerunner to the merciful hands of Nurse Lindy Cox on Section Thirteen. As Dr. Henry Carter had been a pioneer in defeating yellow fever, Dr. David Minter, in the early 1940s, did extensive research at Providence Cooperative Farm on the use of atabrine in the control of malaria.

All of them came to mind. Recollections of Dr. Minter lingered. When he was working out of Providence, there was one doctor for every four thousand patients. His rejection by the white citizens who gathered that night in Tchula High School made the odds even higher. On my first trip to Providence in 1955, I heard some of the stories. Over the years I heard more. I heard old ones again, and then new ones, on cassette tapes Dr. Minter, vacationing in France not long before he died, had recorded, and Sue Minter had sent me.

There was the beginning. On the day the clinic was to open in the remodeled dairy barn, a couple arrived at the Minter residence before they were awake. The man said his wife needed to see a doctor. "Is it an emergency?" Dr. Minter asked.

The man timidly rubbed his head, pawed the ground, and said, "Wellsuh, I don't 'zactly know 'bout all that. I just knows she needs to see a doctor real bad." Dr. Minter dressed hurriedly and made his way to the clinic for his first patient.

He took the woman's vital signs and found them within normal range. "What's troubling you, ma'am?" the young physician asked in his finest professional voice.

"I'se had a passel of young'uns," she bashfully told him. "A dozen, I reckon." Then straightening up and looking the white doctor she had never seen before in the eyes, she added, "My old man's aggravatin' me nearbout to death every night and mornin'. And I don't want no mo'."

Dr. Minter sat looking at this pathetic Mississippi woman, in the land of the Choctaws, William McKendree Gwin, Colonel Richard Davis, and all the Gwin dynasty, and innocently inquired, "What can I do to help you, ma'am?"

"He made me come see you," she replied, nodding her head toward the waiting room where her husband sat. Dr. Minter patiently explained some methods of birth control to her, then called the lustful and impatient husband into the room and graphically instructed him on ways to be aggravating without adding to the passel.

He said he never saw them again. Dr. Minter logged his first case in the new clinic as an emergency. I reckon it was.

Seven degrees above zero. A man came to the doctor's house on foot. His wife was having a baby and he didn't think she was going to make it. Dr. Minter's car wouldn't start so they walked three miles, the man carrying one of the doctor's bags, he carrying the other, facing a freezing wind. He found the woman lying on a bed of rags in the middle of the room. Water that had spilled beside her bed had frozen right up to the hearth where a pine-knot fire was flickering its last. Telling the husband to stoke the fire, Dr. Minter pulled the bed closer to the fireplace and within an hour delivered a healthy boy. He estimated the weight as five pounds. Then he walked home, carrying both bags himself, in as cold a weather as he had ever experienced. "At least the wind was at my back going home," he said.

Infectious diseases were common in summer and winter. Most recovered with only symptomatic treatment without complications. One, Dr. Minter remembered, developed encephalitis from a severe case of measles. When a toxic psychosis made it impossible to control the man at home, he was sent to the state hospital, euphemism for insane asylum. He was treated there as crazy and died.

Poliomyelitis left many of his patients crippled for life. Others survived with withered arms or legs. Dr. Minter did what he could for those with respiratory damage. But with no iron lung available, sometimes he could do no more than make them as comfortable as possible while they died. Saturdays, when people could more easily leave the fields, were especially busy. One memorable Saturday Dr. Minter and Nurse Cox began work at 5:30 in the morning and closed the doors after midnight. Ninety patients, including three house visits, had been seen.

A man with excruciating stomach pains was found to have an intestinal obstruction requiring surgery. The blockage was found to be a mass of hard mud. Eating clay was common among the poor and uneducated. No one knew why. Some suspected iron-deficiency anemia, but it was never proven. Some people just thought eating a little clay every day was good for them. Like one of my uncles who sipped a bit of kerosene every day. He said everyone should. He never said why. "It's just good for you." My uncle died of old age. Dr. Minter's patient died of peritonitis.

The flu epidemic of 1951 was the busiest season the Providence clinic experienced. Early one morning a man, sick himself, brought three children to the clinic, all seriously ill with flu and bronchial pneumonia. They were treated and sent home. At three in the afternoon the man returned with five more children. Because the man was too sick to drive home, Mrs. Cox and Mrs. Booker put them to bed in a room that had housed students from the summer camp school until the father recovered enough to drive. As the winter wore on, Dr. Minter and Mrs. Cox realized they could not hold out against successive days and nights without sleep. Since few of their patients had telephones, a family member would drive to Providence to summon the doctor. Instead of driving his own car, he would crawl in the back seat of the person's car, wrap himself in a blanket, and sleep going and coming. Mrs. Cox took naps in the clinic.

When times were not so busy, there were programs of medical education. Mrs. Cox, in conjunction with their practice among sufferers of diabetes, heart disease, and hypertension, organized a Dieting Dames Club, precursor of the successful and lucrative Weight Watchers empire. Mrs. Cox, of course, had no fee. One extremely overweight man, a diabetic, joined the Dieting Dames to the delight of his jesting neighbors. I thought of the obese Richard Davis, an earlier inhabitant of these acres believed to have been diabetic also, who might have profited from the nurse's program of diet and exercise.

Careful charting of their work was useful to the larger medical community as well. When Dr. Minter read an article claiming the low incidence of high blood pressure among Southern Negroes was due to their relaxed, carefree lifestyle, the Providence clinic could refute the nonsense of the claim itself, for just the opposite was true; the incidence was greater in this group. Dr. Minter saw one probable cause as the suppressed tensions forced upon them.

Dr. Minter spoke kindly of the medical community in Lexington, said two of the county's busiest doctors came to Providence the day after the mass meeting at Tchula High School to show their solidarity. "One always took my emergency patients," he said. "And never asked me if they could pay." On one of his tape recordings, he talked of a patient having her sixth child. The family lived ten miles in the hills and half a mile off the gravel road. It was a rainy winter night and his car would not make the half-mile muddy drive, only the man's truck. There were five children asleep in the far end of the one-bedroom cabin. After preliminary preparation, he stretched out on the floor for a few minutes' sleep. The quiet in the room awakened him. Finding no fetal heart tone, he reasoned the uterus had ruptured during a heavy contraction, smothering the baby. The mother, too weak to push with abdominal muscles already flaccid from other deliveries, was helpless, the baby no longer struggling. Using a sling fashioned from a bed sheet, he was able to simulate contractions and deliver the child. The placenta stubbornly remained, and Dr. Minter knew surgery was necessary. There was no choice but to leave the five sleeping children in the cabin with their dead sister. The woman had to be taken to the gravel road in the husband's truck, then in the doctor's car to Lexington. The friendly physician there responded to the 3:00 A.M. call, and the woman's life was spared. Dr. Minter returned to Providence for a busy day at the clinic.

There were times when the medical team was asked questions of national politics. Dr. Minter recalled making a house call at about one o'clock one winter morning. An elderly black woman, known by blacks and whites as Aunt Cindy, was reportedly near death. She lived in Tchula in a one-room house with a lean-to kitchen. After parking his car on the dirt street, he had to walk across a narrow plank over some backed-up water. There were two double beds in the large room, a fireplace for heat, a kerosene lamp the only light. There were fifteen or so people in the room, making a thorough examination difficult. He found the frail, ninety-pound or less woman very sick with pneumonia.

When he finished the examination, penicillin injection, and instructions to a relative on further care, he started to leave. Outside someone told him Aunt Cindy wanted to see him again. Thinking she wished to tell him something with no one else hearing, he leaned his ear to her mouth. "Doctor, do you think the president is going to get that civil rights bill passed?" Dr. Minter, with his busy schedule, was not even aware that President Truman was trying to get a Fair Employment Practice Act through Congress. A dying old black woman in Tchula, Mississippi, knew well.

From allergies and aneurysms to yaws and zoonosis, with a little politics thrown in, such was the life of a country doctor and nurse, David Minter and Lindsey Hail Cox. With no such thing as Medicaid or Blue Cross. Bills were sent out once a year. With no bill-collecting agency to follow up.

CHAPTER 11

Less than a month after the grim rains struck Providence, a feat of nature reordering ancient claims, another tragedy made its visitation to Section Thirteen, one over which the inhabitants had full bridle and command.

"It come about right in that old store," an elderly black man told me. It was on another of my visits to the area. I had stopped to ask directions but tarried when he told me his father had worked on Providence Plantation for Mr. John Gwin. He asked me not to use his name, said he didn't want to get in trouble with the white folks. When I pointed out we were talking about something of a long time ago, he shrugged and said, "Meanness got a long memory."

"We talking about the very same store your Mr. Cox used to run," he continued. "The co-op store. It was the plantation commissary back then. Had been since old Colonel Dick Davis had it, I reckon. This all happened when Mr. Champ Taylor had the place. Colored fellow killed a agent over on another plantation." I wanted to ask him what he meant by "agent" but didn't want to hinder the flow of his story. I supposed he was referring to a white overseer.

"It happened right after that big wash you said Mr. Hampton told you about," he said. I sat listening to his story, making notes, trying to remember every word of his colorful locution.

After the murder, the man who had done the killing ran, along with a friend who had been with him at the time. A mob had formed when the news went out and for several days and nights had chased the two. With finely honed storytelling skill, the old man took me through the Black River swamps, up and down the new and still swollen banks of Chicopa Creek, across the teeming water back and forth, sometimes wading downstream for miles to lose the scent from the dogs.

"They had bloodhounds?" I asked, almost apologetically. Waving me off with his hands, and without a pause he answered, "They wouldn no bloodhounds. Just dogs. This wouldn the law. Huntin' dogs. A colored man wouldn nothing but a animal back in them days. Just huntin' dogs. Chasing them with the same dogs they hunted coons." I thought I saw him flinch as he said "coons." Or maybe I flinched.

He took me on the chase up the Loess Bluffs and again to the flatland. One minute we were combing the woods with the mob, hearing their yells, eavesdropping on their strategy, and what they would do when the killers were found. Then we would join the hunted, run when they ran, stand watch while the other one slept, the mob uncannily close. I realized I was sharing the old man's predilection for the escape of the fugitives as he described the dispirited assortment of their relatives and friends gathering to pray night and day in the fields and cabins back on the plantation.

Just at sunrise the two men stumbled out of the woods, hope hours gone. They came from the direction of the still-flawed gravel pit to within sight of the store. "Old man Champ Taylor tricked 'em. He just tricked 'em. He was a settin' outside, on one of them cement blocks Mr. Dick Davis had between his house and the commissary, cause he couldn walk from the house to the store without restin'." A bee buzzed, then kissed the old man's lips, tasting, I supposed, the licorice in his tobacco. He waved it off without complaining. He digressed to tell stories about Colonel Davis. I marveled at his skill in taking the most ordinary happening and translate it into legend.

"He seen 'em coming. Said he smelled 'em coming. You know how white folks talk like that about colored folks." He paused for several seconds, as if thinking of a way to amend or apologize for what he had just said. Finally he added, "Some white folks, I mean. This was around 1920 or so." Then he went on. "He told them if they would give theirselves up, he would call the sheriff and they'ud be safe from the mob. Tole 'em to go on in the commissary and he would be in dreckly. But 'stead of that, he tipped off the mob and they come got 'em." He eyed me cautiously as I scribbled. He asked me again not to mention his name if I ever told someone else what he was telling me. I assured him I wouldn't and he finished his story, the first of many he would tell about his days at and around Providence Plantation and Providence Cooperative Farm. He told me Champ Taylor had been the high sheriff in Leflore County before he bought the plantation and knew how to tie someone up with a rope. He took some well-bucket rope from the commissary and tied the hands of the two men before the mob got there. "See, they trusted him to do what he promised. Thought, I reckon, he was just gon tie 'em up for the sheriff. So's he wouldn put the handcuffs on 'em." He paused again, his expression and eyes seeming to ponder the hundreds of years of similar deception, as if wondering why the two black men trusted Champ Taylor in the first place. Then, as if to explain their error, he said, "Course, they was awful tired at the time."

From then on he seemed unwilling to finish the story. I had to prompt him, ask specific questions, and promise again I would respect his wish not to be quoted directly.

I heard the screams and struggling of the two men as he described them being dragged from the store building, heard with him their prayers, the wailing of their mothers who were kept informed by the grapevine, and knew, as he told me, that their sons would not live the day. And the beastly, incomprehensible noises of the mob, the grunts, guttural sanctions, the heavy, near orgiastic breathing, heaving, pushing against each other trying to touch one or another of the Negroes. The work of a mob—a collection of men who, each alone, would have found what was happening unspeakable, yet together devoid of reason or decency. Soon each would return to hearth and household, there to resume the role of loving father, devoted husband, faithful in church and Sunday school, constant in all good works.

It was the same spot where A. Eugene Cox, another white man, had counseled the local folk in the ways of peace. I thought of another scene. A nearby schoolhouse where five hundred men, similarly on leave from their individual civility and rationality, had ordered the gentle Gene from the state. I wondered how many of them were issue of those whose deed I was hearing.

The two black men were taken to a grove of trees near a church on the Pinchback Plantation, where Eliza Stuart and her white planter husband had lived with their mixed-blood children. There they were tied in trees and their bodies riddled with lead pellets from shotguns until their cries and pleas no longer filled the morning. "I remember all that plain as if it was yesterday," the old man said. "My daddy was runnin' up and down the roads, gettin' all the colored folks back to their houses. He was afraid the Ku Klux would turn on us and wipe us all out."

He seemed faraway when he finished, and we sat in silence. There were other things I wanted to ask him about Section Thirteen and Providence Plantation but for the moment felt some memories should best be left alone. I would wait with him until he was ready to go on. When he was, he looked me straight in the eyes, something black folk didn't do with whites in the days he was recalling, and said, "I've seen a heap in my day." I said, "Yessir, I'm sure you have." Then we talked of things even more painful to both of us, for they were of us directly.

He started to tell me of the fire that came, he thought, about a year later. I knew that the plantation house Richard Davis had built with slave labor, under the supervision of Tobit, had burned down long before Providence Cooperative Farm had come. I knew nothing of how it happened. I was pretty sure the two events didn't come that close together, but remembering that storytellers of his age, and mine, sometimes have a strange field of time— tomorrow might be six months from now and yesterday five years ago—I let it go. The old man was fuzzy on details, but as he talked many things came back.

"There had been this hard freeze," he began. "It was, near as I recollect, the coldest it had been since the winter of ninety-nine."

"Yessir, I know about that one," I interrupted. "That was in February. February the eleventh." His expression inquired but he didn't stop me as I began a sort of soliloquy, not really thinking.

In the second week in February, 1899, a violent and devastating timber freeze and winter storm settled over the piney woods country. Colder than anything the early settlers had ever seen. So cold ice on ponds and lakes would support the weight of a full-grown man. Massive boughs of trees, groaning under the burden of ice and frozen sap, crashed to the ground, jarring the earth around them as they landed. Trunks of giant virgin longleaf

pine trees that had stood for hundreds of years split from freezing,
the cracking echoing and reverberating over the hills and valleys
like gunfire. Eggs in hen's nests expanded and popped with the
ease of soap bubbles. Milk in pie safes was as solid as hoop
cheese. And then, morning came and the sun shined forth and
the thaw began.

My venerable host, untutored but wise, sitting with me on the front porch of his modest house in Holmes County, Mississippi, studied me with what I remember as the eyes of a trained analyst. Something was about to happen and I wasn't sure I was going to like it.

"You don't remember all that," he said, looking at me in what I felt a patronizing fashion. "I don't remember that far back, and you don't remember that far back. You telling me something, Mr. Will. What you telling me?"

I had put my notebook on the floor. I sat clicking my pen in a fidgety on, then off, position, looking at him, not sure why I had said the words I had. It was my mission, to interview him, learn as much as I could about the history of a piece of geography known as Section Thirteen, a portion of Providence Plantation, and later Providence Cooperative Farm, the latter too ecumenical and racially careless for Delta ways of the fifties. He had recollections of both eras, something few living people had. Now he was the interviewer, leading me on in an air of competent innocence, up to nothing but kindness, I was sure.

"Go on, Mr. Will. You telling me something. I been telling you stuff. Why don't you just tell me what you're telling me?"

It seemed a reasonable request, but whiteness, or something, resisted. My impersonal stance had been penetrated. The man who had been my subject knew there was a reason I knew what had happened on a certain day more than ninety years earlier.

In a bumbling fashion, I tried to regain the journalist advantage. "Aw, nothing. I just happened to know that." His response was a dubious smile. Then I blurted it out. "That's the night my daddy was born." I felt childishly vulnerable. I was sitting a few feet from a black man I had never met before and had stopped to see by chance. Now suddenly I was under his control.

I knew I was repeating some words I had said at my father's funeral a year earlier but hadn't thought about it raising any questions. When there was a question, I was surprised the words were etched so indelibly in my mind that I could recite them verbatim to a stranger without really meaning to.

"When your daddy die?" he asked sympathetically yet with the sternness of the therapist he had become. My resistance had not deterred him, whatever his purpose.

I told him it had been about a year. "You preached the funeral," he said. It was not as a question. I nodded yes, then added, "Well, I gave the family eulogy. We felt someone in the family should say something, and it fell my lot to do it."

"I'd be much obliged if you'd tell me the rest of what you said."

"Aw, well, to tell the truth, I'm not sure I can remember the rest of it," I said, feeling closer now but still constrained.

He looked into the distance, down the bluff toward the land we had been talking about, the land of Providence. When he spoke again, the air of professionalism I had found disquieting was gone. Now he appeared crestfallen, almost pleading. "How old your daddy was?" I told him almost ninety-two. "Mine was fifty-two. So they told me." He paused for a long time again. I sat thinking his daddy was as old to him at fifty-two as mine had been at ninety-two.

"I didn't even get to come to my papa's funeral," he said, looking back at me. "Let alone say something. I was off in Detroit City working and didn't get to come and be with the rest of them. Fact is, like I tell folks, I was kind of wild back in them days, and they didn't know where to get holt of me till he'd been dead and in the ground more than a month." He took his cap off in what I thought was an act of reverence. "But I sure 'nuf loved my old papa."

He told me later that he had been a freight-train hobo for part of the years he was gone, and sometimes a bare-knuckled boxer for a traveling carnival. He said once in Toledo he fought for thirty-seven rounds before he knocked out his opponent. I asked him if he ever fought Jack Johnson. He said he never did but he wasn't afraid of him. Said he never saw him.

Now the old hobo and bare-knuckled fighter sat with his hands in his lap like a child at prayer. I wasn't sure what he said next but I thought it was, "I'd be powerful pleased if you'd go on."

I picked up where I had left off, pausing often to remember, pausing at other times to go on, still not sure why I was doing it. Just because he asked me, I supposed. He sat fixed on the ladder-back chair, leaning slightly toward me, listening hard to my stammering rendition of a year-old tribute to a man he never knew, and yet knew well.

> *And just at daybreak on February 12, 1899, the birthday of the Great Emancipator, the news spread about the community by men on horseback and women over garden gates, that Miss Bettye Campbell had another little boy, and had named him Lee Webb, for her Georgia kin. Time was marked from those two fortuitous events—the birth of a tiny baby, and the most destructive winter storm the piney woods country had ever known. We grew up hearing the stories from the old timers: Uncle Fork Baham, Cousin Ed Cockerham, Mr. Zius Newman, and others. When there would be an unusually cold spell we would hear them say, "I believe this is the coldest it has been since the night Lee Campbell was born.*
>
> *And then, almost a century later, lying not many miles from the spot of his birth, the pain now gone from his elegant features, he went fearlessly out to meet his maker, on as calm and quiet a summer evening as those same piney woods ever knew.*

I suppose I expected, wanted some word of encouragement from him, some sign that he wanted me to continue. But there was just a blank stare. I went on.

> *Those two circumstances of transition—entering the world at a time of great turbulence, and leaving at a time of quiet tranquility—suggest to us that he accomplished that which should be the desire and ambition of us all: to leave the world a little better place than the one we found.*

He nodded his head slowly but that was all. Again I had hoped for some spirited Pentecostal egging on, in the fashion of traditional black religion of the rural South. I considered stopping there but felt his presence in what had become mutual homage to our treasured dead.

> *He made the Biblically allotted threescore years and ten, with a tidy bonus to spare. But we shall mourn him nonetheless, for sweetness of the visit is not measured in terms of its longevity. Yet in our mourning there is the knowledge that kinships such as ours do not end with "so-long," and life does not end with what*

the clinicians call death. In that we can, and do, exult. We could never say that he belonged to us. Nothing that has life belongs to another. It comes as a gift, a matter of grace, like the tiny baby, and when it is gone, with all our technology, know-how, and striving, we cannot preserve it.

"That's right!" I heard him whisper. It was the only sound he had made to suggest he was listening to me at all. And the only verbal response I would hear from him.

I am not able to sum up his near-century amongst us. Each of you must write your own epitaph, in your own heart, and based upon your own memories. But there are some words which do sum up his faith, his philosophy, his very life. I think you will agree that they are also a succinct summary of the Christian movement in its entirety. For they acknowledge the Deity, they speak of mercy, of thanksgiving, sin, forgiveness, restoration, and end with the benedictory AMEN. And perhaps the only appropriate thing to be said at the passing of such a one is a hearty amen. His life has said all else. I close with those words he repeated at his table three times every day, no matter how lavish or how sparse the fare. They are words he learned early in his life, and were among the last lucid words I heard him speak. They were his words, and now they are ours, for he has left them as our legacy.

And I leave them with you.

"O LORD, LOOK DOWN ON US WITH MERCY, PARDON AND FORGIVE US OF OUR SINS, MAKE US THANKFUL FOR THESE AND ALL OTHER BLESSINGS, WE ASK FOR CHRIST'S SAKE. AMEN."

So AMEN, sweet Daddy. Well done!

AMEN!!

When I finished, I was even more ill at ease than at first and didn't know how to get the conversation going again. Then I realized the old man sitting across from me was crying. And I was close to doing the same. Then, seeing him, I was. Two grown men, two old men, weeping together for their sires. Two chasms, one called "now be a man," the other called "white folks/black folks," chasms seldom fully crossed, had been challenged and bridged in a litany of tardy grief. I had not viewed my father's body when he died. And had not cried. Now, as I saw him plainly in a black face contorted with grief, I knew it had been a mistake. But one I need never again regret.

We sat for what seemed a long time, each looking at the other, earnest and commending. At times our whimpering became the deep sobs of privacy abandoned, neither apologizing to the other for being little children.

In that moment I knew something I had never known before. Death is *that*. Friend is *friend*. And macho is a *goddam lie*.

I had never thought of "integration" as being something one felt. Now I was learning that is all integration is.

When we gained our composure, each one taking an identical red bandanna from his pocket and fiercely blowing his nose, my new friend quickly bowed his head. "Amen," I heard him say, his voice firm and clear. He had let his father go, as I had let mine go.

The communing had introduced a sluggishness in both of us and I knew the story about the Providence House fire would have to wait for another day. As I started to drive away, he came and opened the car door, shook my hand again, and said, "You can use my name if you want to." *Integration is trust.* I told him, no, I had made him a promise. Integration is promises kept.

It was almost a month before I got back to Mississippi and visited with him again. He said he had been missing me and I told him I had missed him too. "So how've you been?" I asked as he poured coffee from a percolator pot that had been bubbling briskly, a friendly sound automated coffee makers have all but taken from the morning ritual.

"Oh, just waitin' around for my severance pay," he replied, laughing. Then after a bit, serious again, "I reckon you want to hear about the time Providence burned down." He poured some of the steaming coffee into his saucer, blowing and slurping it in a kind of cadence.

Before I could answer he said, "You got a wife?" I told him I did. The same one for forty-four years.

"Mine passed five years ago. She could make coffee a heap better'n I can." I said the coffee was fine. "Too much of that bitter chicory, seems like," he said.

"That old house made quite a fire," he began. "Folks said they could see the smoke way the other side of Tchula." He talked again of how cold it had been. "Just such a time as when your papa was born. I'm talking about cold."

One of the workers on his way to the gravel mine saw a wisp of smoke coming from underneath the eve of the half-story. It was not unusual for the Franklin furnace that heated the water to pour smoke from its belly, but that furnace was near a vented wall on the bottom floor. The man thought he should sound a warning. He knocked on the back door, routine for Negroes at white folk's houses, and when Mrs. Taylor peered through the slightly opened door, he told her of the smoke. The woman didn't tell the man her husband was not at home, also routine. She told him the early morning sun was probably melting the frozen roof, causing a fog-like vapor. "I'll check on it directly." Half an hour later the worker told his white foreman he was afraid Providence House was on fire. By then they could see billowing black smoke swirling over the rooftop. By the time the foreman got all the crews out of the mine and off the dummyline and across the fields to the house, half the top-story roof was engulfed in flames.

The foreman, cousin of Taylor's wife, jerked open the back door, cursing loudly, screaming, "Woman, you must be crazy as a bedbug!"

Within minutes the roof collapsed, sending a shower of cinders in every direction, the men fleeing the torrid breath of Satan. Mrs. Taylor, in hysteria and wearing only a light kimono over a cotton nightgown, was struggling to break free of her cousin's fierce grip to go back inside for some prized possession she wouldn't name. Horses, mules, and cattle, still stalled, were frantically trying to escape, their raging cries sometimes drowning the calamitous roaring, crackling, hissing sounds of the burning house.

Without further warning, the entire structure split apart as if a mighty charge had been detonated beneath it. The mounting pressure inside the fortress-like perfection of Tobit, the builder, had, like a combustion chamber, yielded to outside forces and exploded, everything falling in upon itself, an inferno, consuming in one hour what it had taken an elderly slave who had been offered to Richard Davis as a bonus two years to construct.

What W. C. "Champ" Taylor saw when he returned was a smoldering ruin. Even the sturdy brick chimneys had disintegrated in the spontaneous eruption. Iron stoves and bedsteads had softened in the heat and were twisted into puzzle-like caricatures, costly chandeliers and melted window glass draped over them like a Picasso painting. The only thing left upright was the stile at the end of the long cement walk. The white and blue lettering seemed a boasting omen: GWIN. The taunting pyre flickered as grim reminder of the psalmist's warning: That life is suffering and sorrow, that we all come forth like a flower and are cut down and are of a few days and full of trouble, and that all flesh is like grass and we are all here dying together.

And his wife lay whimpering on the floor of the commissary beside an unstoked cast-iron heater.

We sat as if watching the last of the dying embers. "What do you suppose caused it?" I asked.

"I imagine, when the water froze and wasn't running through the pipes behind the heater, it just got too hot. Started scorching the dry wood and it finally flamed up. That's what they thought anyhow."

"Maybe if she had listened to the first fellow who told her he saw smoke they could have put it out," I said.

"He was a colored fellow." And that was all he said.

> God gave Noah the rainbow sign;
> No more water, the fire next time.

Two years later there was a brief meeting in a lawyer's office in Tchula. W. C. Taylor and John Gwin discussed the matter of arrears, and Taylor signed a document. They shook hands and went their separate ways. The Snopes who would be a Compson had failed, the planter Grail beyond his reach. Providence Plantation was back in Gwin hands.

John Gwin had in mind moving back to Providence, building an even bigger house than the one his Uncle Dick Davis had built, and operating the plantation. But when the foreclosure was done, he drove his wife to their patron acres where he expected a scene resonating precious memories. Instead there was a bleakness about the place. It was not so much that the house was not there to resurrect what they remembered as the magnificent past. They were prepared for that. But the trees were gone. The surplice of big gum, oak, elm, beech, and sycamore that had encompassed and embraced the old house with gracefulness and dignity were no more, cut down for marketable timber, the crude, rotting stumps standing like a cynical tableau on ground that had once been lavish shade, beckoning kin and neighbors to pleasant evenings. The naked gullies yawned in mockery of the pitiful strands of Johnson and Bermuda grass struggling to right the mayhem of nature and stupendous wrongs of the keeper of the land, stoking the melancholia gripping the once-proud planter and his bride.

GWIN. The white and blue lettering on the mounting style seemed sad and alone against the backdrop of the cold and surly remains of what had been the site of their highest hopes, conjuring thoughts in the head of Annie Kelly Gwin from which plantation ladies were presumed exempt by proper breeding. Section Thirteen was not the same. The beautiful and socially conscious Annie had looked to the city with longing eyes for many years. Here was an opening to move to Jackson. They did, but stayed one year in the grand mansion they purchased and moved back to Holmes County.

Rather than reorganize the plantation as a sharecropping operation, John Gwin rented, leased, or sold it to a nephew, Samuel Donnell Gwin Hutton, brother of Charlton Hutton, who had told me so much about the history of Providence and the Gwin family. Charlton Hutton believes his brother bought Providence. Because there is no record in the chancery court records of transfer of title from Gwin to Hutton, I think it was a handshake agreement. John Gwin, with no blood child of his own, was partial to the nephew who carried his father's name and doubtless wanted the young man, then twenty-seven years old, to have the plantation. But I don't believe it was ever in his possession.

Samuel Donnell Gwin Hutton was an ambitious and hardworking man. Although a child of an urban manse, his father the learned pastor of Jackson's hegemonic First Presbyterian Church, the young Hutton was always of the earth. He loved the Delta, and being one of its planters was his dream from childhood. Providence was one of the earliest plantations in Holmes County and had been in its day the pride of the countryside. Being its lord, although only from January until December in the ill-fated year of 1929, must have made him proud. Still a bachelor when he went there, as was his uncle Dick Davis, he worked as hard as any of his workers. And like Richard Davis, he was almost starting anew. That he failed is not to his discredit. His two sons, one bearing his name, the other the name of his father, remain, farming the Cooper Plantation nearby.

The year 1929 began with promise and prosperity for Samuel Donnell Gwin Hutton. It ended on a note of gloom and fiscal despair. He made what was said to have been the best cotton crop ever on Providence Plantation. In early June the lush, waist-high foliage was filled with the little triangular offshoots called squares. Within two weeks the squares open to become a dazzling white blossom. The second day the flower is a dainty pink, deepening to a pleasant lavender or purple before drying and being pushed from its nest-like nook by the tiny beginning of a boll. Although my most lean years were those spent as a member of a yeoman cotton-farming family, straits to which I hope never to return despite the security I knew there, I have never seen a more lovely sight than the floral offering of a cotton field—the progression and profusion of white, pink, and purple blossoms waiting their turn, diamond dewdrops sparkling on the rich green, succulent leaves in the first morning rays of a summer sun. Even the bustle of ravenous insects, drinking greedily from the nectaries or sinking their spiteful snouts into tender stems and fruit, adds to the enchantment. That so much evil and ugliness have been attendant to the drama of cotton is one of life's lamentables.

By July Hutton's cotton plants were heavy with walnut-size bolls, damp seeds and fiber inside like an impatient fetus, waiting for the August sun to deliver them, burst them open, ready for picking, gins, and looms. The heavy bolls met in the middles, their weight too much for the stalks to support. Two bales per acre was the estimate on the Delta land, better than a bale per acre on the hills. A good price was predicted.

The Great Depression began instead. Banks were failing as the infant Cotton Kingdom financial establishments had done ninety years before. Wall Street was in panic. A bushel of corn went for a can of Prince Albert and a Baby Ruth. Hundreds of cotton bales, queued up for wealth on a warehouse dock in Tchula, rebuffed by the errors of America's commerce, sold as low as a nickel a pound.

Samuel Donnell Gwin Hutton could have been a rich man. Instead, he didn't clear enough to pay for his seeds and fertilizer. John Gwin did what he could to convince his nephew to stay on, assuring him he was an excellent farmer, a prudent steward of the land who would do well in other years when the financial crisis passed. But the usually persuasive John Gwin did not prevail. Hutton read the times correctly and did not choose to invest his most productive years in a depression-ridden cotton economy. He moved back to Jackson, returned to his job with the Mississippi Power and Light Company, where he remained for ten years.

So far as Providence was concerned, the Gwin dynasty was at an end. It had begun with the brilliant and restless William McKendree Gwin, son of a Tennessee Methodist preacher who was friend, chaplain, and troop commander of Andrew Jackson. He bought Section Thirteen and the surrounding property in a preemption sale following the Treaty of Dancing Rabbit Creek.

On October 11, 1930, Carl Parrish, a local bookkeeper and manager of a neighboring plantation, bought Providence from John D. Gwin. Parrish was suffering from severe diabetes and rented the property to a relative. He was treated at the preeminent Mayo Clinic, but the disease killed him. Before it did, he sold Providence Plantation to a little band of Christian visionaries, apostles of Sherwood Eddy and Reinhold Niebuhr, two men as far removed ideologically from the measure and merit of white Holmes countians as East from West. The delicate nuances were disturbing to those who still reeled under recollections of Reconstruction's legacy. "Why did he sell Providence to those people?" they pondered. Whether under the spell of charity, an act of attrition, a mortal effort at prevenient grace, or simply the money, he did it. And took his reasons to his grave.

Those who came to Section Thirteen under the aegis of northern liberals—the Coxes, Minters, Bookers, Morgans—would be seen by many as no more than a beguiling interlude, changing nothing. They would be greeted by others with a facade of good humor, some with alleged Old South manners and civility, a delicate membrane of friendship that would soon join the cavilling white majority. Sons and daughters of ex-slaves, the numerical majority, still bowed by the weight of servitude, offered the same hearty greeting they had extended to others who had teased them with charitable overtures. The ideologues would keep the name Providence because it so nearly indicated what they were about. The generally churlish Loess Bluffs welcomed them. Chicopa Creek, though once more in nasty disarray, seemed more disposed to fellowship than it had been since Luther Cashdollar and Jesse Furver partook of its hospitality. The young votaries came with zeal and a commitment to innocent hard work. But in eighteen years they would be gone, swept up in the vortex of the times. *Providence* did not prevail.

Providence Cooperative Farm paid six dollars an acre for 2,880 acres, close to the amount William McKendree Gwin had paid for the same land almost exactly a hundred years earlier. On one occasion it had commanded $750 an acre.

Section Thirteen, like the old man who told me of the lynching and big fire, had seen a heap in its day. During the next fifty years, from the creation of Providence Cooperative Farm until the same government that had wrested it from the Choctaws would again hold clear title, it would see a heap more.

CHAPTER 12

"It's just some poor land that has broke a lot of people."

Those words of former congressman Frank Smith kept coming back. Why did this parcel have such estimate while adjacent lands flourished? Maybe the flood that came, confined as it was but wreaking such havoc, confounding the surveyors' instruments with ambiguous boundaries for years to come, was the weeping of the land itself, a lament for the fights that happened no matter who claimed control, portent of things yet to come.

Even those whose purpose was laudable were no exception to the rancor that seemed to track and possess all who came. The demise of Luther Cashdollar's people was but the sad beginning. Maybe judgment still.

It was time for me to look at some more recent events in the history of Section Thirteen. I had communed with the Choctaws, engaged the early aristocracy, walked with slaves, witnessed the Civil War and Reconstruction, but spent little time with the founders of the cooperative farm. Perhaps those I should have known most closely I knew least. I had known the Coxes and Minters since 1955 but not the founders of Delta and Providence cooperative farms. I knew little of the first years of the cooperative endeavor. In 1955, when I was introduced to Providence, that phase had ended. Gene was organizing credit unions, operating the co-op store, and doing his informal teaching. Dr. Minter and Lindy Cox were running the medical clinic, which, though largely a missionary enterprise serving mostly black patients, was not a radical threat to the county.

I went to the University of North Carolina Archives where the early records were stored to get a more accurate view of the budding years of Providence Cooperative Farm. That search was to be the most dispiriting portion of my pilgrimage. I had held the Coxes and Minters in such esteem that I was not prepared for what I found.

The most influential founders of the cooperative, Reinhold Niebuhr, Sherwood Eddy, Dr. William Amberson, and Reverend Sam Franklin, were gone when I discovered the farm in 1955. I had not bothered to ask why it was so. Why had they gone? Neither had I considered their deportment while they were in charge. Maybe I didn't ask because I suspected stories I didn't want to hear. Heroes are too few and hard to come by to risk their loss.

I knew that Sam Franklin had been resident director at Rochdale and then at Providence. I had known of problems, had heard accounts of discontent when promises—that the land would one day be owned not by the cooperative but by individual families investing their time and energies—had gone awry. More than once I had heard the slur "paternalistic feudalism." But that was generally from detractors. Or so I had thought. I accepted the inevitability of such things, for the odds against them were great. Now I was examining primary sources, looking within, exhuming accounts of things that pained me. At times I wished I had left them interred in the deepest recesses of Wilson Library and not found them at all. But they were part of Section Thirteen's story and must be told with the rest.

I had chosen not to think that the fathers of so high-minded a project might have fallen prey to the same soul-molesting hubris that does so easily beset us all. I had not reckoned that in modern times, as in Biblical days, even the best of us go to Baal of Peor and become like unto the things we detested. As I searched the chronicles of stalwart men of goodwill and good intentions and saw them behave more and more in the old plantation mode when the house they were endeavoring to build was threatened by forces within and without, I was saddened.

Trouble came quickly. Complaints began soon after Delta Cooperative Farm was founded at Rochdale in 1936, and they followed the founders to Holmes County and Section Thirteen two years later. Curious as it must have seemed, the approach to some of the problems appeared to make a mockery of the original ideals. Often they centered around activities of the Southern Tenant Farmers Union. It had been the folk of the union who had paved the way and first dreamed the dream of black and white farmers living and working collectively, enjoying the fruits of their labor. The STFU, interracial in rank and file from the beginning, had grown rapidly since it began in 1934 with eighteen members. Within two years it had reached thirty-five thousand, who promised ten cents a month dues but often could not pay. With H. L. Mitchell and Clay East as spearheads, Norman Thomas and Howard "Buck" Kester as godfathers, and women like Willie Sue Blagden suffering the same flogging as men because they were equally feared by the planters, Myrtle Lawrence writing songs and asking regularly for the most dangerous assignment, Evelyn Smith sparking a feminist movement whose militancy has not since been duplicated, the STFU was for a time a powerful force, standing for everything the Delta Cooperative Farm and Providence Cooperative Farm stood for. The co-op farms were children of the union.

From Arkansas, the union spread immediately into Mississippi, Missouri, Louisiana, Oklahoma, and eventually to the West Coast. Wherever there were tenant farmers being evicted from the land, the union was heard—welcomed by the sharecroppers, hated by the planters. Only the Oklahoma Choctaws, who had been evicted from their land in Mississippi a hundred years earlier, saw the STFU as too conservative and irrelevant. When H. L. Mitchell met with the Tribal Council, he spoke through an interpreter, a Cherokee from Muskogee. Mitchell thought he had made a favorable impression until the response of the chief was translated. Politely and ceremoniously the chief had told him:

> The white man talks well. Our brother from Muskogee talks well. But Choctaws don't need organizing. We are already organized. When the white man and the black man are ready to take back the land, just let us know, and we shall get our guns and come too.

Sins of the fathers. . . . Mitchell understood.

Since it had been spawned by the Southern Tenant Farmers Union, one of the social articles in the cooperative farm's Statement of Basic Principles was: "We believe that farm workers, like industrial workers, should organize themselves into unions for their own protection and betterment. We welcome the establishment of the STFU on the farm, and wish to cooperate to the fullest extent with it." The article was soon tested. When the cooperative was advancing members sixty-six cents a day for chopping cotton while the traditional plantations were paying a dollar a day, co-op residents who took their hoes to neighboring fields to get the higher rate were punished. Victims of what they called "sanctions," the violators were not allowed credit at the cooperative store and could not receive gift clothing sent by well-wishers from afar. When it became evident that enough of the residents, especially women, were working elsewhere, or picking blackberries to show their displeasure, and the cooperative farm crop would most likely be lost from lack of hoeing, workers were trucked in from Clarksdale and paid the prevailing rate. The ugly words "strikebreakers" or "scabs" were not used. Even so. . . . And when a leader of the Southern Tenant Farmers Union urged the local union members to demand five dollars per day advance, Sam Franklin, as farm director, told them it would break the farm. Perhaps so. And yet. . . .

The Christian virtues of equality, love, and forbearance seemed to wane when the institution itself was threatened. It is not a new story in the history of humankind. Institutional survival, even institutional well-being, becomes sacred. We search in vain for exceptions.

Oliver Hotz, a graduate student at Eden Theological Seminary who had been a volunteer at one of the cooperative farm work camps, and who went on to become a prominent United Church of Christ preacher in the Midwest, offered a critique in a poignant letter to Reverend Franklin in 1940. He was discussing correspondence he had with Reinhold Niebuhr in which he took Niebuhr to task for moralizing to the people of the farm before "investigating conditions more thoroughly." He submitted a detailed audit of his own firsthand observation of those conditions. Addressing Reverend Franklin directly, he wrote:

> *I also maintained that ministers should remain ministers instead of seeking to enter the economic field and become supervisors of farms, especially when they have control over other human life and destiny. I mentioned you as an example of an excellent preacher but a failure as a farm director. What I meant by that*

last remark was that your fine personality has become hardened
by the economic problem for which you knew no answer so that
you no longer treated the people with their grievances as persons
but as less than yourself. They do not love you but fear you.

The young seminarian then discussed at length the manner in which four black union members who had a different view as to how the farm should be run were treated. He concluded with some hard sayings:

It isn't that the Farm has failed and retrenched along all lines.
That isn't hard to take considering the difficulties. What hurts is
that you have become an obstacle and hindrance to those people
ever understanding what Christianity and its genius of repen-
tance and faith really mean. What did the term "humility"
connote to you when you played God who sees all, knows all, and
judges all in the matter of peoples' grievances as due largely to
these four men? I hold no brief for them except that your dogma-
tism in regard to them and their activities confirms my suspicion
that your mind and heart have played you tricks so that without
knowing rationalized your position.

Another basic principle that seemed to fade when tested was that management was to be democratic. A council was elected by the cooperative membership by ballot. An exception was made that seemed to negate any real authority of the elected council. "The trustees, through their representative, must approve all actions of the council." Reverend Franklin, as farm director, was the representative of the trustees. This gave him veto power. When that power was exercised in ways many residents thought was less than judicious, Mr. Niebuhr, chairman of the Board of Trustees, at one point recommended a censure of Mr. Franklin. Other trustees, for the sake of harmony, voted him down.

It was a cooperative. But the collective aspect led at times to the greatest dissension. The director and manager were seen by some who knew well the ways of the plantation as "riding bosses," little different from what they had known on other plantations. Preachments of social equality fell on deaf ears. Survival was of the heart. Their own plot of ground they could farm on their own was their preference. They saw assignments and decisions made by someone whose knowledge of farming they questioned. And they saw payments made to them from the trustees' secretary-treasurer, Sherwood Eddy, out of New York City and wondered why they were separated by such distance from funds they were told they controlled. Conflict was inevitable. Black sons and daughters of slavery and centuries of white ascendance could not be easily convinced that all was well, especially when chinks in the armor of goodwill were visible. Nor could white sons and daughters of a sharecropping system that had pitted them against the blacks but left them in their same plight be expected to have a different view of the promises.

Revolt of the poor whom the missionaries had come to save was not alone among problems. There was internal contention at the top as well. When the creamery at Providence had a lien on it that the farm could not pay, Sherwood Eddy bought it. It was his understanding that it was his gift to Providence Farm. When debts were incurred in the operation of the creamery, Reverend Franklin's reasoning was that the creamery belonged to Mr. Eddy. Therefore, Mr. Eddy owed the money. After many letters and memoranda, Mr. Franklin's logic continued to baffle Mr. Eddy's bookkeeper.

By then the festering sore erupted in volcanic proportions with the resignation of Dr. William Amberson from the trustee board. He had been one of the founders of the experiment. He was a scientist, a professor of physiology, not a theologian. An agnostic, not a Christian. It had been a strange alliance from the beginning. He had long quarreled with what he saw as unilateral decisions of Mr. Franklin and had repeatedly asked the Board of Trustees to devote itself to a search for effective techniques of fundamental democracy on the farm. In a previous letter he had said, "I cannot give allegiance to plans and programs launched without my knowledge, and in whose preparation I have had no share." His six-page letter of resignation was filled with serious allegations regarding the financial and ideological failures of the cooperative venture. He insisted that it would have been better to say that all decisions would be made by the farm director than to mislead the elected council into believing that they had authority. He said the democratically elected council had authority only until the members chose to exercise it. "It is sociological ventriloquism at its dreadful worst," he wrote. He blamed Mr. Franklin and Mr. Eddy for not admitting to a losing venture, rather than claiming glowing successes in appeal letters for contributions.

I have never been able to fathom the mental processes which demand that we must pretend to successful operation when the basic reason for our financial appeal is that we are not yet successful. We are in great need of money, yet we dare not admit it. Failing, we must seem successful, so that, by garnering new contributions, we may stave off the time when we must successfully fail.

He challenged Sherwood Eddy's proposed appeal letter that said that a fine spirit prevailed in the personnel on the farms. Amberson stated that they were instead

depressed and almost despairing. A feeling of futility grips them. Some of our key rank-and-filers are ready to leave, believing that we have not meant and do not mean to make good on our early promise to sell them the land. Our position in this matter has shifted greatly.

Again he chastised Mr. Franklin, farm director, and Mr. Niebuhr, board chairman, for not bringing the people along with them and for the most blatantly undemocratic practices:

This Board has drifted into that very hypocritical attitude which its Chairman once so ably exposed and denounced. (Reinhold Niebuhr—"Moral Man and Immoral Society.") Unthinkingly, unwittingly perhaps, we look down from our great heights upon these miserable people whom we started out to serve, and we despise them. Or at least we completely discount them. They are so incompetent. We must do everything for them, make all the plans, handle all the money, maneuver all the more important elections.

Nor did he spare Dr. Eddy:

Dr. Eddy lives in a dream world, all his own. There is no hope in this confused brain. The tragedy is that he should be trying to run our business, and bringing the cooperative name into disrepute. If by some miracle he gets through to economic success we will have not a cooperative, but a corporative farm. Cooperation cannot be reached by dictation or coercion such as he and Sam are trying to use. . . . Criticizing absentee landlordism, we have ourselves created its most vicious forms.

In response to Mr. Franklin's assertion that the subterranean rumblings had been launched by "instigation from outside," Dr. Amberson replied:

> From "outside instigator" to "outside agitator" is only a step, and the pattern of plantation thought which he had meant to break, rises up again to grip his own mind. Than this no tragedy can be more dreadful.

Before concluding his words to his former comrades, he renewed his vows to his own academic discipline:

> I shall struggle no more with that dark spirit of untruth which is blighting every chance we ever had to make a success of this work. I cannot maintain the pace of your frenzied philanthropy. Never before have I seen with such blinding clarity the essential and irreconcilable conflict between the scientific and the ecclesiastical approach to social problems. Never before have I become so deeply committed to the scientific search for knowledge as opposed to all other methods.
> Gentlemen: . . . I bid you farewell.

When I finished Dr. Amberson's long letter of resignation and rebuke, I felt a sense of betrayal. After all, for thirty-five years I had been a member of the Providence board. I could argue that when I went on the board, even when first I heard of its existence, those battles were over. And technically Providence was no longer a cooperative when I arrived. In 1946 Providence took the corporate name Delta Foundation, Inc., with a Mississippi nonprofit charter. By then, all the founders and early residents except the Bookers, Coxes, and Minters were gone. But that change was the effecting of one of Dr. Amberson's prophecies. Corporation, not cooperative. It was not that being a corporation made the work they did any less worthy. In some ways the change unshackled the Coxes and Minters to be about what they did best. Dr. Minter and Nurse Cox could practice medicine in the traditional fashion. Since money had never been their purpose, their healing was not impeded by a change of charter. Mr. Cox could stand behind the counter of the Providence Plantation commissary and teach, exhort, counsel, and befriend in the posture of a country storekeeper. Still they were haunted by the dream of the land some day belonging to the people who worked it. A corporation is not a cooperative. Though the vision was challenged and defeated by expediency, the service of their hands prevailed. Even so, I was depressed as I sat alone in the bowels of that enormous storehouse of information in Chapel Hill, grieving not so much about harsh words and bitter feelings between people, nor even the pitiable victims caught in the quagmire of missionaries become feuding overlords, but grieving that their dispute had the land and its use at its heart. As if the land had feelings, a soul, moods, and tears to shed, like a mother weeping when her children quarrel.

I went outside and sat for a long time on the steps of the huge building, leaning against a column. In my thirty-five years, what had I done or said that might have revived the dream? I could think of nothing. What could I have done or said that would have made a difference? I did not know.

I watched the students, rushing to classes on spiffy English bicycles or on foot. Young lovers sat close on the clean leaves of early fall the way young lovers have always done. What are their dreams? I noted the diversity of messages on the students' T-shirts: SODOMIZE SADDAM. DAVID DUKE FOR GOVERNOR. VOTE FOR JESSE HELMS; KEEP NORTH CAROLINA IGNORANT.

Back inside I spent many more hours going through box after box of records of the failed cooperative enterprise. I found no gainsaying of Dr. Amberson's torrid pages. Instead, in grammatically flawed, sometimes barely legible notes on Blue Horse tablet sheets or scraps of brown paper, I found more of what I had had enough of; pitifully stated evidence of the faltering of the beautiful dream.

Something went wrong. Something not intentional, for these were all men who devoutly yearned for the success of what they had started. What was it? They were all men of note. Reinhold Niebuhr was one the most distinguished theologians of his time. Sherwood Eddy was a social critic and Christian layman, known around the world for his zeal for human betterment. William Amberson was a brilliant teacher, medical scholar, and humanitarian. Sam Franklin was a Presbyterian missionary to Japan, before and after his years with the cooperative farms. What then is one to make of this behavior, which at times seemed a blend of schoolyard scuffle and political party bosses contending for control? Was it nothing more, nor less, than what the theologians among them knew as original sin, that indefinable flaw in the human condition that magnifies pride, ego, thinking more highly of ourselves than we ought to think until it controls all else? Some of the early neighbors had called the principals of Providence "Ecclesiastical Carpetbaggers." Was the scorn more correct than epithetical? What would have been Amberson's scientific diagnosis? Benign narcissism, perhaps. Was he correct in saying only the scientific approach to social problems is to be trusted? Would he revise his thinking today when science and technology seem set on making robots of us all? Would he remind us that religion has offered little by way of corrective?

Was it that, from the beginning to this day, under the system there was no other way to do it? That no matter how highborn the notion, a plantation has a built-in modus operandi. A gasoline engine runs on gasoline. There may be slight octane variations, but there is no real substitute.

Or was the righteous warfare solely the pox on all houses no matter what the mission, sent by the Great Spirit of the people of Luther Cashdollar?

I did not, and do not now, know the answers to my questions. And the asking of them had only heightened my perplexity. It was time to retire from some sad days of inquiry in Chapel Hill, North Carolina.

But wait! I had found much in which to rejoice. The dreaming had been there. Dreams are the stuff of hope and are sometimes their own triumph. The struggling of so many to make the vision real was there. In abundance. The healing and sacrificial hand-prints of Lindsey Hail Cox and David Minter were found in almost every opened archive container. And through it all, A. Eugene Cox had stood like the sturdy oaks on the banks of Chicopa Creek that had weathered the spring freshet. He would not be moved. When others haggled and wavered, his brooding presence was felt. When the last of the founders had defected and moved on, he was there. His was an uncomplicated dream: to do the best he could with Section Thirteen. And for the people. He never saw the promised land. But he kept the faith in the wilderness.

Knowing that, I felt better.

CHAPTER 13

Leaving Providence had been hardest for Gene Cox. The others had lived in various parts of the world. With the exception of the brief time at the Rochdale farm, and his childhood in Texas, Section Thirteen had been his home all his life. He knew every part of it, loved every rock and cranny. So it was with anguish that he walked out of the store that sad day in 1956, leaving everything as it was. He turned a page in his life as he turned the key in the lock, and took his family across the Tennessee state line to a suburb of Memphis called White Haven. The dream of the young Socialists for a cooperative, interracial farm in Mississippi had been truncated by civic folly. But Gene never really left Providence.

Dr. Minter closed his clinic and moved to Tucson. The Hendersons, Morgans, and the remaining families scattered. A stalwart woman—Mrs. Fannye Thomas Booker—remained. The pillar of fire that had guided them in Exodus fashion was flickering low. But Section Thirteen was undaunted. It would endure. To serve Mrs. Booker as she would serve it for years to come. Until she too would be similarly taken away.

Gene Cox did not harness well. He was a man of the soil, and neither regular hours nor life in a big city were to his liking. Being father to his three children was a responsibility he took with great zeal. He had not spent more than one night at a time away from them in their lives. He was equally devoted to his wife. Financial security was not on the agenda before. Providence was more than a name they had inherited from the plantation; it was a watchword. Now he must join Lindy in providing for them as best they could. Lindy could, and did, return to her profession of nursing on a part-time basis. But life in the city was hectic and expensive, and the family routine of the children was important. Yet Gene had to find work outside the home.

The National Council of Churches, a large, active, and effective ecumenical agency at the time, offered Gene a job in rural development in the South. Though the council had become exceedingly controversial during the McCarthy years and many in the rank and file within the constituent denominations considered it too far to the left, it had survived and was staffed by dedicated and courageous men and women who were not bothered by the Coxes' Socialist past. Even so, it was an institution with institutional rules. One rule was that a staff person had to be a member of a local congregation. Being unwelcome in the Presbyterian church in Tchula, Gene's only affiliation was the community worship at Providence, which did not appear on any denominational roster. This meant a delay in his appointment until the legal officer, also a Mississippi expatriate in sympathy with Gene's plight, could devise a way to circumvent the bureaucracy. Gene was without salary for several months.

Because of the National Council of Churches' strong support of the Supreme Court's decision of May 17, 1954, declaring public school segregation unconstitutional, it was even more suspect within the local churches of the South. But one of the few advantages the city afforded the Coxes was anonymity, so the neighbors were generally friendly. In addition, Gene and Lindy had learned to be foxy survivors during their twenty years in Mississippi and had no fear.

His job description was intentionally imprecise, and he was free to carve out his own niche in the Southern struggle. He approached the task with vigor, driving the back roads, calling on old Labor Movement friends, county agricultural agents, small-town newspaper editors he knew to be somewhat sympathetic to bringing the South into compliance with the Court's ruling. Gene, who was seen as a radical activist in Holmes County, Mississippi, now saw himself as a conversationalist, talker, persuader, trying to communicate with anyone who would listen, no matter how antagonistic to his message of reconciliation.

Perhaps it was his vocation as communicator that led to his new avocation, almost obsession—old telephones. Riding the county roads, he would spot old, abandoned telephone wires, lines that had once carried messages when party lines had numbers such as one long and two short rings or one short and one long, where women called "Central" had switchboards with sometimes fewer than a dozen plug-in jacks and you had to first ring Central to communicate with your neighbors, and the switchboard operator knew all the news as it happened and everyone's business. With the coming of rural-electrification modern equipment—though far less advanced than what we have today when one can directly dial Sweet Water, Alabama; Davos, Switzerland; or the Kurile Islands without hearing a human voice until the party answers—those systems were as obsolete as the cavalry in the bombing of Baghdad. Gene would follow the fallen lines or still-standing poles until they finally led him off the road and to a farmhouse where Central had once been located. If the outmoded switchboard was still there, no matter the condition, he would try to buy it. Generally the aging owner could also tell him which farms had been on her system and he would locate them and buy the old phones if he could. Sometimes when he returned to White Haven, his car, at first a Packard as antiquated as the telephones he bought, would be loaded with various styles of the old-fashioned instruments. From the simple desk type to wall boxes with the front looking like a swine snout placed discreetly beneath two mammary-looking bells that vibrated and rang when the turn of the crank from the calling party sent a faint electrical current from two nine-volt, dry-cell batteries mounted inside, to elegant oak or walnut stand-up cabinets with solid brass receivers and transmitters, sometimes with the coat-of-arms of the family or the insignia of the plantation delicately carved into the fine wood. On other trips he would come back with spare parts or pieces that he used in repairing others. From where I sit in my writing cabin, I can see one of his many purchases hanging on the wall. It serves as intercom to the residence and guesthouse where two others are located and to remind me of days when wiretapping would have been an outrage and eavesdropping was an acceptable way of learning your neighbors were in trouble if their phone rang more than twice in quick succession.

Gene did not consider his work finished at Providence. He visited often and continued to look after all business matters. It was in this period that he had asked me to serve on the Providence Farm Board of Directors.

Now all the founders and participants in the Providence Farm saga were getting old. Some were long dead. For years the board had consisted of Gene and Lindy Cox; Sue Minter, who lived in Tucson and never attended meetings; and me. Gene was perpetual secretary-treasurer because only he could attend to financial matters. Lindy and I rotated being president and vice-president each year. After several years of that routine, Gene recommended that we elect someone to the board who lived in Memphis so if some emergency arose a quorum could be quickly convened. He suggested Walter Diggs, a man I did not know at the time. Walter was superintendent of the Memphis Mental Health Institute. He was from a prominent Memphis family, was well educated, energetic and articulate, committed to many good causes. When Gene introduced him, he said we would forgive the poor fellow for being a Unitarian. Mr. Diggs immediately assumed a vigorous role on the board and was soon selected chairman.

Providence had by then lain fallow for many years. The board had annual meetings according to the bylaws. Sometimes the sessions consisted of little more than deciding the time of the next meeting. Others went on for hours. Pressure had been mounting from former members and original founders to do something with the land. The state of Mississippi would have been within its legal bounds to revoke the tax-exempt charter and seize the property years earlier. All through the sixties, when anything slightly liberal on race was considered subversive, I marveled it didn't happen.

During the passionate sixties there were numerous proposals from groups and individuals wanting to use the property. Gene Cox could generally discourage them with dawdling efficiency. If they addressed the board directly, he was equally skilled at parrying the inquiries with recommendations of further study. In 1963 the Student Nonviolent Coordinating Committee sent James Bevel and Diane Nash, two of their more articulate and colorful leaders, to Mr. Cox with a plan to use the facilities for training SNCC voter-registration workers. He was convinced that local whites would not tolerate the presence of a group so visible and leftist. He patiently explained that a long and indigenous follow-up operation would be needed later to authenticate the zealous labors of the civil rights activists, and Providence should keep a low profile until that time came. Prudent or cowardly, the facilities of Providence Farm were in effect red-shirted during the activist years of the civil rights movement. Gene Cox, the old war-horse and prophet of earlier years, considered a dangerous revolutionary by the white populace of Holmes County when he was in their midst, would give the whites quarter in the turbulent sixties. Red-shirting has its hazards. It can be for the benefit of the team next year. It can also be calling the fireman when the fire is out.

Others came with offers. Lilith Quinlan, an assiduous and financially secure young woman with an activist group called Common Ground, wanted to purchase the farm for a Center for Justice, with a view toward organizing the poor of the surrounding communities. They were also involved in the sanctuary movement for Central American refugees. After repeated visits and detailed written proposals, she gave up and backed away. In 1979 Gene invited Professor Wilson Welch of Fisk University, then director of the prestigious Race Relations Institute, founded by Charles Spurgeon Johnson in 1943 as a research and training organization, to submit a plan for Fisk and the institute to use the land. Dr. Johnson, an eminent scholar and educator, had been on the Providence board in its heyday. Dr. Welch and I drove to Memphis, got Mr. Cox, and spent the day at Providence. Dr. Welch was not able to make a concrete offer but cautioned against careless disposition of the property, reinforcing Gene's determination to keep the land. That Fisk would ever make an offer was highly unlikely under its leadership at the time, but the latent potential served Gene's purpose of delay.

By 1983 inquiries and offers were coming with predictable regularity as word spread of its existence. In January of that year, Gene received a proposal (which I did not see until years later) from Tony Dunbar, a young man who had worked in Mississippi during the sixties, who founded and directed the Southern Prison Ministry and the Southern Coalition on Jails and Prisons, and who had written a scholarly and critically acclaimed book, *Against the Grain,* an account of Southern radicals of the depression era. Providence Farm had been prominently discussed in the book. He submitted the following proposal on behalf of an ad hoc group of his friends:

To: Gene Cox, for the Directors of Providence Farm
From: Tony Dunbar

235

We would like to add another proposal to the many you have considered for future use of Providence Farm. It is, I'm sure, more humble than some you have seen.

As you probably know, there are a few people of our generation in the South who know what Providence Farm has meant and care also, as its custodians did, about stewardship of the land and the community of people living on it. If all of the other prospects are found wanting—the church summer camps, the training ground for union organizers, the sale of the property for a worthy cause—please consider us.

Would the idea of passing the farm along to a few younger men and women who care about making the land productive in terms of fellowship—recreational, spiritual, and worldly—have any merit in your eyes? I am speaking of myself, Andy Lipscomb of Shiloh, Georgia; Michael Raff of Jackson, Mississippi; Mike Blackmon of Chalmette, Louisiana; Andy Griffin of Drew, Mississippi, and a couple of others. Good pastors, mostly, whose ideas about the use of the land are in no way superior to yours but who are merely younger, speaking very relatively. About half as experienced and 80% as involved in things as you are.

I do not think that we could make any promises about what we would do with Providence. Most likely it would serve for awhile as a hunting and fishing spot for ourselves and members of the community, like Mr. Woods [who worked on the place for Gene Cox in earlier days]. If nothing else, we would have organized, so far as I know, Mississippi's first interracial hunting club. I haven't much doubt that more new shoots would emerge from that seed. Kids who learned to love the place—troubled young people who found land on which to work and grow. But what we would promise is not to sell the farm, to preserve the land for the wildlife and people around it, to pay the taxes, and to seek ways to make it useful as a place to change people's lives and aspiration. The most accurate way to say it, I guess, is that we are offering ourselves as caretakers for the next generation.

You may have a half dozen proposals in hand that conform better to what you hope the place to be, and if so I'm glad of it. But if you decide to pass it along to people who know the history and will keep the Providence sign on the store, and if you don't care if we start from scratch just like you did, we'll be stewards for the land.

Sincerely,

Tony Dunbar

I was closely associated with all the persons named in Tony's memo. Some would have taken umbrage at his use of the term "pastor" in his second paragraph, for none could claim the title in the traditional sense. Tony had been ordained to the Gospel ministry by a little group of us on the banks of a creek in Talbot County, Georgia. Andy Lipscomb was originally ordained by the United Methodist Church, which later rescinded his orders when they found it impossible to give him a special appointment as a carpenter, a trade he had learned as a means of supporting his family. Michael Raff was a laicized Catholic priest. Mike Blackmon had been declared "Reverend" by a few of us on a telephone conference call to free him from service in the Vietnam War. Andy Griffin was a food caterer. Yet Tony Dunbar's reference to them as good pastors was accurate, for they were all shepherds of discernible flocks, bootlegging the Gospel of caring.

There were numerous other offers. Some reached the board, other were screened by a man who had his own interpretation of stewardship and with whom I seldom quarreled, for, to me, Gene Cox *was* Providence at the time.

As we gathered in June 1989 for another meeting of the board, all of us were prepared to liquidate and put Providence Farm behind us. All except the old patriarch, Gene Cox. He continued to resist any notion of doing anything at all. Especially selling the land. Section Thirteen, and the rest of Providence, had been his life. His body was forced to leave it in 1956. His heart remained beside Chicopa Creek as surely as the heart of the Choctaw's when the last steamboat weighed anchor in Vicksburg or Memphis taking them away. He was no stranger to forced removals and broken treaties.

Gene had undergone a heart bypass operation and was suffering from debilitating hypertension. He spent a great deal of his time with his telephone museum and making bird feeders, giving them to anyone who came by who would promise to use them. As he hammered in his workshop, his mind was concocting schemes to delay disposition of his beloved Providence. A favorite proposal was that we construct a demonstration solar-energy plant. He spent weeks designing and building scale models. Rays of the sun would move a little cart along a track. Stored heat would warm a plate of food or lift a balloon off the floor. Although it was inconceivable that we had the resources to begin such a project, he knew the idea was complex enough to buy a great deal of time just talking about it. When he was caught without a new idea, he would resort to reminding us the earth requires seventeen trees to provide enough oxygen for one person. "Let's just let the land grow trees to give off oxygen," he would say. His arguments were difficult to refute, his spirit too gentle to slight.

On this stormy June evening, we who had gathered in the Cox parlor knew we had to press beyond Gene's recalcitrance. Since I had gone on the board thirty years earlier, I had seen my role as simply supporting whatever Gene Cox wanted. Lindy had been able to let go of the Providence dream. Gene was still as locked to those acres as the day he had arrived from Texas brimming with religious and political idealism. It was his bailiwick and I had no special agenda for it. Now I was growing as impatient as some of the others. At one point I had written the Minters and Sam Franklin that I felt I had been used by Gene all these years. Sam was not on the board but was pressuring us to dispose of the land. I soon regretted the fleeting lapse of goodwill toward my old friend and apologized the next time we were together.

Gene always insisted on following the most formal parliamentary procedure, no matter how trivial the agenda. The meeting must be declared officially convened; minutes read and approved; the chair addressed correctly; motions properly made, seconded, and voted. Because the bylaws said annual meetings of the corporation must be held in Mississippi, we would drive the few miles from Memphis to the state line, stop along the highway, and meticulously certify the matters that had been decided at the Cox residence.

This meeting of the board began with a hint of tension, a stranger to Providence gatherings. No one wanted to offend Gene, sire of one, husband of another, dear friend of the other two. Yet we all knew the patience of the Minters in Arizona, and

Sam Franklin in Maryville, Tennessee, had long since ceased to be a virtue. And we were growing weary of their letters begging us to take some action in their lifetime.

After Gene read the minutes of the last meeting, we elected the Cox's youngest daughter, Ann Cox Belk, to the board. Some routine business was attended to before we reached the primary reason for our gathering: what to do with the Providence land. Gene showed no interest in any of it. He sat in gloomy silence. We were sure he intended to propose yet another scheme of delay. Instead he sat, his hands folded, staring at the floor. It was an uneasy quiet. No one looked at another. Finally Walter Diggs broke the awkward stillness. "Well, Gene, what are you thinking?"

Gene didn't answer for a long time, his gaze still fixed at his feet. Lindy shifted with professional and spousal concern. As a nurse for his health. As mate for half a century, she understood the wrenching in the depth of his soul. With Ann, blood compassion. With me, clemency for an old radical mentor, mixed with renewed anger at those who in 1955 had stripped him of his calling.

"We really don't know where the lines are," Gene sighed at last. The irrelevance of his remark was not up to his adroit parrying of past threats. It had a feeble, desperate ring to it. Lindy, ever strong, smiled at Ann with a "Here we go again" glance. Ann, eyes fixed on the father she adored, said nothing.

"Let's give the land back to the Choctaws," I said, leaning back and glancing about the room for the first response.

When the words came out, they sounded to me more brazen than I intended. It was, however, something I had given a lot of thought to. The notion of returning the land to its original inhabitants appealed to me as a chance for a bit of honor. The wider implications of the gesture excited me.

"Will Campbell!" Ann said.

I wasn't sure what her words meant, thought maybe she was treating my suggestion as comic relief. I expected then nothing more than a chuckle around the room.

Gene got up, crossed the room, and peered through the curtains. "My god, Will," Ann laughed, moving to the window and putting her arm around her father. "You've hit the old man's starter. This is the first time he's batted both eyes at the same time in weeks."

"That might work," Gene said. He seemed to study each of us

239

as he moved back to his seat. I had forgotten his fascination with Choctaw history and culture when I first knew him. I remembered Ann telling me that once when she was a little girl she watched her daddy walk across a freshly plowed field, never straightening up until he reached the opposite side, picking up arrow points with each step. I was with him in Jackson one day when he gave a shoebox full of arrow points, spearheads, broken pieces of pottery to the state archives. He told me he had given others to Mississippi State University. The mood in the room shifted noticeably. It was not one of exhilaration, but we seemed out of the doldrums. Gene's mood was at least mildly refreshed. I decided to let my proposal rest. Walter Diggs, still the correct chairman, nodded to Gene, who was already writing the suggestion in his minutes book.

Sam Franklin, though no longer a board member, had written that he would like for us to consider giving the property to Mary Holmes College, a small school established by the Presbyterian church in 1892 in West Point, Mississippi, for Negro students.

Piney Woods School was suggested. Piney Woods, a vocational and technical high school, was founded in Mississippi in 1909 by Lawrence Jones, a Negro scholar from Iowa who advocated a "head, heart and hands" system of education. The school came to national attention in 1955 when Mr. Jones was featured on the Ralph Edwards television show, "This Is Your Life," and appealed for funds. A few others were talked about as possible recipients of the property or money from its sale. But it was the idea proposed in less than half-seriousness that got the most attention. Ann started to laugh. Suddenly this tough woman of forty-four was a giggling little girl. "That's a great idea. Will Campbell. Where do you come up with such inspiration?" Her flattery made me feel a little cocky. Like the village runt who had just bested the bully. My suggestion wasn't being treated as some more of Will's romantic nonsense after all.

Ann had read somewhere that Johnny Cash was on the Heritage Council of the Choctaws in Neshoba County. I added that the entertainer and writer, Tom T. Hall, known as "The Storyteller," was a close friend with whom I had often discussed our dilemma. I could guarantee he would write a song about something as authentic and dramatic as returning land to its long-ago owners.

We talked of convening another mass meeting. In the very school where Gene Cox and Dave Minter had faced the angry mob in 1955. Only white students attended that school then. In 1989 it was all black. Johnny Cash and Tom T. Hall would be there to sing when we signed a new treaty, the Treaty of Section Thirteen.

Ann Cox Belk, who was nine years old when the mass meeting ended her parents' vision of a better life for the poor of rural Mississippi, began the scenario. "We'll smoke a peace pipe," she said. "Pass it to everybody at the high school. What kind of tobacco, Will Campbell?"

"What about Half and Half?" I said.

"No, no." She gave me a pampering pat on the head. "Rev-e-lation! Deary." I was beginning to feel more silly than cocky.

She began naming men who were leaders in the kangaroo court that had tried, convicted, and sentenced her daddy that night. "Oh, they'll be there all right, Mother," she snickered. "I'll go to the Lexington Nursing Home, and I'll roll their wrinkled asses right up to the front in their wheelchairs." Lindy gave her a motherly look of disapproval, but she went on. "And if they're dead, I'll drag their rotten bones in there too. I saw what they did to my daddy!"

"Ann," Gene said gently, correcting her the way he had done when she was a child, cooling but not staying the party mood.

Walter Diggs, who had not moved from the seat or role of chairman but instead sat smiling good-naturedly at our frivolity, called the meeting back to order. He asked Gene to read the list of suggestions and said we would have to do some research on each one. I was appointed to visit the Choctaw reservation in Neshoba County. Lindy and Ann would visit or correspond with Mary Holmes College and Piney Woods School. Walter told us we didn't need to rush, we would not have another meeting until fall. A few years earlier, we had voted to donate the Indian mound on Providence property to the Mississippi Department of History and Archives. We authorized the chairman to sign the document they had sent, then adjourned the meeting.

When I left the meeting, I became apprehensive about my idea. I realized I knew nothing at all about Choctaw culture, history, or present circumstances. I had been on the reservation only one time and was lost on that occasion, looking for something else.

A few weeks later a friend, Bettye Fürstenberger, who taught

English at Hinds Community College near Jackson, drove me to the Choctaw reservation in the Pearl River community, a few miles west of the little town of Philadelphia. The romance of Section Thirteen reaching a noble plane in its long history of defeats danced in my head as we rode. Yet the trip was not without trepidation. Neshoba County. The place where James Chaney, Andrew Goodman, and Michael Schwerner, three young men who began their civil rights work in Mississippi with the same zeal that had brought the youthful founders of Providence Farm to Holmes County twenty-five years earlier, had been murdered and buried by a bulldozer in a red clay dam in 1964. My last trip there had been during that period. The thing I remembered most of that visit was not the sailors and federal lawmen combing the swamps and woods searching for the bodies of the three civil rights workers; rather, it was the depressing sight of the Choctaws, their shanties along the country roads, grown men lounging on the dirt streets of their villages in demeaning idleness, sometimes drinking from a common bottle, sharing a roll-your-own cigarette, their half-clad children a picture of hurting that would never end. I remembered the scene and dreaded seeing it again. Maybe, I thought, the gift of Providence land would offer some piddling but symbolic relief. At the least, perhaps it would say to them that somebody cared, knew they existed.

My dread was short-lived. That was not the picture we found. We were seeing genuine signs of change, more than a whiff of progress. We had come upon what appeared to be a sizeable industrial park. Just beyond was a modern high school building and stadium, then a newly constructed hospital and nursing home. A little farther what I assumed to be a television transmitting antenna, a swimming pool filled with splashing youngsters, a park and playground. We drove down several paved streets, saw scores of small but neat and ample dwellings.

We circled back and pulled up behind a marked police car. Two uniformed Choctaw officers were talking playfully to a group of children gathered on each side of the car. I asked where we could find Chief Phillip Martin, told the officers I had an appointment. They motioned for us to fall in behind them and led us to the tribal office, a handsome building looking like the prevailing town halls of the region.

Inside, a smartly groomed receptionist said Chief Martin was in a tribal council meeting but should be finished shortly. She said his secretary was expecting me. She invited us to a seat in the hallway where a continuous video was playing. The video answered the questions we had about what we had seen outside.

In the twenty minutes we waited, we heard the story. More than two decades earlier Phillip Martin had returned to the reservation after ten years in the U.S. Air Force. Before that he had attended a Cherokee high school in North Carolina because, although there were schools for Negro and white students in the county, there was no high school for Choctaw children. Following the Treaty of Dancing Rabbit Creek in 1830, the Choctaws who stayed in Mississippi had been squatters, aliens in their own land. Those who had bolted in the overland caravans before they reached the ports of embarkation for removal, and those who had chosen to remain and apply for land under Article 14 of the treaty, survived as best they could. Some as nomads in the wilderness, some as laborers for white farmers after it had been demonstrated that no Choctaw would succeed in getting the land promised, except the leaders who had assisted Andrew Jackson in his quest. Not until 1918 was recognition given that they existed at all. And not until 1945 was land finally set aside as a reservation for them.

Thirty-year-old Phillip Martin intended only to visit Neshoba County and then move on. Anywhere at all. The relative comfort of ten years in the military had exposed him to the good life, and he liked it. Seeing the straits of his people, he was soon involved and compelled by conscience to stay.

Although still a poor state, Mississippi had made remarkable strides in its economy during and following World War II. But the plight of the Choctaws was about what it was at the turn of the century. What Phillip Martin found was the same abject poverty he had left. The red clay on reservation land was never suited for successful farming. Their ability and willingness to work was their only asset. Prior to the Civil Rights Act of 1964, that was of no account. Available jobs were given to whites, then to blacks. The Choctaws, who for 150 years had been neither white nor black, were left where they had always been. Consequently, what Phillip Martin came home to was an unemployment rate of more than 80 percent and the same shanties he had left, few with electricity in a locale that various federal programs had been lighting up since Herbert Hoover, even fewer with indoor plumbing. Automobiles were rare.

Within a few years the determined warrior was elected chief and went to work to upgrade every aspect of tribal life: economics, health, education.

The first move was to start a construction company to build houses and hospitals for the tribe with available federal funds. Soon it began building industrial plants and structures for non-Choctaws.

Getting business names and addresses from the Dun and Bradstreet directory, he mailed out five hundred letters. His was not the banal cry for alms. He did not dwell on past grievances, nor appeal for sympathy for an impoverished people. His was a straightforward business offer, telling industrialists of the potential. There was not one favorable response. Undaunted, he pressed on, writing other letters, calling, visiting.

Within six months an official of General Motors' Packard Electric Division was willing to talk. The upshot of the negotiations was a contract to manufacture harnesses for the electrical system of light Chevrolet trucks. Fifty-seven jobs, a tincture of hope. Within a few years 250 men and women were producing more than thirty different harnesses in that plant alone. He had not rested in his search for other industry to move in. Another plant was built, and Ford Motor Company gave them a paltry contract for twenty thousand dollars. Nothing was turned down. Within six months the Ford contract had evolved to a contract for more than four million dollars. Westinghouse followed. More jobs.

The visionary chief was not through. Unlike an earlier chief who chose to remain in Mississippi while his people suffered and died en route to an alien land, he worked for the advancement of the whole tribe.

Another plant was built for American Greeting Corporation, with almost two hundred people producing greeting cards. Soon others were building radio speakers for automobiles.

The video had started to play again when a young Choctaw woman appeared, greeted us politely, and led us down a corridor to Chief Martin's office. A handsome, bronze-skinned man of medium build, with a full head of black hair and an uncontrived countenance, approached from a large executive desk, shook hands cordially, and offered us seats at a conference table stacked with books and records.

I was searching for words with which to explain my mission as he took his place behind his desk. Bob Ferguson, a white man I had known casually when he lived in Nashville and was a successful music producer for some of Music City's biggest stars, was seated across the table from us, ready to take notes. Mr. Ferguson was also a well-known environmentalist and had done films for the Tennessee Department of Conservation. Many years earlier he left the bright lights of Nashville, choosing to work on this reservation as a Choctaw.

Following a brief bit of visiting, I stated my business. I told Chief Martin I was on the board of an organization that had some land in Holmes County it needed to give away. I explained I was there not to say we intended to give the land to the tribe, but only to inquire as to whether they would accept it if we should, and how they might be able to use it.

I briefly outlined the history of Providence Farm and why we must now dispose of the land.

Chief Martin laced his fingers behind his head and swiveled around to face us squarely. His expression had not changed. "Mr. Campbell, of necessity this tribe has had to accept anything we were offered." He paused for a long time before continuing. It was as if he did not want to offend but still be emphatic. "But never in our long history has anyone ever offered us one foot of land." His impassive stare did not reveal what I surmised he was thinking—that twenty-five million acres had been wrested from them. "So yes," he went on, "we would accept it."

I told him we did not intend to place conditions on the gift, that the recipient would be free to live on it, let it grow timber, sell it, or whatever.

He turned and picked up a small book and pushed it toward me politely. "Mr. Campbell, here is a dictionary of our language. You may search its pages. You will not find 'sell land' anywhere. That is a combination of words not in our vocabulary." This time the irony in his voice was transparent. I saw a trace of a smile as he glanced at Mr. Ferguson. "No, Mr. Campbell. Right now I can't say what we would do with it. But I can say what we wouldn't. We wouldn't sell it." He stood up and walked around the spacious office, voicing hasty ideas. "That's close to Belzoni, isn't it? The catfish capital?" I nodded it was. "Maybe we'll build a catfish farm. Maybe a processing plant. Not many jobs there though. Any cane-brakes there? We still make baskets. Clay? We make pottery too. Older folks still make baskets and pottery. Want to pass it on. Part of our heritage. Baskets and pots." I told him there were cane-brakes and an old clay mine. "Oh, we'll do something with it," he said, moving back behind his desk and sitting down. "Something big, too." He cleared his throat and grinned broadly for the first time. It seemed a grin of anxious anticipation. Maybe, I remember thinking, even absolution. Later, on reflection, I realized that was too much to prophesy.

The ride back to Jackson was relaxed and enjoyable. We stopped at a roadside cafe, far out in the country. It was a scene once familiar to me but one I had forgotten. The motor whined and the tires spun in the mud-slick drive as we pulled in. Raw sewage trickled down an open ditch. Chickens pecked leisurely at a watermelon rind. The building, looking more like a warehouse than a restaurant, had no screens on the open door and windows, and the rough siding was a dull brown from weather and age, unpainted. A hand-lettered sign above the door announced: ABSOLUTELY NO ALCOHOLIC BEVERAGE ALLOWED. It seemed incongruous. Somehow I couldn't imagine this place on a Saturday night with iced tea and Nehi orange. Remembering bootleg places of the past, I motioned to the sign and added, "Unless you buy it from the fellow hiding in the thicket in back." The place had the markings of Delta blues, but I could tell from the raucous country-and-western sounds blaring from the juke box, and the three little children playing near the drainage ditch, that the clientele here was white.

When I started to get out, my friend gave me a dubious, city-bred look. I told her they would probably weigh us at the door to keep us from fighting out of our division, but I was sure the food was all right.

Inside were several bare-top tables. Behind a long counter was the kitchen area. Several men in work clothes, one with a carbide light, the kind possum hunters use, fastened to his cap, were playing pool. They leaned on cue sticks as we entered, paying more attention to Mrs. Fürstenberger than to me, grinned timidly, but did not speak.

A very fat, middle-aged woman wearing a skimpy sundress stood sweating near a short steam table. She was yelling through a window at the children as we sat down at a table farthermost from the billiard players. "Y'all want some young'uns?" she greeted us, followed by a boisterous laugh.

"Got anything to feed 'um?" I replied.

"I heard that," she laughed, then asked what we wanted. I ordered a hamburger and iced tea. Bettye, still not sure we should have come in, asked for hot coffee.

Balls of cotton hung over the windows and front door. Bettye asked me what they were for. I told her it was an old remedy for houseflies. "I guess it works," she said, shooing several away from her place at the table. "These seem pretty healthy."

We drove to Nanih Waiya, climbed to the top of it, discussing Choctaw history. And our own. We exulted in the thought of doing one small deed to say we were sorry.

Bob Ferguson had told us the site of the Treaty of Doak's Stand was not far off our route back to Jackson. I wanted to go there, though I wasn't sure why. I had seen the historic marker on the Natchez Trace, but Mr. Ferguson said that was far from the actual spot. He didn't remember the name of the family who owned the land but gave us directions as best he remembered. He said the man trained and raced trotting horses. He cautioned us that where we were going bore no resemblance to the neatly manicured Natchez Trace Parkway. He understated.

Several miles off the parkway we stopped at a large country roadhouse. The muddy gravel yard was crowded with vehicles, most showing signs of age. Dozens of men and boys were standing around the cars and trucks. They were white, black, and Choctaw, the clusters mixed. Inside the place was a combination pool hall, beer joint, and grocery. Except for size, and thriving business, it reminded me of the cafe where we had lunch. Also, from occasional remarks we overheard in the cafe, Choctaws would not have been welcome there. Here—the men playing pool, eating, drinking beer together while the boys bought candy and sodas, tousled, and laughed—everyone seemed at ease. I asked the young white man at the cash register if he could direct us to where the Treaty of Doak's Stand had been signed. His quizzical expression indicated he had never heard of any sort of treaty, and I didn't trouble him further by trying to enlighten him on American history. The barroom sounds all around me made it seem inappropriate. Instead, I asked an elderly black man who was finishing the last of his beer if he knew anyone who trained trotting horses.

"You mean pacers?" he asked. I said, "Yessir."

"You must be talking about James Smith. Runs a club. On down this road. He don't stay there though. He stay way off the road.

Way back in the woods. You talking 'bout a colored fellow, ain't you?" I told him I thought so. "Well, you go on down this road till you see a sign say 'Junkyard One.' That's where you turn at. Stay right on that road and you'll come to where he stay at. It's a pretty good little piece though. That where he stay at though."

A few hundred yards down the road we saw a building similar to the one where we had stopped. A huge sign in front said, JUNKYARD TWO. It was not a salvage business as I assumed but another country tavern. I supposed Junkyard One was the original. A twelve-foot woven wire fence completely surrounded the building, with a lot of yard space for parking. A few miles further we saw the sign pointing to Junkyard One. On a narrow and twisting road, we passed dozens of run-down mobile homes with lean-to rooms added, dilapidated dwellings where lots of children and dogs played in dirt yards cluttered with abandoned cars, trucks, and farm equipment, scenes that might be seen in the average third-world country. "My god!" Bettye Fürstenberger exclaimed. "*Every* house is a junkyard. How will we know when we get to Junkyard One?" I was about ready to give up the search. But I said, "We'll just know."

Suddenly we saw it. We topped a hill and looking up at us was a sizeable compound—untidy barns, smaller outbuildings, a fenced-in arena, and a cumbersome, rough wood building we assumed to be the Junkyard One Club. As we got closer, we saw two log trucks, a bulldozer, and an assortment of well-worn heavy equipment strewn about in no seeming order. Beside the road, as we turned in, was a neat brick residence, partly hidden by nursery shrubs and huge evergreens, seeming somehow incongruous to the cluttered surroundings.

"You sure we want to stop?" Bettye asked. I said I was sure.

Despite the unkempt, almost abandoned appearance of the rest of the area, there was a warm, homey feeling about the house as we pulled up near a carport that seemed out of proportion to the house. The shrubs and small cedars had strings of dismantled colored lights lying beside them. I had noticed larger trees, even the deciduous ones, with the bulbs still strung on them as we turned in. There was a life-sized picture of Santa Claus hanging on the carport wall. Too early for this year's December and too late for last, I thought, imagining what the place must look like at Christmastime. Underneath the carport were two cars, one with a Mississippi National Guard license plate. I thought of how recent it had been that black people would not have been allowed to join the Mississippi National Guard. On the paved drive outside was a Lincoln Continental and a fashionable customized van. The barking watchdogs I expected did not appear. There was no sign of life in any direction. Everything was quiet. "You sure we want to stop?" my friend asked again. I said, "We've come this far."

I rang the doorbell and stepped back. I felt eyes seeing me from behind the drawn curtains, but there was no response. I tapped sharply with my pocketknife on the aluminum storm door. A woman, barely grown, opened the door enough to see out. When I asked if Mr. Smith were home, she looked me up and down for several seconds, then asked curtly, "Who's calling?" It was more like, "Who wants to know?" I recalled a day when black young people didn't talk that way to white adults. Maybe bad manners is one of the by-products of progress, I thought. Or maybe it is inevitable that the victors accept the gods of the vanquished. White people were rude to them first.

I gave my name, told her I was looking for the place where the Treaty of Doak's Stand was signed. She looked me over again, hesitated, then said, "Yeah, seems like I heard them talking about that one time. Just a minute." I stepped back and waited. A stocky, good-looking man of about forty-five walked out, greeted me a bit suspiciously and asked, "What can I do for you?" I told him what I had said to the young woman. He pointed to a distant hill. "Right by that gate. They tell me its right by that gate." We talked a few minutes and he offered to lead us to it. He went inside to put his shoes on, came back out making no effort to conceal the medium-sized pistol he was carrying.

We followed his Lincoln out the drive. A sign at the gate said, HOPE YOU HAD A GOOD TIME. COME AGAIN. Bumper stickers read, "Junkyard One Racing. Fri. Sat. Sun."

The hurried conversation on the short ride went something like this. "Is he going to shoot us?" Bettye asked. "No, he's not going to shoot us." "Then why does he have a gun?" "He doesn't know he's not going to shoot us. So just in case." "Just in case what?" "Just in case we need killing."

He stopped beside a deeply washed gully on the highest hill in the area and we pulled in behind him. I was pleased he left the pistol in the car. Across a rusty barbed-wire fence was the burned-out skeleton of a mobile home. The ground around it was littered with empty quart-size Colt 45 Malt Liquor bottles and other debris apparently thrown from passing cars.

He told us he had never heard of the treaty when he bought the land, said an old woman had bought thousands of acres back when land was fifty cents an acre. He bought the last 150 acres from her. He said they used to play here when they were children and heard stories about what was under tiny grave markers. He pointed to where they had been. "All gone now though. Don't know what became of them." Some schoolchildren from the reservation had come some years earlier, and their teacher told him about the treaty. There was no marker, nothing to indicate the historic significance of where we were standing.

I tried to imagine the scene in these sinuous woods in early October 1820 when Andrew Jackson arrived astride a fine steed, ready to do battle with those who had fought beside him at the Battle of New Orleans and against the Creek Nation.

I listened for the grumbling of Chief Puckshunubbee, who refused to let his men accept the allotment of beef, corn, salt, and liquor, knowing he would refuse the treaty offer and not wanting to be beholden. I envisioned the ball games, wrestling, races, and heavy drinking by the Choctaw citizens while their chiefs and captains discussed the business at hand.

I strained to eavesdrop on the Calvinist missionary, Cyrus Kingsbury, as he adamantly counseled against the treaty.

As the crow flies, we were not more than forty miles to the southwest of Providence Farm, where Gene Cox and David Minter had faced similar odds. It was an unsettling feeling, knowing I was standing exactly where General Andrew Jackson and General Thomas Hinds, with free liquor to bribe and soften the Choctaw hearts, had, first by honeyed inveigling, difficult for even the most sophisticated to contest, then by threats and at the last by fits of vociferous anger, frightened the beleaguered Choctaws into giving up five million acres. Jackson had called the expanse "that useless little slip of land," but within two weeks the Port Gibson *Correspondent* described it as "fine as any in the United States, . . . exhibiting at once the most pleasing variety of hill and dale, prairie and grove, and furnishing a variety of soil, and a salubrity of air, not surpassed by any other region." The thirteen million acres in the West the Choctaws were promised could not even be identified until a new treaty was held five years later in Washington. It was that treaty, Luther Cashdollar had told Jesse Furver, that cost the Choctaws the lives of their most notable chiefs. The great Pushmataha died in Washington before the treaty was signed. Puckshunubbee died en route.

I had read of the treaty site as a flat, grassy knoll, replete with the beauties of nature. This scene, with incredible erosion, sparse new growth on the cutover hills, shabby and abandoned houses in view, the red clay accentuating the abjection conspicuous in the scene itself, seemed a sober indictment of what happened here in the fall of 1820. In half an hour we were riding along the twisting shoreline of the Ross Barnett Reservoir, that miniocean of thirty thousand acres of once Choctaw land reaching into five counties and named for a governor who, with an incorrigible lust for power, took on the federal establishment to block one black citizen from entering the University of Mississippi, the citizen from Kosciusko, seat of Attala County, the town named for a Polish patriot and a general in America's Revolutionary War. Attala. One more name echoing a vanquished people. Young lovers lolled on narrow white sandy beaches, the sand seeming somehow misplaced. Precocious geriatrics maneuvered their sails perilously close to looming cypress trunks that had given up their battle for life with the deep waters, the two together punctuating the descending legend of time.

At dusk we saw the Jackson skyline. Jackson. A city named for the one who more than any other man was responsible for where we had been that day. In Hinds County. Thomas Hinds. The general who helped him with his mischief at Doak's Stand.

We drove past LeFleur's Bluff, site of Greenwood Leflore's father's trading post. A billboard sign, LEFLEUR'S CADILLAC, stood as a grim boast of implacable wrongs.

Returning from a past still present to haunt the future, we agreed that we had been about something right.

Two weeks after my visit and conversation with Chief Martin, the Providence board received a letter from the U.S. Department of Interior. They wanted 540 acres of Providence land for a game-management program. They offered almost three hundred thousand dollars for it. "That's a lot of money," Lindy said when she called to tell me about it.

It was incredulous news. Why now? After all these years? The Department of Interior, the agency that dogged not only the Choctaw but every other native tribe and nation since it took over their management in 1849. Of the 370 Indian treaties the U.S. Senate has ratified, provisions in every single one have been violated. Since 1849 the Department of Interior has been a party to each one broken. On the eve of the quincentenary celebration of the arrival of the Christ-bearing colonizer, would we really consider selling Providence land to them? I couldn't believe we would. After five hundred years of consistent deceit, did we not hold in our hand a tiny gesture of confession and beg for pardon? A chance to say we are heartily sorry for our misdeeds?

I knew something of game-management programs. There was already one adjacent to Section Thirteen called the Morgan Canebrake Game Management. One had to pass the entrance to it to reach Providence Farm. Since 1955 we had permitted local people to hunt Providence land. We knew many of the black people hunted for food, not for sport. Once I had stopped at the Morgan gateway and picked up some of the Department of Interior pamphlets that contained regulations and application forms for anyone wanting to hunt there. I recall thinking many citizens who hunted our land would not be able to complete the detailed questionnaire nor afford the fee. These would be the guns of autumn from the cities, in quest of trophies more often than food.

My paranoia was deviling me. Asking questions. Perhaps preposterous but nagging still. Did they know? How could it have been possible? "Mole" was a new buzzword in governmental circles for one who leaks classified information. Who might it be within our small circle? Certainly no one. Even if they did know, why should they care? Did they begrudge some innocent precedent that might undo even the tiniest thread of their misdeeds? I didn't know.

The Providence board agreed to meet with a delegation from the Choctaw reservation on August 7, 1989. Expecting no more than a representative of the tribal council and a secretary, I was surprised to find Chief Phillip Martin waiting for us at the Tchula post office where we were to convene. With him were Bob Ferguson, William Richardson, who ran the Economic Development Office for the tribe, and Nell Rogers, education and development planner.

As soon as I could, I maneuvered Chief Martin and Bob Ferguson aside and told them of the Department of Interior letter. "Hmmm," was the only sound I heard. It was Chief Martin.

Bob Ferguson simply looked into the distance. I couldn't think of anything to say; had nothing to add. Chief Martin started walking around the tiny town. Although we had passed lush fields of cotton and soybeans, watered by sprinkler systems reaching as far as one could see, with attractive residences and evidences of a prosperity for those who lived in them, what we saw as we walked was a combination ghost town and skid row. It was reminiscent of what I had seen on the dingy street of the Choctaw reservation twenty-five years earlier. I wondered if Chief Martin might be thinking the same thing, thankful it was no more.

No one said anything during the several minutes it took to tour the area. Just before we arrived back at the post office where Lindy, Ann, and Walter Diggs were waiting to drive us to Providence Farm, Chief Martin stopped walking, turned to me, hesitated a moment, then, gesturing back to what we had seen said, "Mr. Campbell, if this was my town, it wouldn't look like this. These people need help."

I had heard him rattle off potential uses of the land when we were in his office two weeks earlier. But at that time I was thinking, at best, that the bequeath would mean additional jobs, more revenue for the tribe. Now, as we stood on the indigent streets of Tchula, I realized the romance of the gesture had become a consuming fantasy for me. Not such a noble notion after all. I realized there was more than that in it all. Whether of me or not.

Nell Rogers, the educational and development planner, had been on a Tchula tour of her own. As she joined us she began sharing ideas about what she could accomplish in Holmes County if given the chance: Department of Education literacy grants, vocational education, substance-abuse prevention, employability training so skills could be acquired that would attract industry. She kept looking back at the squalor she had seen. "I was born and reared in Neshoba County," she said. "Lived in Mississippi all my life. Been all over the state. It's been a long time since I've seen anything like this."

I told them some of our people favored selling the Department of Interior the land they wanted, to establish a scholarship fund for poor black students. Chief Martin still had not responded to the Department of Interior's offer. Now he said, "We've known those folks for a long time. Since they took over managing us from the War Department in 1849. They have a lot of money. And if they were dealing with us for the land, we'd get a lot more than what they're offering." He did a quick survey of the area we had walked, shook his head, and continued. "You can send young people to school from here. But when they graduate, they won't come back here." Nell Rogers nodded in agreement.

I knew they were right. There was nothing to come back to. Maybe if some factories were built, they could come back and run them. And people could afford to send their own children to college. It seemed a logical extension of the Providence dream, helping people to help themselves. When Sergeant Phillip Martin returned from the Air Force, that was what he told his people they must do. Now he, a Choctaw, was offering to help black people, on land controlled by white people, do the same. On land that had once belonged to his people. Surely God is looking with favor upon all this, I thought.

Listening to Chief Martin, Miss Rogers, and Mr. Ferguson outline their plans for the impoverished people on whose behalf Providence Cooperative Farm had been established, I realized for the first time that the Choctaws didn't need our help. We needed theirs.

We joined the others and drove the few miles to the property. Chief Martin asked questions as we moved along. He spotted a canebrake and asked if it were on the land. He asked about the location of the clay pit. As we drove through dense woods, he said it would make a fine recreation park or campground. "Rent cabins and camping spots to rich people from up North who want to rough it awhile," he laughed, his black Cadillac grinding through the mud.

When we reached the old Providence community center, he stopped and unrolled some intricately drawn maps of the area. He asked for a description of the acres the Department of Interior wanted. Walter showed it to him on a sketch he had. Mr. Richardson located where he guessed it to be. "Hmmm," the chief smiled knowingly. Then, glancing up at the bluffs overlooking where we stood, he said, "Looks like they want the bottom land."

Must be a familiar story to him, I thought. White man gets the bottom land. Red man gets the bluffs. Or nothing at all. But I didn't say it.

For more than two hours we walked and drove around the property that, years earlier, had been a bustling interracial, cooperative farm and medical facility, swelling with promise. As we talked, some of us were envisioning a renewal of the covenant, inevitable Providence, the promise complete. I was convinced the Department of Interior was the only barrier. I also knew that was a formidable hurdle before "*Chahta hapia hoke!*" could be heard once more reverberating down the slope from where we stood.

We covered every part of the property we could reach by car. And some on foot. Not only Section Thirteen but the other property Providence Farm owned as well. Each time we moved from one place to another, Chief Martin took the lead, the rest of us following. It was as if he knew every foot of it, had been here before. That, I knew, was impossible, for he would have been a hundred years from birth when the last of his people were escorted out of these woods by armed horsemen, soldiers of a government that gained title to it at the creek where the rabbits danced, for the benefit of white settlers, and now wanted a portion of it back to benefit white hunters.

Walter Diggs asked the Choctaw delegation to submit a proposal, which the board would consider. The chief said he would.

CHAPTER 14

Providence was once more becoming a subject of controversy. This time without acknowledged antagonist. Since the Second Removal had forced the abandonment of Providence as an interracial venture in 1955, there had been unanimity among the board members. All of us were about our own pursuits and were content to let Gene Cox manage the limited activities from his base in White Haven after Mrs. Booker moved into town. The second generation was even more scattered than we were. From Mexico to Washington, D.C.

Ten days following our visit with Chief Martin and his party at Providence, the board received a letter from him outlining a proposal for tribal development of the land. He said, "The Mississippi Band of Choctaw Indians is very interested in pursuing minority economic development in the Tchula area." He reminded us the tract was "historically Choctaw Indian land" and said if deeded back to the tribe it would be placed under Federal Trust status, i.e., designated as an Indian reservation under the jurisdiction of the Mississippi Band of Choctaw Indians. He said the tribal economic development program had a history of creating jobs for all minorities, not just Choctaw. This fact, he said, had resulted in 1,500 new jobs since the late 1970s, representing a capital investment of more than twenty-two million dollars. He stated they would work with local minority leadership and felt that with their proven expertise in Neshoba County they could do the same in Holmes County. He discussed their concept of an "agriculture related, value-added manufacturing facility," given the location and proximity to railroad and highway transportation. He offered no foolish claims and made no boasts exceeding what we knew of their accomplishments.

The Cox family owned 190 acres of land adjacent to Providence Farm. For some years Gene had expressed a desire to trade it for a tract on Providence land where his children's roots were. At a regular board meeting, I moved that this be done, whatever the disposition of the remainder. The motion carried and a survey was authorized to effect the exchange. It was a simple swap and had no bearing on other proposals. I hoped that the survey would show at least a few of their acres on Section Thirteen. I knew that part of that section had previously been sold to High Cotton Plantation.

Although I was not an officer of the board, I had known the members as family for more than three decades and saw nothing imprudent in sharing my views with Sam Franklin and the Minters, knowing of their anxieties. Sue Minter had asked that I call her as soon as possible after the meeting.

She was not receptive to the idea of returning the land to the Choctaws. We did not quarrel, but it was clear we disagreed. When she said that to expect the Choctaws to improve the plight of the poverty-stricken blacks of the area seemed patronizing and condescending to the blacks, I countered that I saw it no more so than when white people came in the thirties for the same purpose. She responded with a news story about Navaho chief Peter MacDonald, who had been convicted recently for misappropriation of tribal funds. She said we couldn't be too careful. I didn't argue. She also suggested that we should consider the NAACP or the United Negro College Fund, two organizations all of us approved.

Sam Franklin was more forthright. He had been the most assertive of all in pressing for the disposition of the land before the end of the year. I had assumed he would settle for anything the board agreed upon. And his first letter after the board meeting was amiable and casual. He wrote, "It is interesting how, when you set your mind to make a decision, new ideas emerge." But he added that though he had no question as to the stark and terrible need of Native Americans in many parts of the country, from the start the cooperative project had been involved with the terrible tragedy of black people in the Deep South. He concluded the long letter on a cordial note. "I think the Spirit is working among us and I have no doubt that other ideas and insights will be given. Let's keep in touch."

Sam's next letter could only be described as furious. With a perfunctory "Thanks for your letter," it began: "Your idea of giving the Providence land to the Choctaws to enable the latter to 'industrialize' that part of Holmes county and thus benefit the rural Blacks is the most bizarre yet."

It was another lengthy letter, one that I interpreted as a personal assault. I had tried to make it clear in my letter that the rationale for returning the property to the Choctaws was Chief Martin's proven ability to work cooperatively with local minority folk, government agencies, and industry. And since he had made it clear it was highly unlikely that anyone from the tribe would move to Holmes County, resulting jobs would be filled by local people. Sam's position was that it would be an affront to local blacks, who had seen the founders of Providence Farm as their friends. He acknowledged that local poor blacks had no apparatus in place to attract industry but saw selling the land to the federal government as the only acceptable option.

I began to realize our major difference was that my concern was for Section Thirteen; his was for the reputation of the original venture. No special charity in either position, I suppose.

Undoubtedly, though, what disturbed me most was his remarks about the Choctaws:

> The choice of the Choctaws as our surrogate would not be a
> happy one for historical reasons. The portion of the tribe that
> remained in Mississippi was conservative, bent on maintaining
> racial identity. They refused to let their children attend a black
> school. I have the impression there has never been any love lost
> between them.

My first impulse was to take pen in hand and challenge his interpretation of history. Then to say, "Sam, I'm sure we all have our favorite ethnic minority. And least favorite. But damned if you ain't sounding like Andrew Jackson when it comes to your attitude toward the original owners of this land." And finally, "You're into a hefty binge of stereotyping." I dismissed all such thinking when I remembered the pouch of Red Man chewing tobacco in my pocket with the archetypal feather-bedecked Indian chief on the front. "None righteous," I mused.

Upon reflection I decided that Sam Franklin, Presbyterian minister, was quite within the example and tradition of his progenitor, Cyrus Kingsbury, Presbyterian minister, teacher of my fabled friend, Luther Cashdollar, in holding out for selling the property for educational purposes. Although it chafed to hear Luther Cashdollar's people maligned, I could not hold Sam responsible for my fantasies. Reverend Kingsbury made many compromises, and sacrifices, for his primary cause: education. Sam thought, and strongly inferred, that I had taken leave of my senses if I could not see the value of accepting the money from the Department of Interior for the same end. I could disagree, and did, believing with Chief Phillip Martin that the scholarship fund would do nothing in the long haul to improve the economy of the area. But I could not question the Calvinist consistency. Reverend Franklin was in the lineage of Reverend Kingsbury, though I never knew the latter to speak so harshly of the Choctaw people.

I suppose I knew the die was cast. We would play out the drama, but the people who lost Section Thirteen in 1830 would not get it back in this encounter. Still I did not give up completely. Despite Sam Franklin's passionate protest, he did not have a vote on the board. Actually, after leaving Providence in 1943 to enter the Navy chaplaincy, he never returned to be a part of what was left of the original endeavor. Sue Minter was in Arizona, and I thought Walter Diggs had said proxy votes were not allowed under the bylaws. He had continued in the role of impartial chairman, and I had no reason to cross ideological swords with him. I remembered the enthusiasm at the meeting when the proposal was offered, and Gene's passion for Choctaw history. Ann Cox Belk and I had always been buddies, and I had no question of her genuine interest in proceeding with Chief Martin's proposition. Lindy Cox, though upset by the hostility developing among old friends and colleagues, had no ego investment and wanted only what was best for the people of Holmes County. In addition, Piney Woods and Mary Holmes College had been ruled out. Ann and Lindy, in their research, had learned Piney Woods was the most heavily endowed black secondary school in America, and Mary Holmes would have no use for the land except revenue from its sale. Sue Minter had not succeeded in her overtures to the NAACP and Negro College Fund. The choice now was between the Choctaw Band and the U.S.

Department of Interior, traditional enemies from the outset of America's resolve to make the territory available to white settlers. The moral choice, to me, seemed clear-cut.

Walter Diggs and I had several frank discussions about it. When I said I saw it now as a matter of honor, that to decline to deal with the Choctaws would be tantamount to repeating the way white people had dealt with them since Hernando De Soto, he expressed no disagreement. Nor when I insisted that to sell the bottom land to the government and give the Choctaws the bluffs would be a similar replay of history; the white man gets what he wants, the red man gets what's left. My repeated harangues about past performance and accountability of the Department of Interior went unchallenged. I regained a degree of optimism.

There were several months of silence. Then an inquiry from the Nature Conservancy, a national organization with an admirable reputation for reclaiming wilderness land for the preservation of endangered species of birds, fish, and animals. Walter Diggs wrote that Mr. Roger L. Jones, Jr., Mississippi director of the Nature Conservancy, along with former governor William Winter, had met with him, Ann Cox Belk, and Gene and Lindy Cox, where the offer was discussed. He enclosed a copy of the option for purchase. He said he understood my uneasiness with selling the property to the Department of Interior, a statement I interpreted as meaning the Nature Conservancy might be easier for me. He was right. He explained that the gathering was not intended as an official meeting of the board and that he would convene another session with Mr. Jones with me present to answer any questions.

I knew and admired the work of the Nature Conservancy. However, their agenda would do no more for the poor of Holmes County than a game-management program of the Department of Interior.

What we had seen of Tchula's distress when we were there with Chief Martin was a picture that stayed with me. I was certain that there were honorable people there, white and black, who would join the chief in his desire to better their lot.

There was another meeting with Mr. Jones. He was gracious when I stated I had no problems at all with the Nature Conservancy but had an abundance of questions concerning the Department of Interior. He smiled and said they had had their own problems with Interior.

The price they were offering for 833 acres of Providence land was $299,600. I said something about the amount having a $999.99 used-car sale ring to it, pointing out that another $400 would round it out to even money. I was being flippant, but Mr. Jones gave me a serious, bureaucratic explanation.

One of the stated conditions precedent to the sale was receipt of a letter of intent for repurchase by John Turner, director of the U.S. Fish and Wildlife Service of the Department of Interior. My understanding of that condition was that the Nature Conservancy intended to sell some of the wetland to Interior at a profit, then utilize the remainder for their own program. Except for the gnawing reality that neither agency would put bread on the tables of the poor, the idea was difficult to contest. At least the land would be preserved. The white planters who had been responsible for the demise of the cooperative, interracial venture would not win in the end by getting the site, and the trees would not be strip-cut for lumber. Walter Diggs had announced this was simply a meeting for information and not an official meeting of the board. So I stated my position again but didn't ask precisely what the letter of intent for repurchase by the Department of Interior meant. The mistake was mine.

A few weeks later we convened again. Now we were gathered for an official meeting. The vote would be taken this time. We had the usual pleasant lunch, everyone casual. The mood changed abruptly when we began the business. Gene read the minutes, and preliminaries were taken care of. Walter was the same professional, noncommittal chairman he had always been. He stated the order of business, said he had Sue Minter's proxy and would cast it according to her instruction. Then he said he would entertain a motion on the Nature Conservancy's offer. No one moved or spoke. The silence was riddled with tension. Eventually Walter said a proxy could make a motion, and he knew the position of his proxy. He did not reveal what it was. The quiet persisted.

I remembered one of my father's favorite stories about a church business meeting. We called them church conferences. There had been a long and heated discussion about a committee recommendation that the church building be painted. But no one would make a motion, fearing the wrath of those who would oppose it. Finally one of the deacons said he would make the motion. The pastor, called the moderator during conference time, asked whether the motion was to accept or reject the report of the committee. The deacon said it didn't make any difference to him. Finally the exasperated moderator said, "Now, Brother, if you're going to make a motion, it has to be one way or the other." The response was, "Hit don't make no difference. Either fer or agin." To him the logic was plain. Let's just get it on the table. Remembering the story, and feeling some sympathy for our patient chairman, I asked if it was acceptable to make a motion, then speak and vote against it. The chairman said it was. So I did.

It was quickly seconded, and I made the speech the others had expected—about the poor of the area, the signal we would be sending to the previously conquered Choctaw, and my grave misgivings about how much good a few scholarships would do. I talked some more about the poor land-stewardship record of the Department of Interior, repeating that Interior already owns five hundred million acres of land. Giving them more land would be like giving more money to the IRS. I really didn't want Section Thirteen to be added to the Interior's holdings. To them it would be like a turnip patch in the state of Texas. It seemed to me one final sanction, one more insult to a piece of ground that had suffered enough. Everything, everybody, is entitled to one grand gesture. Since the going of the Choctaws, everyone else had failed on the gesture. The land deserves better. It merits the Choctaw's return. My speech was over.

There was no other discussion. Walter said as chairman he could vote only in case of a tie. He called each of us by name.

"Will."

"Nay."

I knew my negative vote had heightened the stress within the others. They are not people who would offend a friend. And we were friends. In the deepest understanding.

"Record one nay, Mr. Secretary," Walter said. Gene took an inordinate amount of time writing in his minutes book.

"Ann." No one looked at another. Ann sat mute, gazing at the floor. Somehow I wanted to reach out to her, recalling her exuberance as she talked of plans for the transfer of title to the Choctaws—another mass meeting in the same school, Johnny Cash and Tom T. Hall singing their songs, the peace pipe we would pass around for all to puff, those who had been so mean to her daddy sitting down front in their wheelchairs.

Walter softly called her name again. Her pain was glaring and contagious as she sighed deeply and whispered. "Aye."

The chairman was quiet as Gene methodically recorded the vote of his daughter.

"Lindy."

She hesitated briefly. Then, "Aye."

Again there was the wait for the work of the man who had recorded the affairs of Providence Farm for fifty years. Soon it would be his time to cast a ballot. He had resisted casting it since 1955. I thought of the many creative, though at times nonsensical, ways he had maneuvered and manipulated to hold on. Now the end was near. I remembered my own impatience with him at times, wanting to just sell the land and be done with it. Now I knew he had been right all along. I wanted to tell him again that I was sorry I had once questioned him.

I saw again the handsome, wavy-haired stranger approaching Mac Bryan and me with the bulge of a lethal weapon under his arms on an autumn afternoon in 1955. A kaleidoscope of our brotherly odyssey jammed my brain for a moment. I heard the imperturbable chairman call his name.

Gene didn't answer. He pretended to write in his book. At earlier meetings he had been confused at times, sometimes not sure if he had dreamed something or if it had actually happened. This day his thinking was clear. His medication had been changed and his recovery was easily noticeable. The same Gene Cox was back with us.

I wondered what was going through his mind. All those memories. All that devotion to every tree and rock and person. A part of me wanted to scream at him, to say, "Gene Cox, you are likely the most morally literate man I have ever known. Don't do this, for it is wrong, wrong, wrong!" I wanted to recount the many fights waged over the years on Section Thirteen: whites fighting Choctaws, slaveowners fighting slaves, landowners fighting banks and banks fighting back, landlords fighting sharecroppers. And even to remind him that some of the most vociferous battles of all had been directed by Providence trustees against each other: Franklin the Christian fighting Amberson the agnostic. Day, Treadway, Eddy, Niebuhr, and others, Christians all, bickering over the use of this precious and tragic piece of land. And Sam Franklin and me in our own heated exchange in which Sam exploded, "It is not our purpose to venerate the land." And my angry comeback, "Well, it is by god *my* purpose to venerate it! Everyone since the Choctaws has ravished it. And that includes us. We of Providence Cooperative Farm. Not since the Choctaws has there been real peace on this ridge. Let's by damn give them a chance to restore it. Let this land again know solace. It has known grief enough."

I was quickly dissuaded from my glandular upheaval by directing to myself some humbling words that Oliver Cromwell sent to the Church of Scotland in 1650: "I beseech you in the bowels of Christ, think it possible that you may be mistaken." Another part of me wanted to direct Cromwell's words to my adversaries in the room, people I loved even as I was losing.

Still another part of me wanted to embrace Gene and tell him how I had admired him over the years, and that I understood. I didn't do that either. I had made my speech and cast my vote. Others must do what they would.

Before us sat a stoic. An old man hanging from the low limb of a transitory tree, where longevity is only shadows of yesterday. He who, thirty-five years earlier, had endured an overblown citizen's arrest and trial where there were five hundred judges, five hundred prosecutors, five hundred plaintiffs, and two defendants, with no counsel at the defense table that night in the Tchula High School save the principles for which he was prepared to die. He had not cried out then and he would not now. He would not show what he was feeling. It was his ache and he would bear it. As he always had.

Now Ann and Lindy looked at each other, their eyes doing the talking. It was as if each wanted the other to intervene, or somehow save their spouse and sire from his affliction. Walter repeated the bid for his vote, calling his name again. There was still no response.

"Gene, we're waiting for your vote," Lindy said, breaking the silence, smiling sympathetically.

Without taking his eyes from the paper he had been writing on he answered abruptly, as if propelled, like roosting quail flushed from a thicket.

"Aye!"

The room fell silent again. The man who had given his whole self to Providence Farm returned to his night watch, perhaps realizing in the stillness it was now history. And that nothing is ever quite one's own. For a few minutes we sat with him. And yet without him. Section Thirteen had begun a new chapter in it's trek toward forever. The meeting ended and we turned to small talk—Ann, ever the joker, chattering away, me assuring the Coxes I wasn't mad at anyone.

Then for some reason I thought of the question I should have asked earlier. "Just what does the Nature Conservancy plan to do with the land?"

Walter answered quickly, as if he had anticipated the question. "Nothing. They don't have any interest in that land."

"Then what th—"

"They're selling it to the Department of Interior. It was a convenient shortcut. Nature Conservancy works faster than the federal government. No, they don't have any interest in the land. Except to sell what Interior doesn't want so they can buy Sweetbay Bogs Natural Area in Stone County."

Well I'll be damned!

CHAPTER 15

Well, I run to the rocks
to hide my face.
The rocks cried out,
"No hiding place."
There's no hiding place down here.

I wanted to go back one last time. In another way I never wanted to see Providence again. I wanted to put all that behind me and let it be. I had had many projects in my life. In some I had succeeded. Or thought I had. In others I had fallen far short. I had learned to deal with the failures. Many of them were against formidable odds. Reality told me the successes were often fortuitous. In this I found neither hiding place nor comfort. It was a defeat that continued to plague me. I didn't understand it.

Why had I taken it so seriously? The Mississippi Band of Choctaws had been doing very well without me, without my trying to give them something they really didn't need.

I tried to make something lofty of it now, as I had in the beginning. Despite the fact the Choctaws did not need the land, there was, I thought, something beyond the original romance of the idea. Something about justice, fairness, honor. Had not my ancestors wrested these acres from the Choctaws in the most devilish fashion? Accounts of oppression, deceit, bribery, connivance are now routine lessons in the most conservative history books studied by our young. Would not this simple act be an addendum, therapeutic perhaps to the chronic illness of our evil conscience? Might not this small deed serve as modest oblation to quell the wrath of the primordial gods of that vast wilderness who, after all, were not sent west by the Treaty of Dancing Rabbit Creek and must surely seethe in anger still? Much as the wine and wafer we offer our own Divinity?

Ye who do truly and
earnestly repent . . . and
intend to lead a new
life . . .

And what of the issue of those African people sold by Wiley Davis of Section Thirteen to Andrew Lee? Andrew Lee, his executors, administrators, and assigns were to own them *forever.* And what of those included in the sale of the land to Richard Davis? The sales are still recorded on the record books of the probate court.

Do we not have something to say to their heirs as well as to the surviving heirs of Doak's Stand and Dancing Rabbit Creek? That we are sorry for our misdeeds?

And what now of the executors, administrators, and assigns of Andrew Lee? Are they not the ones who live in the big houses on the edge of town with the lush fields and prosperous businesses who continue to profit from the children of those sold? Are they not the ones who gathered in Tchula High School in 1955 and ordered the people of Providence from the county, and will be the ones to profit from the Department of Interior's agenda? Could we not say to them "forever" is about to end? Granted that the notion of returning the land to the Choctaws so they might help the impoverished blacks was a convoluted, even patronizing and condescending one toward them. But not, I insist, imperialistic. And what does an empty belly care or know of ideology?

So might the shout of them that triumph die. Or have the hearts of even the good among us hardened beyond remorse?

Such self-righteous musing, brazen judgment of friends I had known and loved for years, jarred me to other more likely reasons for my disconsolate mood.

I never liked losing. Maybe it was nothing more than my own fantail ego. Yes, possible.

Perhaps my members were saying the sands of time were running out on me, that I would not fight many more battles, and that I was not up to licking my wounds, parlaying my winnings of the past and moving on.

Could it be that from the time the subject was first broached in the home of the Coxes, refugees from this land as surely as the people of Pushmataha and Luther Cashdollar, I had been trying to orchestrate the final chapter of a book? A new treaty, peace pipe, and a popular country ballad? Yes, possible also. For it would have made a tidy ending to the tale.

The only thing of which I had been certain was that I very much wanted to return these acres to a people who had once known them as their own. I was now certain of one other thing. It wasn't going to happen.

Whatever was bothering me, as I rented a car in Jackson and headed north on an interstate highway with garish displays of what the white man did to the land of Nanih Waiya, I knew I was going back to Section Thirteen because of something of which I had no sure knowledge, and over which I had little control, but which, like some ancient witchery, was compelling me. This square mile of geography that had challenged me painfully, that had set my life on a new course thirty-five years ago when my first visit attracted the ire of the powers of Mississippi in whose employ I had until then been content, was now inviting me back in a manner I could understand only as some mysterious and magisterial subpoena I should not resist.

I had considered calling my old friend Mac Bryan, who was with me on that first adventurous journey to Providence in 1955, and asking him to make this last trip with me. But the years of my involvement with those of Providence since that October day had not been his.

It was a cold December morning. On I-55, typical of the thoroughfares of the Kennedy-Johnson years, this one built by hands that by day accepted federal money and by night damned government intervention in local affairs, I might as well have been in Colorado or New Hampshire. But the scene changed abruptly when I turned onto state Highway 17 and headed west. A British Petroleum service station and quickstop market overlooked the interstate. The British were here before, I thought. Now they're back with power. Oil power. Just down the road was the Richland cotton gin, followed by single and doublewide mobile homes where sharecropper shanties once stood.

I stopped at a historical marker, the Little Red Schoolhouse, and read the inscription:

> IN 1849 ROBERT MORRIS, MASON, SCHOOLMASTER, BEGAN
> MOVEMENT THAT RESULTED IN CREATION OF THE ORDER OF THE
> EASTERN STAR. SCHOOLHOUSE HAS ALSO HOUSED MASONS, AND
> COMPANY C, 15TH MISS. INF. C.S.A.

Robert Morris started an auxiliary for our foremothers' pleasure. He couldn't get away with that today, I thought.

As I pulled back onto the highway, a local affiliate of National Public Radio was playing Beethoven's Eighth Symphony, a favorite. I tried to relate it to where I was and what I was about. I couldn't. Leonard Bernstein and the Los Angeles Philharmonic followed with William Schuman's "American Festival Overture." That was more relevance than I wanted to deal with, so I switched stations and heard Roy Rogers and Clint Black's duet of "Hold on Partner, Good Things Coming Your Way." Then, without interruption, Kenny Rogers with the robust lyrics, "Let's go out in a blaze of glory. All good things must end." Where's the glory? I wondered.

Not far from the schoolhouse was a new brick house with a sign in front stating it had been built by Habitat for Humanity, an organization started in Americus, Georgia, at Koinonia Farm, a communal and interracial venture similar to Providence Farm. Habitat is supported vigorously by former president Jimmy Carter. The sign had fallen down halfway. I stopped and copied the words:

HOLMES HABITAT FOR HUMANITY
A DECENT HOME FOR GOD'S PEOPLE IN NEED
NO PROFIT
NO INTEREST
NO GOVERNMENT FUNDS

It took me back to an incident in 1958 when Koinonia Farm would not have been indulged a roadside sign to announce their good works, for they were under siege by both the law and local citizenry. A total boycott prevented their buying food and supplies for the farm or getting medical or dental attention. Begun in 1942 by Clarence Jordan, a graduate in agriculture from the University of Georgia with a Ph.D. in Greek from the Southern Baptist Theological Seminary in Louisville, his wife, Florence, and one other couple, the farm had been popular when Clarence was teaching new and better ways to farm the Sumter County loam, although they had been an interracial community from the beginning. Their acceptance waned as World War II became a near unanimous cause; Clarence taught a strict New Testament pacifism and practiced a communal economy. But it was not until the racial mores were challenged in the mid-fifties that they were totally isolated by the white community. In addition to being unable to purchase supplies and equipment, they were the target of relentless violence. Barns and warehouses were burned, gasoline tanks for farm implements destroyed, buildings and grounds riddled with machine-gun bullets.

It seemed no coincidence the shooting always occurred on Thursday nights, the time when the Army Reserve and National Guard units had their weekly drills. In my naiveté I thought it might be helpful to visit the FBI office in Albany, Georgia, to report the abuse. I asked three friends who taught at Mercer University in Macon to accompany me. They went on the condition that they were speaking as individuals and not as representatives of the university, a Christian school still rigidly segregated.

It was a Saturday afternoon on a beautiful late fall day. Since FBI agents must always meet in pairs, we had difficulty convening the meeting at all. One was on the golf course, the other entertaining houseguests. Our interview with them was closer to slapstick comedy than serious talk.

One of the professors taught religion, another history, and the third one chemistry. After asking and noting our names and addresses, the agent in charge asked the profession of each one of us. I stated I was a Baptist preacher from Tennessee. The religion professor said he, too, was a Baptist preacher. I was becoming concerned as to how the other two would identify their means of livelihood without naming Mercer University, which, we had agreed, no one would do.

"And what about you, Sir?" the agent asked the chemistry professor. "Are you a clergyman too?"

"I'm a chemist," he replied. I was sure the agent would name some of the chemical companies with plants in the area and inquire as to which one he worked for, but he didn't. He turned instead to the teacher of history.

"Are you a chemist?" he asked the waiting history teacher.

I eyed the others nervously. How is he going to get out of this one? I wondered. Without flinching, as if ready for the question from the beginning, he answered. "No, sir. I'm a historian."

The agent made no further inquiry as to our employment, moving instead to the nature of our visit.

My innocence, and total ignorance of the mindset of this federal agency, did the thinking and talking for me. I spoke of the pacifist, communal, interracial philosophy of the founders of Koinonia Farm, certain I had a liberal and sympathetic audience from the federal establishment, dedicated to the principle of liberty and justice for all.

Neither agent showed the slightest emotion. They just sat looking at us. I explained that down south we had this instinctive fear of "the feds." And I figured if they would simply show up on the streets of Americus, maybe ask a few questions, just be a couple of strangers around town, the word would get around that folks had better straighten up or President Eisenhower and Attorney General Brownell were going to get awfully riled, and somebody was going to be in a peck of trouble.

I leaned back, laughed modestly at my luminous bit of strategy, and waited for their nods of approval. Instead, one of them asked, "Why do you think any federal law has been violated?" I sat squeezing the red fifty-caliber tracer slugs I had brought along in a fashion the professors later described as Humphrey Bogart's Captain Queeg in *The Caine Mutiny*. I had told the agents about the tracer bullets found plentifully on the premises, even adding what I was sure these men, skilled in crime busting, would see as a foolish redundancy. "You know, you don't walk into your friendly neighborhood hardware store and buy fifty-caliber tracer bullets," I had told them. We had also reported the attacks always came on Army Reserve and National Guard nights. Still they had asked why we thought federal law had been violated. We sat in disbelief as the agent continued. "You really don't have any probable cause, do you?" Adding, "Mr. Hoover doesn't want the bureau to become a national police force."

That ended the meeting. We laughed a lot driving back to Macon. In later years, it wasn't so funny. Riding along now on Mississippi Highway 17 thirty-two years later, heading for Providence Farm one last time, remembering those of Providence got no more of a hearing from "the feds" than those of Koinonia, I remembered my days of nescience.

After copying the words of the sign, I drove into the yard of the Habitat house. The grass and weeds looked as if they had not been cut all summer. A screen door at the side entrance was swinging clumsily in the wind, half off its hinges. An abandoned automobile, stripped of everything that could be removed, was in the backyard. Litter was strewn all around. I went to the front door and found it open. The knob was gone. Inside I found garbage and more rubbish. Everything had the appearance of trashy folk having lived there. It was the stereotype I had heard many times, of what *they* will do with a nice house even if you give it to them. I was sorry I had stopped.

A little further down the road was another sign, billboard size:

TOP $'S FOR YOUR TREES
1-800 6TIMBER

Across the road I saw a large bow of yellow ribbons, the popular announcement of support for soldiers in the Persian Gulf War, long over, on the door of a tarpaper shack. A black, middle-aged woman was hanging clothes on a barbed-wire fence. I recalled there were no yellow ribbons at the British Petroleum station.

Suddenly, around a sharp curve lined with dormant crepe myrtle bushes and giant pecan trees, I heard a blaring siren. Glancing in the rear view mirror, I saw the whirling blue lights of a police car. Certain the officer had seen me driving unsteadily as I jotted notes on the slim reporter's notebook, I pulled to the shoulder and stopped. The car darted past me. Realizing I was not the culprit, I sped after it. A few miles down the narrow road I found two black deputy sheriffs who had stopped a stout, neatly dressed white man. They were calmly making what appeared to be a routine arrest. The man, who appeared to be drunk, was stretched spread-eagle against the recent-model car, one of the officers patting him down. They had stopped him where a gravel road led to the little church house where the black cavalrymen from Grierson's Raiders had roundly trounced a company of Confederates.

I remembered one of the first stories I heard from the Minters and Coxes, about a black man being shot by the county sheriff because he had not obeyed his command. Hazel Brannon Smith, a moderate newspaper editor of the county, had reported the incident, was sued for damages by the sheriff, and Dr. Minter, who had examined the man, had testified for the editor as to the nature of the wound. The testimony made Dr. Minter even more unpopular. Hazel Smith continued her paper, was boycotted and financially ruined, but won a Pulitzer Prize for her gutsy journalism. Lying now in a geriatric fog in an Alabama nursing home, she would have applauded the scene I was watching. On the other hand, Hazel was a tough and sometimes vindictive woman, and

I wondered if she would have found it in her heart to forgive the white sheriff. And how would she react to hear the sheriff's son was chosen to survey Providence land for the Department of Interior's purchase?

I waited for half an hour in front of the Holmes County jail in Lexington, still eleven miles from Tchula, to watch the black lawmen bring in their white prisoner. Near the jail I saw the First Baptist Church. On the bulletin board were the bold-lettered words WE SUPPORT OUR TROOPS. And the First United Methodist Church with "M. E. Church, South" still chiseled in stone above the chancel doorway. I could see St. Thomas Catholic Church from where I sat. It had been there since 1898. Marcella O'Reilly Davis had helped to build it. Looking for the jail I had just driven by Beth El Synagogue. Beth El. *House of God.* In Lexington, Mississippi. Earlier I had asked one of the members how there came to be a Jewish congregation in so small a Mississippi town. He said a dozen or so families had come there when the Cotton Kingdom was in the development stage. Thinking stereotypically—peddler wagons and fruit stands—I asked him what business they were in. "They were planters," he answered. "Plantation owners." Remembering the European persecutions when Jews were not allowed to own land, and expecting a discourse on some ancient Diaspora, I asked from which country they had migrated. He hesitated a moment, smiled, then answered, "From Georgia. They came in here from Georgia." Hmm. That's where my people came from. And Jesse Furver's people. About the same time.

The deputies brought in their prisoner without incident. I should have known. Now the sheriff of Holmes County is a black man.

While I had waited, I recalled bringing Vernon Eagle to this town to visit Hazel Brannon Smith during the turbulent sixties. Vernon had lost a leg while flying for the Royal Canadian Air Force during World War II. After the war he had become an investment banker and from that was executive director of the New World Foundation, the philanthropic arm of the McCormick Reaper empire, an agency heavily involved in civil rights activities in the South. We engaged in casual banter as we strolled around the courthouse square on a late afternoon in August.

"Old Man Cyrus Hall McCormick took more Negroes out of the cotton fields than Abraham Lincoln," Vernon told me.

"Yeah. Well, actually Mr. Lincoln didn't take very many out of the fields, and I'm not sure Mr. McCormick did them much of a favor with his mechanical cotton picker he stole from the Rust brothers," I came back.

Vernon tapped his cane, tipped his Panama hat, and spoke cordially to everyone we met. "Good evening, Sir. And how are you today?" he would say in his crisp Yankee accent. It didn't matter if they were white or black. I wasn't anxious to call attention to our presence. "I think I'll ask one of the locals where the liquor store is," he said, looking at his watch.

"I don't think that's a good idea."

"Why not? They may be closed when we get to Jackson."

"No. The liquor stores won't be closed in Jackson."

"What makes you so sure? It's almost six o'clock." He was still greeting everyone we met. "Nice to see you, Sir. And how are you today, Ma'am?"

"I'm sure they won't be closed because there aren't any," I told my New York friend.

"Campbell!" he almost shouted. "Are you telling me we're in a dry county? Then how in hell are we going to get a drink?"

"I didn't say anything about dry," I whispered, getting more uneasy as the stranger's greetings attracted attention from bystanders. "I said, there aren't any liquor stores in Holmes County. And there aren't any liquor stores in the state of Mississippi. The bellhop will take care of us when we get to the Robert E. Lee Hotel."

I'm not going to admit to this Yankee that saying sir and ma'am to Negroes in my home state is dangerous right now, even if we both get lynched.

"Why the devil does anybody live in this backward ass place?" he exclaimed, laughing out loud.

"A lot of people live here because there aren't any liquor stores. And a lot of people live here because it's home." He sighed deeply, looking at his watch again. "By the way," I said when I saw we were not within hearing range of anyone. "If it's all the same with you, you just tap your cane and tip your hat from now on. I'll do the howdying." He told me later he thought he was just pursuing Southern good manners.

"Old Vernon was a good one," I said to myself, remembering the many times he had been generous with the McCormick money he controlled. And remembering the beautiful requiem in the Cathedral of St. John the Divine in New York not many years later. "Yep. Vernon Eagle was a good one. *Requiescat.*"

I left the county seat town and continued toward Tchula. A wrought-iron sign on the edge of town asked, IS JESUS CHRIST LORD OF LEXINGTON? I wondered if the sign had been there in 1955, how the congregation of Beth El felt about the matter.

As I began the sharp descent from the Loess Bluffs to the Delta, the deep clay gullies, markings of poverty, laced with winter-dead kudzu vines, the shrouded banks looking like masses of cumulus clouds, overlooking the miles of flat brown earth, the sleeping fields like an endless and affluent vat of chocolate, I dreaded seeing again the human counterparts. I noticed leaning and rotting telephone poles with no cross-pieces, some with single strands of wire dangling from them, and remembered Gene Cox following them to find antique telephones. I wondered why no one had bothered to remove the useless poles. Perhaps they were discouraged by the unyielding ropes of kudzu wrapped around them. I passed a sign pointing to a Salvation Army camp. The summer before, noticing the sign for the first time, I had driven down the narrow macadam road and toured the area, a summer camp for urban children. Black and white children were playing ball, swimming, attending arts-and-crafts classes together in obvious comfort and enjoyment, unaware that a few miles away some good people had been exiled thirty-five years earlier for a more tame violation of racial mores. I drove into Tchula and eased down Dr. Martin Luther King, Jr. Drive, the same mile of U.S. Highway 49 that had so moved me when Chief Phillip Martin and his entourage had met us here. I wondered how many streets and boulevards in America bear the name of the young preacher who was thrust to fame by the meanness of my people.

I recalled the legend of the young Choctaw maiden named Tchula who was in love with a Cherokee brave. Her father, the chieftain, opposed any marriage outside the tribe. The determined young Cherokee stole her away, unaware the chief was watching the canoe as he paddled from shore. When the bold lover would not heed the chief's command to turn around, he sent an arrow sailing straight to the Cherokee's heart. The brokenhearted maiden joined her plighted one in the dark waters of what was known thereafter as Lake Tchula.

I swung diagonally and moved slowly by the grocery store, watching the idle but willing and able-bodied dozen or so black men milling around. Aimless, their jokes seeming raucous, their laughter loud but hollow. Dr. Minter had treated their ills when he was here. Gene Cox had offered them a glimmer of hope. How would they respond if they were told a new hope for them had been vetoed in deference to the longevity of endangered wood storks and round pigtoe mussels, along with a preserve for rich folk to hunt by permit? What would be Luther Cashdollar's thinking on the matter?

I remembered the young black teenagers Chief Martin had noticed passing the whiskey bottle and Pepsi-Cola back and forth. Surely they wouldn't be standing in this wretched wind. And they weren't. I caught a glimpse of three boys and one girl huddled in the back seat of a car that, with all but one of the wheels missing, appeared not to have been driven for a long time. I didn't stare. It was clear they were about something other than whiskey to fight the cold. And entitled to as much privacy as the open street could afford. I thought of Chief Martin's words: "Mr. Campbell, if this was my town it wouldn't look like this. These people need help." And the help he offered to bring.

A long HAPPY HOLIDAY banner reached across a vacant store window, the empty shelves and counters inside accentuating the sardonic announcement. I looked back and saw the greeting had its own purpose. It was held in place with duct tape, the banner covering a smashed hole in the glass. Merry Christmas, Red Fox! Happy Hanukkah, Beth El!

A sign on a dusky wall advertised barbecue ribs. The store was a combination grocery and hardware. Ribs seemed a good idea for lunch at Providence. The lady at the counter said they just had them on weekends. I settled for Vienna sausage and a Moon Pie.

As I turned off Highway 49 toward Providence, I stopped at the hunter's permit station on the edge of the Morgan Canebrake National Wildlife Refuge, the one joining Providence land, now secured by the Department of Interior, and picked up a brochure detailing regulations for hunting. It was a mistake, opening old regrets and resentments I had vowed not to nurture. There were twenty-one regulations, most, it seemed to me, designed to exclude the poor of the area who had been allowed to hunt the land for food since it was purchased by Delta Cooperative Farm in 1938. The brochure itself was complicated and would have discouraged me if it had been my intention to apply for a hunting permit. I had to search the fine print to determine just how to go about applying. The introduction stated the right to hunt on wildlife refuge land was set forth in Title 50, Code of Federal Regulations, and applicable state regulations. My Anabaptist genes did an anarchic balk as I wondered how many of the local poor we had allowed to hunt the land would be familiar with Title 50. Regulation 3 directed that all hunters must wear a minimum of five hundred square inches of unbroken florescent orange visible above the waistline. How much is five hundred square inches? I imagined an illiterate farm worker asking. One whose coat would cost less than the five hundred inches of florescent tape. Regulation 10 stated all terrain vehicles are permitted to retrieve dead deer. Fair enough, I thought. Fair for the guns of autumn. The use of horses is forbidden. Unfair, I thought, for a poor local who owns an old mare but not an ATV. Number 15 said no mandrives for deer. Not knowing what "mandrive" meant, I concluded I would be hard pressed to get a permit, stuffed the folder in my pocket, and drove on. But not before recalling the offer of Tony Dunbar and his little band of environmentalists to make Providence Mississippi's first interracial hunting club.

As the engine groaned, the wheels spinning in the wet sand of the road, a small fawn darted directly in front of me. She seemed to catch my eye when she hesitated. She appeared tired and confused as she made her way through the open field, aiming for the relative safety of the deep woods. "Where's your mama, little girl?" Shot dead, perhaps, in the land of Providence. But it was all quite legal, little deer. So take heart. All along the roadside, like vaunting mockery of a vanquished foe, were recently placed signs proclaiming NATIONAL WILDLIFE REFUGE, U.S. Department of Interior. My god! I'm trespassing.

The hard frozen ground allowed me to drive directly to the steps of the old school and community center. When I opened the door, it seemed even colder at Providence than it had been on the dreary streets of Tchula. I decided to sit in the car a while longer, letting the heater warm me thoroughly before going in. I sat looking at the old building now going to wrack and ruin and tried to envision the plantation house that stood here many years ago. I had learned that the nearby land the Cox family had traded the Providence board for some Providence Farm acreage would include the schoolhouse. I was glad. The Cox daughters will bring their grandchildren here and tell them stories of Providence.

I thought of some of the people I had encountered in my search for the story of Providence. There was Greenwood Leflore, the Choctaw chief who had helped to educate and Christianize his people, then sold them out at Dancing Rabbit Creek. Most of the local citizenry still believe he once owned these acres. I suppose as chief he did. Damn you, Greenwood Leflore. I don't like you. I wondered for a moment why I had forgiven the several hundred white citizens who had assembled in the Tchula High School thirty-five years before and abused two good men and their families but somehow couldn't forgive Greenwood Leflore. Maybe later on, I thought. And maybe I should. For I remembered one of his lineage. Wiley Branton, the skillful civil rights attorney who had won the celebrated court case that gained admission of the nine black children to Little Rock's Central High School. He had once come here with me when he had a case in federal court having to do with Holmes County. He, a black man, had been referred to by the state's attorney as "outside counsel for the plaintiff." He laughed as he told me he was the great-grandson of Greenwood LeFlore, so how could he be an outsider in the chief's old district?

I remembered Luther Cashdollar and Jesse Furver, fancied seeing them riding the back of Fičik, racing to the Indian mound that we deeded to the Mississippi Department of History and Archives.

Andrew Jackson was on the banks of the nearby Yazoo again, bargaining but failing with the Choctaws. Then at Doak's Stand halfway across the state, at first toadying and cajoling, then threatening and yelling, succeeding this time with his deception. The final blow to a noble people. Andrew Jackson, I don't reckon I'll ever forgive you.

The obese Richard Davis sat right there on that stile which still wears the name GWIN. I see the blue and white lettering through the bushes grown up around it. This is the spot where John Gwin stood after he had to take the land back from Champ Taylor, seething at the scene of cherished beauty gone. William McKendree Gwin, a young physician from Tennessee, bought it as part of an empire. Another young physician, David Minter, came with an empire of the heart. I thought of these and many more before I opened the car door again to face the cold.

As I walked inside the old school and community center, I felt a strange urge to call Mrs. Fannye Booker's name. I saw the drawings and writing of her Head Start children on the mildewed bulletin board. Where are they now? These little five year olds who eagerly gathered around this giant of a woman on mornings such as this one, learned their ABC's, listened to her stories, and absorbed a notion of freedom. They would be beyond thirty now. Might I have seen them in front of the grocery store? Or would I have to go to Chicago, Detroit, or Harlem to find them? Not Harlem. No, they would not have gone there. Mrs. Booker would have told them early not to go there. She would have seen her children as too soft. She would have told them. And they would have heard and remembered.

"Miss Fannye!" I called her name and it rang through the cold of the empty rooms. She didn't answer. I pictured her proud, gentle face, the dark beauty of her skin. I saw her again seated with the Cox family in the big Presbyterian church in White Haven as I presided at the wedding of Carol, their oldest daughter. She was fifteen when they were forced to leave this place. Mrs. Booker was happy one of her little white children had turned out well and was marrying well. The man she was marrying, Roger Nooe, would one day be dean of the School of Social Work at the University of Tennessee. I looked down from the chancel of that rich edifice as Carol approached on the arm of Gene, her adoptive father who had been father as few blood fathers are, and saw Mrs. Booker's tears streaming down her knowing face, sparkling as diamonds set in ebony. She, dressed in the clean, white, and stiffly starched uniform of a domestic, outwardly still attuned to the mores of the Old South—that black people are welcomed to such occasions if dressed as domestics—yet thinking such free thoughts I could only imagine.

"Mrs. Booker!" I called again, feeling a little silly. But Mrs. Booker did not answer.

The rain that had blown through the forced-open door was frozen. It cracked beneath my steps, snapping the linoleum into irregular pieces as I moved.

In the second of the large rooms I saw big pictures of Abraham Lincoln, Franklin D. Roosevelt, and once-governor Paul B. Johnson arranged in a triangle between two windows. Why a governor of Mississippi and not Martin Luther King, Jr.? Three white men and not one woman nor black person to serve as role models for these impoverished black children. Then I remembered. It was Paul B. Johnson who, in 1940, provided free textbooks for all children, legislation of inestimable effect for those long held in educational peonage, deprived of ownership of a single book. I remembered my own family's struggle, their bartering with neighbors for second-hand school books for us during the Great Depression.

Yes, Paul B. Johnson, racist though he was, deserved a place on the teaching wall. Still, what of Dr. King? It came to me she would have waited for history to declare him hero and entitle him to a place on the wall. He was relatively unknown when the pictures had been put there. Anyway, she was an educator, not a crusader.

But wait! Further down the wall, in the very corner, a darkened corner, was a much smaller picture. It was of a frail-looking black woman. I recognized her. Sojourner Truth. I recognized it as being exactly like the one I had seen in Mrs. Booker's museum. Underneath, in a beautiful script that I assumed to be from the pen of Mrs. Booker, were Sojourner Truth's celebrated words spoken in 1851 at the Women's Convention in Akron, Ohio:

> *I have plowed, and planted and gathered*
> *into barns and no man could head me!*
> *And ain't I a woman?*
> *I could work as much and eat as much—*
> *when I could get it—and bear the lash as well.*
> *And ain't I a woman?*
> *I have born thirteen children and seen*
> *most sold off to slavery, and when I cried out*
> *in my mother's grief, none but Jesus heard me!*
> *And ain't I a woman?*

Yes, a woman. What a woman. And so was Fannye Booker. Crusader too. In her own way. In the fullness of time. As the little children followed along behind her, studying the wall, Sojourner Truth would be the last face they would ponder, would be the last story she would tell them. Underground railroad! Rolling on. Sojourner Truth. Engine and caboose. And Fannye Booker. Valiant daughter of Sojourner. "The wind bloweth where it listeth. . . ."

A small storeroom was cluttered with old posters, crepe paper, and books. I picked through the stack. All civics books. *You and Your Inheritance,* by Hollingsworth, Beck, and Burgess. *The Government of a Free Nation. Journey into America.* They were stamped as being the property of the Santa Clara School System. Inheritance. Free Nation. Journey. All familiar themes to children in California. Perhaps not for Miss Fannye's Camp School children of Providence. Yet she would take the second-hand books and offer them dreams and they would reach out.

I tried to piece together the events that brought the books all the way from the West Coast to Section Thirteen, Township Sixteen, Range One East, Holmes County, Mississippi. Maybe some Quaker lady had, as a child, taken part in one of the work camps years ago, and was now on the school board in Santa Clara. Maybe it was an alternative to shredding obsolete texts. Hand-me-downs. Whatever—here they were, like John Brown's body, moldering in the grave.

I stepped outside and headed for the old shop where James Henderson, Otto Morgan, Gene Cox, and others had labored to keep things working. I stopped to scribble some notes, using the hood of the bright red, rented Mercury Topaz for a desk. The car looked as out of place as it was, parked three feet from the concrete stoop from which fancy ladies of the plantation mounted the sidesaddles, the blue ceramic lettering GWIN still claiming title.

The wind had stopped, and for a minute everything around me. There were no sounds at all. Nothing moved except the discordant Monte Blanc pen a friend had given me. Different, I thought, from the goose quill Greenwood Leflore had used to assign this ground to the white man 170 years ago. The bright winter sunlight glittered on the gold clip of the pen and blurred my vision on the snow-white paper.

As I wrote, I was not aware that my shivering hand was leaving the notes barely legible. Suddenly the still was broken by what I was instinctively sure was machine-gun fire. Infantry drill sergeants of 1943 yelled commands and I obeyed. I crouched behind the car, frozen in place, ready to exert myself. With a writing pen that cost more than the M1 rifle I would have held at the time but hardly as reliable against the odds. I sheepishly realized what I had heard was a woodpecker, drilling for beetles in a nearby pine. Not wanting the ghostly silence to return, I opened the car door and let the chimes sound as I moved hurriedly to the long-neglected farm shop.

The inside walls and ceiling were lined with years of dirt-dauber nests, the long mud cylinders stretching several feet long, each summer's construction piled on top of the last, the heat from the metal roof serving as a kiln, the hard-baked structures resembling the ruins of a pueblo.

All serviceable tools and equipment had long since disappeared. Bits and pieces of metal plows, harrows, and harness were strewn about the dirt floor. Parts of an old cream separator, and the large milk tank from the dairy, stood in place against the far wall. I wondered why the stainless steel tank had not been stolen along with everything else. Too heavy for hurried thievery, I supposed.

Useless items—rusty pieces of chains and wire, broken pliers and wrenches, fan belts, punctured radiators with rotten hoses attached, piston rings, and assorted parts of a crankshaft—hung on the walls, some of them touching and merging with the work of the daubers.

In a smaller room were half-finished horseshoes, a broken steelyard, empty oil cans, jars that still held a medley of rusty nails, screws, nuts, and bolts.

Dozens of shoes were scattered in the mud in both rooms. I seemed to dwell on them. Empty shoes. Of many sizes and styles, not a match among them that I could see. Odd shoes for men, women, and children. Years of flooding, freezing, and thawing had left them encased in the mud. Why were they there? It was if the wearers had walked out of them and kept on walking. Never to return. I recall hoping they somewhere, somehow, found new shoes to better serve them. And more friendly turf to trod. The dirt was frozen as solid inside the shop as the ground outside, the icy mud holding every shoe firmly in place, giving the shoes, if not the feet that once had filled them, a hint of permanence. I was conscious of my own shoes and station as I left the shop and walked toward the ramshackle building that had been the general store, office, and gathering place for the residents and neighbors of Providence Farm, as well as the plantation commissary that had spawned a lynching. Pausing outside the building, I thought of Phillip Rushing, a young black man whose hand I had insisted on shaking in 1955 to prove I was not a bigot. Insisted until Gene Cox whispered to me that Phillip had no hands nor arms. They had been burned off when he grabbed a fallen electric wire following an ice storm. He was sixteen years old when it happened. Born on the plantation of Senator James O. Eastland, he had nothing of value to his world except two strong arms. With that gone, poor, uneducated, and provincial like the generations before him, he had no purpose in life. "I was," he would later say, "a disfigured colored boy, no longer able to plow a field, saw a log, or embrace my girl, Diana." Unsound at sixteen, as Jacob sold as "unsound" at thirty-one to Richard Davis of Section Thirteen, Phillip was without hope. Providence Farm gave him hope in the summer Camp School, and gave him many acts of friendship. Though unable to use the artificial arms and hands Providence had arranged for him, from Providence he went on to graduate from Stillman College, do graduate work at Lexington Theological Seminary and the University of Kentucky, be declared in 1965 one of Ten Outstanding Young Men in America, and write an important book called *Empty Sleeves*. The miracles of Providence were of little consequence. Unless one happened to be a poor, disfigured colored boy named Phillip.

I stopped beside the gasoline pump, the kind with a handle that would draft up to ten gallons into a glass container mounted on top of a stand, from there to be siphoned with gravity into car or truck tanks. The price was still legible. Eighteen cents per gallon.

I moved inside and saw that most of the wide boards of the floor had been pried off the hand-hewn joists. The long counter, the length of the store itself, was the most sturdy thing left. I imagined Gene behind it, advising customers on finances and crop planting, or just talking about mules and the weather. Even some day coming when they would be allowed to register and vote. I imagined the screams of terror of the two black men who had been tricked by Champ Taylor, dragged through that very door, taken to a plantation, the Pinchback Plantation, a plantation far more "integrated" than Providence had ever been, there tied in trees with plowlines and shot dead, one more listing on the interminable roster of betrayal.

I recalled the bolts of gingham for dresses or shirts, muslin for sheets, underwear, curtains. Canvas for cottonsacks. The hoop of cheese sold by the slice or by the pound. The contraption for slicing plug chewing tobacco. The glass display for spools of thread of many gauges and colors. Things all gone. As were the inevitable cracker barrel and potbelly stove. I remembered where they stood.

A few items remained. Small brown bottles that had contained vanilla extract and root beer flavoring. The screw-on caps had rusted, letting the bottles empty onto the ground. Other bottles that had held Camphor Balm, Dr. Tichenor's Antiseptic, or Milk of Magnesia. Bruton Snuff cans were there. And more shoes scattered about. Chesterfield, Lucky Strike, Picayune, and Camel cigarette posters covered the front wall, and the smiling dwarf with his buttoned uniform and round cap still called out for Phillip Morris. I thought of how, unwittingly and unmindful of soon-to-come findings of the surgeon general, these early con-servationists, environmentalists, and healers were selling death to the people they had come here to help as surely as Greenwood Leflore, at Dancing Rabbit Creek, had peddled death to his people and their legacy.

I picked up a child's bracelet made from Orange Crush bottle caps, slipped it over my wrist, and left the building.

"*Afammi hopakih čaš*," I said aloud in my childlike Choctaw. It meant, "distant years ago." When we had first discussed returning this land to the Choctaw Band, I resolved to learn the language. At least enough to carry on a simple conversation. After the Department of Interior made the transfer unlikely, I lost interest. Bob Ferguson had sent me a cassette and manual, and for a while I had worked hard on it. Most of what I learned was, I thought, forgotten. Now some of the words and phrases came back, as if this ground itself were prompting me.

Yes, *afammi hopakih čaš*. Distant years ago indeed. I thought of Luther Cashdollar, who left this haunted glen more than a century and a half ago, to die in an Arkansas cypress swamp. And of his friend Jesse Furver too. I'll never know his end. Little Pinky, P. B. S. Pinchback, crossed my mind—the twice-elected, never-seated U.S. senator of Louisiana who for forty days and nights was governor. A month earlier in Louisiana, David Duke, former Ku Klux Klan leader, had been in a hotly contested runoff for that office on the same party label that had produced Pinchback following the Civil War. *Reconstruction*. Politics as Messiah. Then William McKendree Gwin, doctor, lawyer, marshal, planter, senator, founder of a dynasty, who dabbled in dreams and real estate and died rich. And alone. All had been here *afammi hopakih čaš*. Still others more recently, now history too. Sherwood Eddy once stood here in front of neatly painted houses with screen doors and windows, looked out over lush cotton fields worked by white and black men side by side and said, "This is good!" For a moment I grieved for Sam Franklin, who correctly, courageously, and with compassion diagnosed the evils of tenancy but saw hope dwindle and his dream die in one decade, his antidote no better than the others. All were here. All are gone, and soon I as well.

I realized I was still shivering from the cold. "*Katima čih?*" I asked the clouds that had moved in during the past hour. When will it snow? "*Onnakma,*" I answered, continuing my silly game. No, not tomorrow. Today. The forecast had said it would snow today or tonight. I tried to remember the Choctaw word for tonight. "*Himak toffa,*" I said tentatively. *Toffa* means summer, I recalled. I smiled at the bumble. Tonight is "*himmak ninak.*" It will snow *himmak ninak.* I have to get out of these woods. I'll freeze to death in here and some Department of Interior engineer will find me when spring comes again. Well, that would be a dramatic ending to my story, though not the one I had in mind. Neither is this one. Never mind. Let it be.

I was heading in the direction of the old medical clinic. "*Alikči čiuaho?*" "Are you a doctor?" I looked to see Dr. Minter coming out his door to meet me. But Dave Minter was dead in Tucson. Of Parkinson's disease and a stroke. The gentle warrior who had fought many successful battles for others lost his own, weakened, perhaps, by the years of sacrifice. I thought of the little dogwood tree I had planted in Tennessee as a memorial to him. And of the scholarship his family has endowed at Meharry Medical College in Nashville, a school that still trains nearly 40 percent of the black medical practitioners in America. He and his wife had bought a tract of land near Providence, and when he died the family felt that the land should be sold to contribute in a small way to health care among the poor.

I stopped under the overhanging limbs of the giant oak tree where Mac Bryan and I had parked the first time I saw this building. There was a dignified quality about the structure then. Now it stood in humiliation and defeat, looking much smaller, with only its memories of bustling days and sterling deeds to keep it standing at all.

I tarried briefly where I had been when Gene Cox approached that day to inquire if we were there on a friendly or hostile mission, the bulge of a .38 Special under his armpit encouraging a speedy response to the handsome stranger. Big acorns cracked underneath my feet as I made my way to the door.

I walked slowly down the hallway, trying not to glance into the rooms, as if I might invade a patient's privacy, or disturb Dr. Minter at his work. I did a hasty review of the years of Providence.

I followed Luther Cashdollar and Jesse Furver along the banks of Chicopa Creek, heard the bones of the brilliant young Choctaw crying out from a cypress swamp in Arkansas. I stood outside the courtroom and listened as Wiley Davis and William McKendree Gwin argued for possession of Section Thirteen, which Turner Brashears had legally earned and heired, and remembered anew the Gothic politics of the Cotton Kingdom. I imagined the voice of Major William Pinchback reciting poetry to his mulatto children and saw him rushing off to Philadelphia to free the black woman he loved, saw her desperate and destitute in Cincinnati when her white in-laws had robbed her and the children she had borne the major of their inheritance. The Coxes and Minters came rushing out to embrace me as they had in 1955 during my frequent visits between the mass meeting in the Tchula schoolhouse to expel them and the time of their departure. I thought of other doctors who had preceded Dr. Minter on these acres. Alexander Talley, the Methodist missionary, was also a physician. So was William McKendree Gwin. And Marcella O'Reilly Davis bathed the faces of the dying here in 1878 when her home was a makeshift hospice.

I thought of the contributions to religion of those who passed this way: Alexander Talley, who preached to the Choctaws on the banks of Chicopa Creek with Greenwood Leflore interpreting. Slaves praying on the levees for deliverance. Marcella O'Reilly Davis using it as a base to help launch St. Clara's School. Mrs. Samuel Donnell Gwin giving the diamond ring her husband had given her as her contribution to the building of the Methodist church. And A. Eugene Cox, on Sunday afternoons, preaching to young black people about Jesus and trees.

The story I had not wanted to write would not now turn me loose. I heard the groaning of the land itself telling me there were many old stories I had not found and new ones to come when the Department of Interior and a place called the U.S. of A. shall be but footnotes in books of ancient history, for this too will pass away, and how are the mighty fallen, and the present rulers will die and sleep with their fathers and others will reign in their stead, creating, leaving stories for still others to tell in a thousand years.

The square tiles had come loose from the concrete floor and shifted under my steps. Square tiles come loose. Each one reminded me of a square mile, my square mile—Section Thirteen—that had come loose yet again.

This was the same passageway the cows had walked to their stalls for feed and milking when the building was a dairy barn. And the same hall thousands of Holmes County residents had walked to be treated, sometimes as many as seventy-five in a single day.

I walked the length of the hall again, counting the rooms. Twelve of them. It seemed an appropriate number. The first two were waiting rooms. Back then they were supposed to be marked WHITE and COLORED. These doors were not marked. And never had been. Such visible reminders of discrimination are all gone now. But in 1940, not posting the signs was a bold gesture, in violation of local mores and state law. Even so, segregation was voluntarily observed. Whites sat in the room on the right. Blacks on the left. At least they were spared the humiliation of signs mandating their place when they were sick.

I entered and explored each room, trying to visualize what went on in each one. This was obviously an examining room, for the old table was still there, the steel still shiny. Not something vandals could easily destroy. Across the hall was an antiquated x-ray machine. Lindsey Hail Cox, who had processed thousands of pictures of broken bones and diseased organs here, had told me the machine was given to them by the Alpha Kappa Alpha sorority and had belonged to Provident Hospital of Chicago. She said it was outmoded when they got it. But they were grateful and it served them well. I wondered what the Department of Interior would do with it. Bury it in a hazardous waste dump probably. Many of the heavy plates that held the film were scattered around the room. Ann Cox Belk had marveled they had not been taken, as so much else had been. She said she was sure the thieves didn't know they were made of nickel. X-ray photographs were scattered about, covering the floor like autumn leaves. I examined some of them. Most told me nothing. Others were obvious to my untrained eye. Here was a crushed pelvis. This one a strangely curved spine. Another showed a lung with a darkened area bigger than a grapefruit. "Too many smiles from the uniformed Phillip Morris dwarf," I diagnosed.

Two rooms still held wooden cots with cotton mattresses— makeshift hospital beds. Several Norway rats scampered from a rip in one of the mattresses when I poked it with my cane. I remembered Lindy's stories of patients too ill or too badly injured to make it home who would be left in the clinic until they died or could be moved.

I spent a longer time in the office where records were kept. It had been the feed room of the dairy barn. Several Physician's Log Books were on the floor. I picked one up, brushed the dirt off as best I could. It was a heavy book, bound in black leather, inscribed as the "Personal property of Dr. David R. Minter." I felt intrusive as I thumbed through it.

Each page was lined, with spaces for the day and hour, patient's name, service rendered, charge, cash received, and due on account. I turned to the first entry, January 1, 1940. The clinic was at Rochdale in 1940, but now the records were part of the still and soundless history of Section Thirteen. Lee Moore had been treated for a scalp wound. A New Year's Eve fight, I surmised. On the other hand, he might have been in an accident on his way to church, for New Year's Eve was on Sunday. Dave didn't note what had caused the wound. But then it wouldn't have mattered to this veritable son of Hippocrates. The patient was charged twenty-five cents. Didn't pay. There were ten entries that day. A day when other medical clinics would have been closed. Throughout his years, Dr. Minter was either at the clinic or on call twenty-four hours a day. Every day.

There were three house calls to Annie Belle Billington, each one two hours apart. No charge was recorded for the first two visits. Fifteen cents for the third. It wasn't paid. I assumed the woman had died. But on January 2 Annie Belle came to the clinic for what was listed as a check-up. Again on the fourth. Then on January 6 Jim Billington paid three dollars and fifty cents. The log said, "Delivery." I guessed Jim was Annie Belle's husband, that she had false labor on Monday, wondered what had happened to her on Tuesday, and finally had her baby on Saturday.

Dr. Minter treated seventy-five patients the first week of January. The log showed he received five dollars and ten cents for his services. Total cash for January: forty dollars and eighty cents.

Many of the patients in the log book had more money listed under "Due on Account" than the charge for the service had been. I figured Dr. Minter would examine them, make his diagnosis, then give them cash to pay for the medication he had prescribed.

I leafed through other log books, all the way through 1955, when the doctor was forced to abandon his practice. Whooping cough. Tuleremia. Sickle cell anemia. Luetic heart disease. Circumcisions for fifteen cents. A life-saving tracheotomy for half a dollar. Then, in the fall of 1955, rewarded by a mob demanding that he leave the county for subversion. He had served his country for four years in the jungles of New Guinea during World War II, but that reckoned as of no account. The charge against him was correct. He really was doing his best to subvert the ways of his time.

Nellie Thomas. Elnora, who didn't know her last name. Baby Sellars. Nolly Bivora. Esther Lou Rondry. I read their names from the daily log of Dr. David R. Minter. A man who knew them and their needs.

Where are they now? Gone too. Just walked out of their shoes and left.

It was time for me to be gone as well. Soon darkness would cover this valley. And the bluffs overlooking it. The clouds had become heavy, in marked contrast to the bright sun that greeted my arrival. A fine mist was falling, already freezing on the windshield, leaves crunchy underneath my steps. I was scheduled to catch a plane at the Jackson airport in two hours.

I tried to pull the front door shut. The rusty hinges and buckled floor resisted. Just as well, I thought. Leave the door open, as it always was when Dr. Minter and Nurse Cox were here. Open for black and white, for anyone in the Yazoo basin who needed health care. I recalled a political discussion on health care I had watched the night before. CSPAN, I believe it was. Lindy and Dave would have had no patience with such babble. They already knew the solution to the nation's health-care crisis. Doctors, nurses, and providers who care.

I opened the car door, started the motor, then got out and stood in the cold. It was as if a brief moment of suffering on the cold earth would be my personal oblation.

So here we are, Section Thirteen. For a few more minutes just the two of us. Soon I'll be gone and it's just you. I don't even know for sure who owns all of you now. They tell me you've been all chopped up again, with the U.S. government holding title to most of you. Just as it did on that dreary morning when Luther Cashdollar left this spot on the back of Fičik, destined to death. But you know all that. And being Section Thirteen wasn't your idea in the first place. You were content to be a tiny portion of the universe. Three men with a chain and transit told a Choctaw named Tunapinachuffa and a white boy named Jesse Furver that they were standing on Section Thirteen. Some other white people, with good intentions, had already told Tunapinachuffa his Christian name should be Luther Cashdollar.

So. Good-bye, Providence and Section Thirteen. I won't be back. This is my last trip. I did what I could for you, and for those gallant souls who loved and served you as long as they were allowed by the misguided denizens who also, in their way, loved the land. I'm afraid what I did was never much. You gave me more than I gave. But I have loved you. And finally them. And love you still. It has been thirty-five years since first we met on another somber occasion. I wanted a new life for you. A new life with new sounds. A new life with old sounds. Choctaw sounds. Sounds you have known before. I think it would have been a happy issue out of your affliction.

But I failed. It was not to be. The powers and principalities against which we wrestled prevailed. I still don't want the damnable Department of Interior to own one foot of you. But they do. Land with an absent lord is never whole. You know that better than I.

I do believe your greatest ambition was to meet the needs of the brothers and sisters near at hand. Feed the hungry. Clothe the naked. I wish for you a good life now. I know you will keep the faith and triumph. You will harbor the creatures you always have, give birth to grass and seed-bearing herbs, and fruit trees after his kind. The two lights of the firmament will shine upon you, and you will bring forth the living creatures after his kind—the beasts of the earth after his kind, fowl that fly above the earth in the open firmament of heaven; fish that swim in the waters, and everything that creepeth after his kind. For God created you and saw that it was good. You will battle intruders with your vines and thistles and sawbriars. You have healed yourself since time began, surviving fire and flood and pestilence. And so it will be. I have no fear for you. Your forbearance I honor. Your longevity I covet. Though this is good-bye, I won't forget you.

While I waited for the defroster to melt the ice on the windshield, I fetched a small Evan Williams bottle from my briefcase, took a hefty pull to stay the chills, then poured the remainder on the ground, stretching it in all directions as far as it would go.

Baptism crossed my mind. Then unction. Neither seemed appropriate. Baptism for *earth* came when time began. Unction for *earth* is not liable to mortal surmise.

The ritual was over. It was neither sacrament nor eulogy. Just two old friends having a parting drink.

Will D. Campbell is the award-winning author of ten books, including *Brother to a Dragonfly, The Glad River, Forty Acres and a Goat,* and *The Convention.* Most recently he received the first Alex Haley Award for Distinguished Tennessee Writers. He and his wife of forty-six years, Brenda Fisher, live on a farm near Mount Juliet, Tennessee.